F
LC

G. K. CHESTERTON

A Bibliography

G. K. Chesterton. A Study by James Gunn, 1932

G. K. CHESTERTON
A Bibliography

by
JOHN SULLIVAN

With an Essay on Books by
G. K. CHESTERTON
and an Epitaph by
WALTER DE LA MARE

UNIVERSITY OF LONDON PRESS LTD
WARWICK SQUARE, LONDON EC4

Printed & Bound in England for the UNIVERSITY OF LONDON PRESS LTD.,
by HAZELL WATSON & VINEY LTD., Aylesbury and Slough

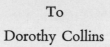
To
Dorothy Collins

ACKNOWLEDGEMENTS

THE dedication of this book is intended to indicate something of the enormous debt that it owes to Miss Dorothy Collins. In her capacity as literary executrix of G. K. Chesterton, Miss Collins has given me the fullest access to the Chesterton papers, to all her voluminous and carefully indexed records and press cuttings and to her extensive collection of Chesterton material. Her enthusiastic support no less than her detailed answers to my endless questions have been of the greatest assistance. That one who knew Chesterton so well and has herself done so much to preserve his memory should be intimately concerned with this book has greatly increased such value as it may have. In saying this I would add that the responsibility for any errors or omissions that the critical reader may detect is mine alone. More specifically I have to thank Miss Collins for permission to reprint the essay by G. K. Chesterton, *On Books*, which now appears in book form for the first time, and for the illustrations facing pages 24, 32, 48, 112 and 160. To Miss Collins also and to the Literary Trustees of Walter de la Mare I am indebted for permission to print the epitaph by Walter de la Mare on page 195.

To my friend Mr. Patrick Cahill, the bibliographer of Hilaire Belloc, I am indebted for much help and advice throughout my labours. His high standards of bibliographical scholarship have proved a salutary check to my own somewhat romantic enthusiasm, and I have drawn deeply upon his profound knowledge of the works of both Belloc and Chesterton.

For permission to reproduce the study of G. K. Chesterton which appears as the frontispiece I have to thank the artist, Mr. James Gunn, and the owner, Miss Dorothy Collins. I have also to thank Miss Collins and Mrs. Eric Gill for permission to reproduce the silhouette of G. K. Chesterton by Eric Gill which appears on the dust-jacket. For the illustrations facing pages 96 and 144 and for valuable information on some specific points I am indebted to Fr. Kevin Scannell.

I am deeply indebted to Dr. Robert R. Yackshaw and the John Carroll University, Cleveland, Ohio, who have made available to me the catalogue and records of the Robert John Bayer Chesterton Collection. From this source I have drawn much useful information on American editions in particular, but also on a number of out-of-the-way Chesterton items. To Mr. John Bennett Shaw, of Tulsa, Oklahoma, a notable Chesterton collector who kindly placed his records freely at my disposal, I am also greatly indebted; to Miss Patricia Butler, of A. P. Watt and Son, Mr. Richard de la Mare, Mr. Philip Hagreen, Mr. Raymond Kahla, Mr. James Laver, C.B.E., Mr. Aidan Mackey, Mr. Harold Mortlake, Mr. D. F. O'Dwyer, Mr. Maurice Pariser, Mr. J. W. Powell, Mr. Bertram Rota, Mr. K. R. C. Sturmer, Mr. Joseph Sudbery, Mr. H. Sutton, Mr. Grant Uden and Mr. Robert Walmsley I offer my best thanks for much varied and valuable help.

To Mr. D. I. Colley, F.L.A., City Librarian of Manchester, and his staff, and particularly to Mr. S. Horrocks, F.L.A., I am greatly indebted both for the generous facilities afforded me at the Manchester Reference Library and for the personal interest they have taken in this work.

Acknowledgements are due to many publishers who have given me the fullest information at their disposal, and I tender thanks to the British Broadcasting Corporation, the British Council, Burns, Oates and Washbourne Ltd., Mr. Desmond Flower and Messrs. Cassell and Co. Ltd., Chatto and Windus Ltd., Mr. E. W. Wall and Cedric Chivers Ltd., William Collins, Sons and Co. Ltd., J. M. Dent and Sons Ltd., Gerald Duckworth and Co. Ltd., Faber and Faber Ltd., George G. Harrap and Co. Ltd., W. Heffer and Sons Ltd., Hodder and Stoughton Ltd., Hollis and Carter Ltd., Hutchinson and Co. Ltd., John Lane the Bodley Head Ltd., Macmillan and Co. Ltd., Methuen and Co. Ltd., Thomas Nelson and Sons Ltd., Sheed and Ward Ltd., the University of London Press Ltd., and Wells Gardner, Darton and Co. Ltd.

I also thank Miss M. Manley for her patient work on the typescript and Miss Mary Sullivan for assistance with the Index and for reading the proofs.

Finally I wish to thank Mr. H. S. Foster, of the University of London Press Ltd., Mr. R. S. Kirkman, of the Editorial Department, and Mr. R. P. Irons for the keen personal interest they have taken in the production of this book.

SALE, CHESHIRE   JOHN SULLIVAN
    March 1958

CONTENTS

LIST OF PLATES

INTRODUCTION

THIS bibliography attempts a comprehensive description of the published works of G. K. Chesterton. It is offered to meet the needs of collectors, of librarians and, indeed, of all students of Chesterton.

The material is arranged in eight sections, and, since I have departed from standard practice in certain respects, the following notes on the entries and the classification will serve to explain the method and to indicate its scope.

Except where noted, the entries are arranged in chronological order. A reference number, running in sequence through all the sections, is placed before each entry. References in the text to numbers are to these numbers and not to pages.

A. *Books and Pamphlets by G. K. Chesterton*

This section provides full descriptions of the first English editions of all works by Chesterton and of those works published in the United States made up wholly, or in part, of material not published in book form in England. A transcription of the title-page is followed by the size of the page in inches and the collation. The method adopted in describing pagination is as follows:

Pp. vi + 396 = prelims. numbered i–vi, text 1–396, total 402 pp.
Pp. vi, 396 = prelims. numbered i–vi, text 7–396, total 396 pp.

A description of the binding with variants, if any, and the date of publication follows. The date of the British Museum copy is given in most cases. Where it is omitted there is either no copy in the British Museum or the copy there is not a first edition. When all, or part, of the text has had previous publication in a periodical, this is noted and details of the periodical publication can be found in Section C. Notes on the text, on later editions and on other matters of interest, are added where appropriate.

B. *Contributions to Books and Pamphlets*

This provides a record of all prefaces, introductions, epilogues and other writings by Chesterton that appeared for the first time in this form. When these items have subsequently been collected, the reference number sends the reader to the collection.

C. *Contributions to Periodicals*

The entries in this section are arranged, for ease of reference, in alphabetical order of periodical titles and in chronological order under each title.

The extent of Chesterton's periodical writings was phenomenal, and a complete record, even if such were possible, would demand a large volume to itself. In this situation some form of selection was imperative and I have limited myself to a record of all such writings that I could trace as having afterwards appeared in book form, with the addition of a number of items which seem to me worthy of inclusion for special reasons. Thus, I have recorded reports of speeches and debates and controversies. Similarly, the list of contributions to the *Debater* is complete, and all of the broadcast texts printed in the *Listener* are listed although they have not, save in two instances, been collected in book form.

D. *Books and Periodicals containing Illustrations by G. K. Chesterton*

The inclusion of a record of drawings by the author may be regarded as out of place in a bibliography. On the other hand, it seems to me that no record of Chesterton's published work would be complete without some account of his work as artist and illustrator. I make no apology for this attempt to list all books and periodicals which contain illustrations or cartoons by Chesterton, and I regret only that it has not been possible to record his many unpublished drawings.

E. *Books and Articles about G. K. Chesterton*

This section lists, in chronological order of publication, books and articles about Chesterton and his work, and a selection of books that contain substantial references to him. When a periodical article has afterwards been collected in book form, both appearances are recorded with a cross-reference to the book, since the latter is usually the more easily accessible.

F. *Collections and Selections*

This section records the collections of Chesterton's works, and selections from it, in which no new material appears.

G. *Translations into Foreign Languages*

The entries are arranged alphabetically by languages and, within language groups, chronologically. The form of presentation follows that of *Index Translationum*: title, translator (when known), place of publication, publisher.

H.   *G. K. C. Miscellany*

The inclusion of this section is perhaps open to the same objection as that of section D. It brings together a number of items of interest to the Chesterton collector which do not fit readily into any of the other categories. It is in no sense complete: enthusiasts may care to add to it; bibliographical purists may ignore it.

No full-scale bibliography of Chesterton has hitherto been published, although, in the twenty-one years since his death, the need for such a guide has become increasingly apparent. Some check lists and notes on individual items have appeared from time to time in books and periodicals, and a detailed description of forty-five Chesterton first editions is given in *A Bibliographical Catalogue of the First Loan Exhibition of Books and Manuscripts Held by the First Edition Club, 1922*. This last, which claims to be "virtually complete", is to be regarded with caution. Beyond these scattered and scanty items there is little to guide the collector through the Chesterton maze. A glance through the following pages may reveal why this is so. The sheer mass and variety of Chesterton's work, the author's own indifference to the fate of that work once published, the number of his publishers, the destruction of publishers' records, and of periodicals at the British Museum during the war—these and other factors conspire to present any bibliographer of Chesterton with a formidable task. In spite of the assistance I have been given and the exceptional opportunities I have enjoyed, I am conscious that the work leaves a number of questions unanswered and a number of problems unsolved. Nevertheless, this attempt at a map of Chesterton's activities as author, artist, controversialist and broadcaster is as thorough as I have been able to make it, and I trust that it will prove of value to all who are interested in Chesterton and his work. I shall be grateful to receive any notes, corrections or additions.

ON BOOKS

By G. K. CHESTERTON

THE only intelligible human controversy is a disagreement upon a basis of agreement. Our whole trouble in most modern controversies is an attempt to get an agreement upon a basis of disagreement. The old sort of agreement, the old sort of disagreement, were natural; they were like the indefinite branchings of a tree which has a single original seed. The modern agreement is unnatural; it is an insanity, as if a madman were to tie all the tops of the trees together. And in all such modern controversies the primary evil is always the same; it is an evil of cowardice, and the worst part of cowardice is that it is not invariably true that the bully is always a coward, but it is invariably true that the coward is always a bully. There is a modern sham courage which is this: that everyone has the courage to pronounce paradoxes; but the true modern cowardice is that no one has the courage to pronounce truisms. Consequently the chief evil of all modern argument is that it will not begin, like Euclid, with the things that are quite obvious; Euclid is dull during the first four or five pages; not before the third book does he begin to become even feebly brilliant. In short, the characteristic modern controversy has this defect, that those partaking in it have not the courage to be dull, have not the courage to state the things which are only evident to some. Supposing we avoid this modern error; supposing we plunge into unfathomable dullness, as into our native air. Let us begin with truisms.

There are two or three main truisms about the writing, buying, and selling of books which may very well be stated in their baldest form. The first fact is the fact which a child sees when he pulls a book down from his father's bookcase and joyfully tears it to pieces. He sees that a book is a thing, an objective fact of modern industry, with a certain definite consistency and a certain recognisable shape. If we were all in the Kingdom of Heaven, we should possibly see a row of modern books as he does; and possibly tear them to pieces as he does. But the first plain point is this, that when the child treats a book as he does a stool or an umbrella-stand, he is first and foremost quite right. A book is first of all a material marketable object like a chair. I think a great deal of the man who makes a book really by himself; I think a great deal more of the man who makes a chair really by himself. But a chair is first and foremost a thing in which a man can sit; and a book is first and foremost a thing which a man buys in order to read.

The first mistake of this modern controversy is that it invariably confounds the question of books with the question of literature. Literature is a certain attitude or atmosphere, like religion or philosophy; books are things like boots. Even if we put on one side altogether those books which pretend to be literature, there still remains a vast mass of books which are not literature and do not pretend to be literature. I allude, of course, to such things as cookery books, timetables, reports of sociologists, technical handbooks, dictionaries, old-fashioned encyclopaedias, and so on.

If, therefore, we are to consider the real position of publishers and such people, the fairest thing to mention at the beginning is that publishers in general and some publishers in particular exist to publish books much more than to publish literature; in many of their publishing houses literature can only take a place along with grammar, geography, theology, cookery, progress, and a hundred other dull things; in some of their publishing houses literature itself is almost a by-product.

But we may pass from the great mass of books which do not profess to be literary at all; we may come to that considerable bulk of published books, of which the enemy of the publisher commonly speaks, the considerable bulk of books that are supposed to be literature and are not literature; or are at the best ephemeral or feeble literature. In this connection there is an injustice done to the ordinary merchant in books. The business of a publisher is not to produce only the immortal productions of his time, supposing that there happened to be any. The business (the moral business) of a publisher is very much like the business of an editor; it is to produce a real picture of the activities and actualities of his own age. The publisher will not be blamed in the permanent conclusions of history, because he made a mistake about which man would be permanent; he will be blamed in so far that he failed to give a clear and honest picture of his time. When the history of modern journalism comes to be written in a remote age, our editors will not be found guilty upon one single essential point touching what they have published; they will be found spotless touching whatever they have published; if they are found guilty, it will be wholly upon the things that they have not published. They will be blamed for not letting their authors tell us what after all

antiquity has not told us—the things which the age took for granted.
There exists also, then, the great mass of books which have the same
right to exist that newspapers have to exist. It is, as I have suggested, a
grave mistake to confuse an interest in books with an interest in good
literature.

Good literature is a thing quite different from books. And in one
respect books are more important even than good literature. They are
more important than good literature in the same serious sense that the
daily paper is more important than good literature. In a quite serious
sense it is more important to read the newspaper than to read Shakespeare. It is more important because of the very simple truth that
citizenship must be more important than art. A man has a very reasonable desire to mix with the vivid and varied life of his time (indeed,
secrecy is the modern evil); and therefore as things are a publisher is
not to be blamed for publishing the books of the moment; nay, rather
he is to be praised for publishing books, which without art, or bad in
art, produce effect; such books are a great calamity, but they should
be published like a pestilence or a fire. Such has been the character of
nearly all the great typical books of our modern time. They have
really brought things to a crisis; they have really raised a question. But
no artist would have published them; no one but a publisher would
have published them. No literary artist would have published *The
Heavenly Twins*; but it interested everybody because it was the
expression of something special and emphatic in our own age.
Women's rights were not literature; they were not politics; they were
not (in spite of many respectable opinions) either morality or philosophy. But they were two most important things. They were journalism, and they were history. The publisher, like the editor, should not
be discouraged, but rather encouraged, in the business of producing
the more bold and entertaining utterances of his time.

If he begins to agree or disagree with those utterances, he is simply
a censor of the Press. If he lets them through he is what he ought to be,
essentially the editor of a newspaper; that is essentially and simply a
man who brings news.

Lastly, it is urged against the publisher that he comes to grief in
relation to the very best literature, the thing to which alone the name
of literature is really due. Now let it be said again: it is not the business
of the publisher to publish literature but to publish books; a great mass
of books is so avowedly un-literary that publishing is scarcely more of
a literary organ than the post-office. We have no more real right to

expect that all books will be literary than we have to expect that all telegrams will be literary, for publishing, like the post, is primarily not an art but a mode of communication of thought. If a thing is popular, is important, that is, in its hour and age, that is a reason for publishing it.

There remains the case of really good literature. Now, immortal literature was never meant to be paid properly. The sixpence or the six shillings or the six pounds that we give for a copy of Virgil or Chaucer is not supposed to represent its value; it represents it about as much as the woman we love is represented by the gold ring that we give to her. And this cheap payment for perfect words ought to be preserved as the main assertion of the liberty of the artist, for should genius be always inadequately paid, it will remain the better. Genius is nowadays both over and under paid. If ever genius is adequately paid, it will mean that someone has judged and limited genius. Better that *Paradise Lost* should be roughly considered worth ten pounds than that anyone should presume to say that it was worth exactly three hundred and forty-seven, and better that a publisher should fix its market value than that any son of Adam should venture to fix its real value. We may say, therefore, in summary, that the position of the publishers is quite inadequately understood.

The business of selling books is in its nature the most perilous and speculative of businesses. The publisher is not (as the authors say) a robber, but he runs as many risks as a robber, and the authors are very unreasonable if they blame him first for treating men's souls as so much cheese and then for remembering that men's souls are dangerous and incalculable. A man putting his money into new books is like a man putting his money into new religions. He will be certain to make mistakes; he will be likely to commit sins; but the decent writer will not be likely to exchange his human sins for the inhuman sins of a quite alien domination.

Morning Post, October 18, 1906.

A

BOOKS AND PAMPHLETS BY G. K. CHESTERTON

1900

1. GREYBEARDS AT / PLAY / LITERATURE / AND ART / FOR OLD / GENTLEMEN / RHYMES AND SKETCHES / BY GILBERT CHESTERTON / LONDON: R. BRIMLEY JOHNSON / 8, YORK BUILDINGS, ADELPHI / MCM

$7\frac{1}{4} \times 5\frac{3}{8}$. A to G in eights; H is six leaves.

Pp. xii + 112. (i) Half-title, (ii) blank; (iii) title-page, (iv) printer's imprint; (v)–ix dedicatory poem, *To E. C. B.*, (x) blank; (xi) *Contents*, (xii) blank; 1–102 text; (103) advertisement of this book (with "Ballads and Sketches" for "Rhymes and Sketches"); (104)–(109) advertisements; (110)–(111) blank; (112) advertisement of *The Wild Knight* (publisher Grant Richards). Twenty-four full-page illustrations by the author.

Pictorial orange paper boards with buckram spine. The front has a drawing by the author in black, white and lemon of an elderly gentleman on a hobby-horse with title in black and lemon: GREY-BEARDS / AT- / PLAY / Then, in black: BY / GILBERT CHESTERTON / The whole enclosed by a black border with at foot: PUBLISHED BY R. BRIMLEY JOHNSON, LONDON. Spine lettered in black reading upwards: GREYBEARDS AT PLAY

Published in October 1900, at 2*s.* 6*d.* BM 10 Oct. 1900.

2. THE WILD KNIGHT / AND OTHER POEMS / BY / GILBERT CHESTERTON / [*ornament*] / LONDON / GRANT RICHARDS / 9 HENRIETTA STREET / 1900

$6\frac{3}{4} \times 4\frac{1}{8}$. An unsigned gathering of four leaves; A to I in eights; K four; L two leaves.

Pp. viii + 156. (i) Half-title, (ii) *Publisher's Announcement* in panel; (iii) title-page; (iv) *Note*; v–viii Contents; 1–153 text; (154) printer's imprint; (155), (156) blank.

Grey-blue paper boards, vellum spine with raised bands.

Spine lettered in gilt: THE / WILD / KNIGHT / GILBERT / CHESTERTON / GRANT / RICHARDS / All edges uncut.

Published in November 1900, at 5s. BM 20 Nov. 1900.

Poems, some collected from the *Outlook* and the *Speaker*: most appear in print for the first time. The last poem, *Good News* (pp. 152–153), is omitted from the Contents.
The second edition, published in November 1905 by Brimley Johnson and Ince, Ltd., has a two-page Prefatory Note signed "G. K. C. Battersea, 1905".

The fourth edition, "With Additional Poems", published in October 1914 by J. M. Dent, has a wider page (5 in.), a portrait frontispiece, the title-page printed in red and black, and includes three new poems: *The Neglected Child, To a Turk*, and *The Aristocrat*. Spine lettered in gilt: THE WILD KNIGHT / & OTHER POEMS / G. K. / CHESTERTON / J · M · DENT / · & · SONS · LD · Top edges gilt, others uncut.

1901

3. THE DEFENDANT / BY G. K. CHESTERTON / AUTHOR OF 'THE WILD KNIGHT' / AND 'GREYBEARDS AT PLAY' / [*publisher's device*] / LONDON. MDCCCCI / R. BRIMLEY JOHNSON

$7\frac{1}{2} \times 5$. An unsigned gathering of four leaves, 1 to 8 in eights, 9 is four leaves.

Pp. (viii) + 136. (i) Half-title, (ii) blank; (iii) title-page, (iv) blank; (v) note of acknowledgement, dated October 1901, (vi) blank; (vii) *Contents*, (viii) blank; (1)–131 text, (132) blank; (133) advertisement, headed *By the Same Author* of *Greybeards at Play*, a book by Cosmo Monkhouse illustrated by G. K. C. and a book written and illustrated by his father; (134)–(136) blank.

Sage-green buckram with bevelled edges. Spine stamped in gilt: [*rule*] / THE / DEFENDANT / G. K. / CHESTERTON / R. BRIMLEY / JOHNSON / [*rule*] / All edges uncut.

Published in December 1901, at 5s. BM 9 June 02.
Essays, collected from the *Speaker*, with an introduction. Portions of "The Defence of Publicity" appeared in the *Daily News*. See *Note*, p. (v).

". . . But the first connected series of articles, the first regular job in support of a regular cause, was made possible for me by Hammond and his friends of the new *Speaker*. It was there that I wrote, along with many pugnacious political articles, a series of casual essays afterwards published as *The Defendant*." *Autobiography*, p. 119.

The second edition, advertised as having "more matter at half the price", appeared in red cloth at 2s. 6d. in 1903. It contains a new four-page essay, *In Defence of a New Edition*.

The third edition was published by J. M. Dent in 1907. The title-page is slightly altered (lines 3 and 4): AUTHOR OF 'HERETICS' / 'THE WILD KNIGHT', ETC.

1902

4. TWELVE TYPES [*in red*] / BY G. K. CHESTERTON / LONDON / ARTHUR L. HUMPHREYS / 1902

$6\frac{7}{8} \times 5\frac{1}{8}$. An unsigned gathering of four leaves, A to M in eights; N two leaves folded round N2, which is four.

Pp. (viii) + 204. (i) Half-title, (ii) blank; (iii) title-page, (iv) blank; (v) note of acknowledgement, (vi) blank; (vii) *Contents*, (viii) blank; 1–203 text; (204) blank.

Bright-green smooth cloth stamped in gilt. Front: TWELVE TYPES / A BOOK OF ESSAYS / G. K. CHESTERTON / Ruled border. Flat spine stamped in gilt: [*rule*] / TWELVE / TYPES / G. K. / CHESTERTON / A. L. HUMPHREYS / [*rule*] / Top edges gilt.

Published in October 1902, at 3s. 6d.

Essays reprinted from the *Daily News* and the *Speaker* "with certain alterations and additions".

Humphreys later published two selections from *Twelve Types* with no indication that they were reprinted from the earlier volume:

1910. *Five Types*. Contains the essays on Byron, Pope, Rostand, Charles II and Stevenson.

1912. *Simplicity and Tolstoy*. Contains Tolstoy and the Cult of Simplicity, William Morris, Francis and Carlyle.

See also *Varied Types* (14).

1903

5. ENGLISH MEN OF LETTERS / ROBERT BROWNING / BY /
G. K. CHESTERTON / LONDON: MACMILLAN & CO.,
LIMITED / NINETEEN HUNDRED AND THREE [*the whole
enclosed in a thin red ruled border with a rule extending from side to
side beneath the first line and another above the fifth*]

$7\frac{5}{16} \times 4\frac{7}{8}$. An unsigned gathering of four leaves, A to N in
eights.

Pp. (viii) + 208. (i), (ii) Blank; (iii) half-title, (iv) publisher's
monogram; (v) title-page, (vi) copyright statement; (vii)
Contents, (viii) blank; (1)–202 text; 203–207 *Index*; (208) blank.
A single leaf of advertisements dated 20.11.02 following p.
(208) is not included in the collation.

Dark-red smooth cloth. Front and back plain. Flat spine,
stamped in gilt: ROBERT / BROWNING / [*ornament*] / G. K. /
CHESTERTON / ENGLISH · MEN / OF · LETTERS / Top edges gilt.

Published in May 1903, at 2s.

1904

6. G. F. WATTS [*in red*] / BY / G. K. CHESTERTON / AUTHOR
OF "ROBERT BROWNING," ETC. / [*ornament in red*] / 1904 /
LONDON: DUCKWORTH & CO. [*the last three words in red*] /
NEW YORK: [*in red*] E. P. DUTTON & CO

$5\frac{7}{8} \times 3\frac{3}{4}$. An unsigned gathering of four leaves, *a* to *l* in eights.
Pp. viii + 176. (i) *The Popular Library of Art*, (ii) list of the
series; (iii) blank, (iv) frontispiece, *The Habit does not make the
Monk*; (v) title-page, (vi) printer's imprint; vii–viii *List of
Illustrations*; 1–169 text and illustrations, 170 blank; 171–174
Index; (175) advertisement of Duckworth's *Greenback Library*,
(176) advertisement of photographs of works by Watts, etc.
Thirty-two full-page illustrations, versos blank, are included in
the pagination.

Smooth, dark-red cloth stamped in gilt. Front: WATTS
[*ornament*]. Spine: WATTS / [*ornament*] / G. K. / CHESTERTON /
[*ornament*] / [*ornament*] / DUCKWORTH / Back: publisher's
device blind-stamped in bottom left-hand corner. Top edges
gilt.

I may describe him as a Star
My best, my only friend
We wore One Hat, smoked One Cigar
— (One standing at Each End)
I always boldly ate the pears
An let him climb the tree
One hope, one toil
    One pair of boots.
Joined us Eternally —

A page of verse illustrated, *c*. 1893. The opening lines were used in the
dedication to E. C. Bentley of *Greybeards at Play*, 1900

A. As described.

B. Green buckram.

Published in March 1904, at 2s. (cloth) and 2s. 6d. (buckram).

Re-issued in 1914 in larger format in Duckworth's *Masters of Painting* series.

7. THE NAPOLEON / OF / NOTTING HILL / BY / GIL-
BERT K. CHESTERTON / WITH SEVEN FULL-PAGE ILLUSTRA-
TIONS BY / W. GRAHAM ROBERTSON / AND A MAP OF THE
SEAT OF WAR / JOHN LANE: THE BODLEY HEAD / LONDON
& NEW YORK. MDCCCCIV [*lines 1–3, 4–5, 6–8 and 9–10
enclosed in ruled frames and the four frames enclosed in a ruled
border*]

$7\frac{3}{8} \times 5$. A to T in eights.

Pp. x, 304. (i) Half-title, (ii) blank; (iii) title-page, (iv) *Copyright
in U.S.A. 1904. / William Clowes & Sons, Limited, London and
Beccles*; v–vi dedicatory poem, *To Hilaire Belloc*; vii–viii
Contents; ix *Illustrations*, (x) blank; (11)–(301) text, (302) blank;
(303), (304) advertisements. The seven full-page illustrations
are tipped in to face the title-page and pp. 16, 70, 104, 190, 220,
264 and 296. The title-page is mounted on a stub.

Olive-green cloth lettered in black. Front: THE NAPOLEON /
OF / NOTTING HILL / [*picture of roof-tops and water tower in black
and red*] / GILBERT K. CHESTERTON [*All within a double
ruled border.*] Spine: [*rule*] / THE / NAPOLEON / OF / NOTTING
/ HILL / G. K. CHESTERTON / [*figure in black and red*] / JOHN
LANE / [*rule*] [*All within a ruled border*]. Top edges green, others
uncut.

A. As above. BM 22 April 04.

B. Top edges green, others trimmed.

C. Front and spine lettered in red, otherwise as A.

D. As A, but foot of spine reads THE BODLEY HEAD in place of
JOHN LANE.

Published March 22, 1904, at 6s. 5,000 copies.

An inscribed presentation copy from G. K. C. to his wife, now
in the collection of Miss Dorothy Collins, is A.

1905

8. THE CLUB OF QUEER / TRADES / BY / GILBERT K.
CHESTERTON / WITH ILLUSTRATIONS BY THE AUTHOR /
[*device*] / LONDON AND NEW YORK / HARPER & BROTHERS
/ 45 ALBEMARLE STREET, W. / 1905

$7\frac{1}{4} \times 4\frac{5}{8}$. An unsigned gathering of four leaves, A to Q in
eights; R four.

Pp. viii + 264. (i) Half-title, (ii) blank; (iii) title-page, (iv) blank;
v Contents, (vi) blank; vii–viii Illustrations; (1)–(264) text.
Printer's imprint at foot of p. (264). Four pages of advertisements following p. (264) are not included in the collation.

Thirty-two full-page illustrations by the author, on art paper,
versos blank, are tipped in, two of them together facing p. 258.

Red glazed cloth. Front stamped in black: THE CLUB OF /
QUEER TRADES / GILBERT K. CHESTERTON / [*reproduction of
a figure from the illustration facing p. 119*] / Ruled border.
Spine stamped in gilt: THE / CLUB / OF / QUEER / TRADES /
GILBERT K. / CHESTERTON / HARPERS / with a black rule at
head and tail.

Published in March 1905, at 6s.   BM 6 Mar. 05.

The American edition, published by Harpers in April 1905, has
illustrations by W. E. Mears.

Serialised during 1904 in the Idler with the author's illustrations.
The first story, The Tremendous Adventures of Major Brown, was
issued in brown-paper wrappers, 24 pp., stapled, by Shurmer
Sibthorp, London & New York, in December 1903. BM 16
Dec. 03. A registration copy.

9. HERETICS [*in a panel*] / BY / GILBERT K. CHESTERTON [*lines
2 and 3 within a panel*] / [*blank panel*] / JOHN LANE: THE
BODLEY HEAD / LONDON & NEW YORK. MDCCCCV [*lines 3
and 4 within a panel. The four panels within a single ruled border*]
$7\frac{5}{8} \times 4\frac{3}{4}$. [A] to T in eights; U is four leaves.

Pp. x, 312. (i) Half-title, (ii) advertisement of The Napoleon of
Notting Hill; (iii) title-page, (iv) printer's imprint; (v) dedication, To My Father, (vi) blank; vii–viii Contents; (ix) fly-title,
(x) blank; 11–306 text; (307)–(312) advertisements.

Light-red glazed cloth. Front stamped with an ornament in gilt, centre; blind ruled border. Spine stamped in gilt: [rule] / HERETICS / G. K. CHESTERTON / JOHN LANE / [rule] / Back: blind ruled border. Top edges gilt, others rough-trimmed.

Published June 6, 1905, at 5s. 2,000 copies.

1906

10. CHARLES DICKENS / BY / G. K. CHESTERTON / WITH TWO PORTRAITS IN PHOTOGRAVURE / METHUEN & CO. / 36 ESSEX STREET W.C. / LONDON

$8\frac{9}{16} \times 5\frac{5}{16}$. [A] four leaves; B to U in eights.

Pp. (viii) + 304. (i) Half-title, (ii) blank; (iii) title-page, (iv) *First Published in* 1906; (v) dedication, *To Rhoda Bastable*, (vi) blank; (vii) *Contents*, (viii) *Contents* (continued) and *List of Portraits*; 1–297 text, (298) blank; 299–303 *Index*, (304) printer's imprint.

Two plates, each with a tissue-paper guard, tipped in facing the title-page and p. 240, are not included in the collation.

Forty pages of advertisements, dated July 1906, in which this book is announced as "in the press" follow p. (304).

Light-green glazed cloth stamped in gilt. Front: CHARLES DICKENS / G · K · CHESTERTON / Ruled border. Spine: [*double rule*] / CHARLES / DICKENS / G · K / CHESTERTON / METHUEN / [*double rule*] / Back: blind ruled border. Tail edges uncut.

Published August 30, 1906, at 7s. 6d. 1,250 copies. BM 7 Sep. 06.

The American edition, published by Dodd, Mead & Co., N.Y., in 1906, is entitled: *Charles Dickens, a critical study*. The two plates and the index are omitted. In 1942 it was issued by The Press of the Readers' Club, N.Y., as *Charles Dickens, the last of the great men*, with a foreword by Alexander Woollcott.

1908

11. ALL RIGHTS RESERVED [*in italics, underlined*] / THE MAN WHO WAS / THURSDAY / [*broken line*] / A NIGHTMARE. / BY G. K. CHESTERTON. [*short line and point below the last six letters*] / [*publisher's device*] / BRISTOL / J. W. ARROWSMITH, 11 QUAY STREET / LONDON / SIMPKIN, MARSHALL, HAMILTON, KENT & COMPANY LIMITED

$7\frac{3}{16} \times 4\frac{11}{16}$. [1] to 20 in eights; 21 is two leaves folded round 21A, which is four leaves.

Pp. viii, 332. (i) Half-title, (ii) blank; (iii) title-page, (iv) *First published in* 1908; (v) dedicatory poem, *To Edmund Clerihew Bentley*, (vi) blank; vii–viii *Contents*; 9–(330) text, with *Printing Office of the Publisher* at the foot of p. (330); (331)–(332) advertisements.

Red glazed cloth. Front repeats, in black, lines 2 to 6 of the title-page, which are a reproduction of the author's hand-drawn title-page to the MS. Spine stamped in gilt: THE MAN / WHO WAS / THURSDAY / G. K CHESTERTON / J. W. ARROW-SMITH / BRISTOL

A. As above. BM 18 Mar. 08.

B. Foot of spine reads: ARROWSMITH / BRISTOL

C. Blue cloth. Spine lettered as B, but in black. This was probably a remainder binding.

Published in February 1908, at 6s. 4,000 copies.

A copy dated 1907 at the foot of the title-page and lacking the dedication was reported in *Desiderata* (July 1949). The publishers suggested that this might have been one of a small pilot edition printed in 1907 and put on the market as a guide to probable demand, as was then common practice. This advance issue was always regarded as part of the first edition proper.

A dramatised version by Mrs. Cecil Chesterton and Ralph Neale, with a Foreword by G. K. C., was published in 1926 (343).

12. ALL THINGS / CONSIDERED / BY / G. K. CHESTERTON / METHUEN & CO. / 36 ESSEX STREET W.C. / LONDON

$6\frac{3}{4} \times 4\frac{1}{8}$. [A] four leaves; B to T in eights; U four.

Pp. (2) + vi + 296. First leaf blank and unpaged; (i) half-title, (ii) blank; (iii) title-page, (iv) *First published in 1908*; v–vi *Contents*; 1–(296) text. Printer's imprint at foot of p. (296).

Dark-blue cloth stamped in gilt. Front: ALL THINGS / CON-SIDERED / G. K. CHESTERTON / Ruled border. Spine: ALL / THINGS / CONSIDERED / [*ornament*] / G. K. / CHESTERTON / [*ornamental design*] / METHUEN / Top edges gilt, tail rough trimmed.

Published September 10, 1908, at 5s. 2,000 copies. BM 23 Sep. 08.

Essays collected from the *Illustrated London News* with an introductory essay, *The Case for the Ephemeral*.

13. ORTHODOXY [*in a panel*] / BY / GILBERT K. CHESTERTON [*lines 2 and 3 within a panel*] / [*blank panel*] / LONDON: JOHN LANE, THE BODLEY HEAD / NEW YORK: JOHN LANE COMPANY. MCMIX [*sic*] [*lines 4 and 5 within a panel. The four panels within a single ruled border*]

$7\frac{1}{2} \times 4\frac{3}{4}$. [A] to T in eights.

Pp. x, 304. (i) Half-title, (ii) advertisement of *Heretics* and *The Napoleon of Notting Hill*; (iii) title-page, (iv) printer's imprint; (v) dedication, *To My Mother*, (vi) blank; vii Contents, (viii) blank; (ix) fly-title, (x) blank; 11–297 text, (298) blank; (299)–(304) advertisements. A four-page advertisement of the *Works of Anatole France* tipped in between pp. (298) and (299) is not included in the collation.

Light-green glazed cloth lettered in gilt. Front: ORTHODOXY / BY G · K · CHESTERTON / Treble-ruled blind border. Spine: ORTHODOXY / G · K · CHESTERTON / THE BODLEY HEAD / with a treble blind rule at head and tail. Back: treble-ruled blind border. Top edges gilt, others uncut.

A. As above. BM 4 Dec. 08.

B. All edges cut.

Published September 25, 1908, at 5s. 5,310 copies.

The American edition was also published in 1908, but whether before or after September 25 it has not been possible to discover. It is dated 1908 on the title-page and has a Preface by G. K. C.

14. VARIED TYPES [*in red*] / BY / G. K. CHESTERTON / AUTHOR OF / "THE DEFENDANT," ETC. / NEW YORK: [*in black*] DODD, MEAD / AND COMPANY [*in red*] / 1908 [*in black*] [*set across two vertical panels within a ruled border. Floral device in left-hand panel*]

$7\frac{1}{2} \times 4\frac{7}{8}$. No signatures.

Pp. (viii) + 272. (i) Half-title, (ii) blank; (iii) title-page, (iv) *Published September* 1908; (v) *Note* signed, G. K. C., (vi) blank; (vii) *Contents*; (viii) blank; (1)–(269) text, (270)–(272) blank. Portrait frontispiece.

Maroon ribbed cloth stamped in gilt. Front: VARIED TYPES / [*short rule*] / G. K. CHESTERTON Spine: VARIED / TYPES / [*short rule*] / CHESTERTON / DODD, MEAD / & COMPANY / Top edges gilt, others uncut.

Published in New York, September 1908.

This volume consists of *Twelve Types* with the addition of seven biographical essays from the *Daily News*, *Pall Mall Magazine* and *Westminster Review*:—*Bret Harte*, *Alfred the Great*, *Maeterlinck*, *The German Emperor*, *Queen Victoria*, *Tennyson* and *Elizabeth Barrett Browning*.

1909

15. GEORGE BERNARD / ::SHAW:: [*lines* 1 *and* 2 *within a panel*] / BY / GILBERT K. CHESTERTON [*lines* 3 *and* 4 *within a panel*] / [*blank panel*] / LONDON: JOHN LANE, THE BODLEY HEAD / NEW YORK; JOHN LANE COMPANY. MCMX [*sic*] [*lines* 5 *and* 6 *within a panel. The four panels within a single ruled border*]

$7\frac{5}{8} \times 4\frac{3}{4}$. A to Q in eights; R four leaves.

Pp. 264. (1) Half-title; (2) list of three books by the same author; (3) title-page, (4) printer's imprint; 5 *Introduction to the First Edition*, (6) blank; 7–11 *The Problem of a Preface*, (12) blank; 13 *Contents*, (14) blank; (15) fly-title, (16) blank; 17–(258) text; (259)–(264) advertisements. A four-page advertisement of the *Works of Anatole France* is tipped in between p. (264) and the endpaper.

Light-blue glazed cloth lettered in gilt. Front: GEORGE BERNARD SHAW / BY G · K · CHESTERTON / Treble ruled blind border. Spine: [*treble blind rule*] / GEORGE / BERNARD / SHAW / BY G. K. CHESTERTON / THE BODLEY HEAD / [*treble blind rule*] / Back: treble-ruled blind border. Top edges gilt, others trimmed.

A. As above. BM 24 Aug. 09.

B. Top edges gilt, others uncut.

Published August 24, 1909, at 5s. 5,000 copies.

The American edition, issued by the John Lane Company, New York, is dated 1909.

Some copies of the cheap edition, dated 1914, are to be found with a slip before the title-page which reads: This is Number . . . of the Souvenir Edition Presented by Kenelm Foss to commemorate the One Hundred and Fiftieth Performance of *Magic* by G. K. Chesterton and the Fiftieth Performance of *The Music Cure* by Bernard Shaw. (See 30.)

A new edition was issued in 1935 in Lane's *Week End Library* with an additional chapter, *The Later Phases*, "specially written for this edition 1935". This had appeared in the *New York Herald Tribune*, March 18, 1934, as *Second Thoughts on Shaw*.

"This book is what everybody expected it to be: the best work of literary art I have yet provoked."

G. BERNARD SHAW, *Nation*, August 25, 1909.

". . . a characteristic and brilliant commentary by G. K. Chesterton, which is the best book on Shaw that has been written and will probably be the best that will ever be written."

ST. JOHN ERVINE, *Bernard Shaw*, 1956, p. viii.

16. TREMENDOUS TRIFLES / BY / G. K. CHESTERTON / METHUEN & CO. / 36 ESSEX STREET W.C. / LONDON

6⅝ × 4⅛. [A] four leaves, B to S in eights.

Pp. viii + 272. (i) Half-title, (ii) list of two books by the same author; (iii) title-page, (iv) *First Published in* 1909; v–vi *Preface*; vii–viii *Contents*; 1–(272) text. Printer's imprint at foot of p. (272).

Light-red matt cloth stamped in gilt. Front: TREMENDOUS TRIFLES / G · K · CHESTERTON / Ruled border. Spine: TREMENDOUS / TRIFLES / [*ornament*] / G · K / CHESTERTON / [*arabesque design*] / METHUEN / Top edges gilt, others uncut.

Published September 23, 1909, at 5s. 2,000 copies. BM 24 Sep. 09.

Essays collected from the *Daily News*, with a Preface.

1910

17. THE BALL / AND / THE CROSS / BY / GILBERT K.
CHESTERTON / LONDON / WELLS GARDNER, DARTON &
CO., LTD. / 3 & 4, PATERNOSTER BUILDINGS, E.C. [*All
enclosed in a double ruled frame with a single horizontal rule below
line 5 and another above line 6*]

$8\frac{3}{4} \times 4\frac{7}{8}$. No signatures. Twenty-five gatherings of eight leaves
and one of six.

Pp. (viii) + 404. (i), (ii) Blank; (iii) half-title, (iv) blank; (v)
title-page, (vi) publisher's monogram with, below, *1910 /
Entered at Stationers' Hall, London, England / Copyright in the
United States by / John Lane Company*; (vii) Contents, (viii)
blank; 1–403 text, (404) blank.

The title-leaf (pp. (iii), (iv)) and the leaf (pp. 357–8) are cancels.
Erratum slip between pp. 92 and 93.

Green glazed cloth lettered in gilt. Front: THE · BALL / AND /
THE · CROSS / BY G · K · CHESTERTON / Blind ruled border.
Spine: THE · BALL / AND / THE · CROSS / G · K · CHESTERTON
/ WELLS · GARDNER, / DARTON · & · CO. LTD. / Blind rules at
head and tail. Back: blind-ruled border, publisher's monogram
blind-stamped in centre. Top edges gilt, others uncut.

A. As above.

B. The erratum slip is present but the title leaf and pp. 357–8
are not cancels.

Published February 24, 1910, at 6s.   First English edition.

Sheets of the American edition (published by the John Lane
Company, New York, in December 1909) were used for the
first English edition with the modifications noted. The copy in
the BM (December 6, 1909) was deposited three months before
the English publication. It has no erratum slip and no cancels.
The verso of the title-page (p. (vi)) reads: [*publisher's monogram*] /
*1909 / Copyright 1906, by / Joseph W. Darton / Entered at
Stationers' Hall, London, England. / Copyright, 1909, by / John
Lane Company. / Printed at the Trow Press, New York, U.S.A.*

P. 93 has the misprint (line 6) "healthy working man" for
"healthy-looking man" which is corrected by the erratum slip
in the English edition.

The Donkey. —

When fishes flew and forests walked
And figs grew upon thorn
Some moment when the moon was blood
Then surely I was born.

With monstrous head and sickening cry
And ears like errant wings
The devil's walking parody
On all four-footed things.

The tattered outlaw of the earth
Of ancient crooked will:
Starve, scourge, deride me: I am dumb
I keep my secret still.

Fools! for I also had my hour,
One far fierce hour & sweet
There was a shout about my ears
And palms before my feet.

MS. *The Donkey*. Written *c.* 1894. Published in *The Wild Knight*, 1900

P. 358, line 18, reads: "But God blast my soul and body" which, in the English edition, A and B, reads: "But Lord bless us and save us . . ."

Serialised in part in *Commonwealth*, 1905–6.

18. WHAT'S WRONG / WITH THE WORLD / by g. k. chesterton / cassell and company, limited / london, new york, toronto & melbourne / 1910 [*the whole enclosed in a thick and thin ruled border*]

7⅞ × 5. [A] four leaves, B to S in eights, T four.

Pp. viii + 296. (i) Half-title, (ii) blank; (iii) title-page, (iv) reservation of rights; (v)–vi Dedication, *To C. F. G. Masterman, M.P.*; vii–viii *Contents*; (1)–(293) text; (294)–(296) blank. Printer's imprint at foot of p. (293).

Red glazed cloth stamped in gilt. Front: what's wrong / with the world / g. k. chesterton / [*ornamental query*] / Spine: what's / wrong / with the / world / g. k. / chesterton / [*ornamental query*] / cassell / Back plain. Top edges gilt.

Published in June 1910, at 6s. 1,500 copies. BM 16 Aug. 10.

Miss Maisie Ward, in *Gilbert Keith Chesterton* (782), states that both the change of title (from the projected *What's Wrong?*) and the omission of the note of interrogation were the acts of the publishers. If this were so, it is at least odd that the note of interrogation, although omitted from the title-page, appears on both the front cover and the spine. The publishers, whose records were destroyed during the war, are unable to throw any light on this. G. K. C. himself, in the Dedication (p. (v)), says, 'I originally called this book "What is Wrong".' Later editions have no mark of interrogation anywhere.

19. THE GLORY OF GREY / by g. k. chesterton

11⅝ × 9. One gathering of four leaves.

Pp. [8.] [1]–[7] text; [8] blank. There is no title-page.

Dark-grey stiff paper wrappers printed in black on front as above. Sewn.

Colophon, p. (7): "Set in type by W. H. N. West, a student at
St. Bride Foundation Practical Printing Classes, and reprinted
by kind permission of G. K. Chesterton, Esq., from *The Daily
News* of September 3, 1910. Blocks designed by students of
L.C.C. School of Photo-engraving."

Issued in 1910.

The British Museum copy is dated October 16, 1912. The
colophon has "Wm. West" and 'reprinted from "Alarums
[*sic*] and Discursions" by kind permission of Mr. G. K. Chesterton, & Messrs. Methuen & Co., Ltd. . . .'

20. ALARMS AND / DISCURSIONS / BY / G. K. CHESTERTON
/ METHUEN & CO. LTD. / 36 ESSEX STREET W.C. / LONDON
$6\frac{5}{8} + 4\frac{1}{8}$. A single leaf, unsigned, [A] two leaves, B to R in
eights, S two.

Pp. vi + 260. (i) Half-title, (ii) list of three books by the same
author; (iii) title-page, (iv) *First published in* 1910; v–vi *Contents*;
1–(260) text. Printer's imprint at foot of p. (260).

Light-red matt cloth stamped in gilt. Front: ALARMS
AND DISCURSIONS / G · K · CHESTERTON / Ruled border.
Spine: ALARMS / AND / DISCURSIONS / [*ornament*] / G · K /
CHESTERTON / [*arabesque design*] / METHUEN / Top edges gilt,
fore edges rough trimmed, tail uncut.

Published November 3, 1910, at 5s. 2,500 copies. BM 4 Nov. 10.

Essays collected from the *Daily News*.

The American edition, published in 1911 by Dodd, Mead, has
an additional essay at the beginning, *The Fading Fireworks*.

21. WILLIAM BLAKE [*in red*] / BY / G. K. CHESTERTON /
AUTHOR OF "ROBERT BROWNING", ETC. / [*leaf ornament
in red*] / LONDON: [*in black*] DUCKWORTH & CO. [*in red*] /
NEW YORK [*in red*] E. P. DUTTON & CO. [*in black*]

$5\frac{7}{8} \times 3\frac{3}{4}$. An unsigned gathering of four leaves, bA to bN in
eights; bO is two leaves.

Pp. viii + 212. (i) *The Popular Library of Art*, (ii) list of the
series; (iii) blank, (iv) coloured frontispiece, *From "Songs of*

Innocence" 1789; (v) title-page, (vi) printer's imprint; vii–viii
list of illustrations; 1–210 text and illustrations; (211)–(212)
advertisements. The frontispiece and the thirty-one full-page
illustrations, versos blank, are included in the collation.

Dark-green grained cloth stamped in gilt. Front: BLAKE /
[*publisher's device*]. Spine: BLAKE / [*ornament*] / G. K. / CHES-
TERTON / [*ornament*] / [*ornament*] / DUCKWORTH / Back: publisher's device blind-stamped in bottom left-hand corner. Top
edges gilt.

Published in November 1910, at 2s.

A. As above.

B. Smooth red cloth. Half-title reads: *The Popular Library of Art.
Edited by Edward Garnett.*

C. Rough red cloth. Top edges plain. Otherwise as A.

D. Light brown paper boards. Spine stamped in dark brown, no
publisher's device on back. Top edges dark brown.

E. As D, but top edges plain.

I have no evidence of priority and the publisher's records before
1914 no longer exist. D and E, in the cheaper binding, are
probably later issues.

21x. THE ULTIMATE LIE / BY / G. K. CHESTERTON / "***
VERY HANDY TO DRAW AS / A GUN ON THE ULTIMATE
LIAR." / — LINCOLN STEFFENS. / PRIVATELY PRINTED AT
HILLACRE / RIVERSIDE, CONN. / 1910

6⅛ × 3⅞. One gathering of four leaves.

Pp. 8, unpaged. (1) Title-page, (2) *At the Suggestion of Mr.
Lincoln Steffens / A Few Copies of This Brief Essay Have Been /
Printed At The Hillacre Book House For / Private Distribution/*;
(3)–(5) text, with at foot of p. (5), *The London News*; (6)–(8)
blank.

Stiff brown wrappers. On front wrapper a white label lettered
THE ULTIMATE LIE / BY / G. K. CHESTERTON [*all within a
single red ruled frame*]. Sewn.

Issued in 1910.

The note on p. (5) refers to the *Daily News* (July 3, 1909).

1911

22. A CHESTERTON / CALENDAR : : / COMPILED FROM
THE WRITINGS OF / 'G.K.C.' BOTH IN VERSE AND IN /
PROSE. WITH A SECTION APART FOR / THE MOVEABLE
FEASTS. / KEGAN PAUL, TRENCH, TRÜBNER & CO. LTD. /
DRYDEN HOUSE, GERRARD STREET, LONDON, W. 1911
[*lines 1 and 2 in red and underlined in red*]

$8 \times 5\frac{1}{2}$. An unsigned gathering of four leaves, B–Z and 2A to
2D in eights; 2E is four leaves.

Pp. (vi) + 424. (i) Half-title, (ii) blank; (iii) title-page, (iv) blank;
(v) *Prefatory Note,* (vi) blank; (vii) *January,* (viii) quotation
from *Orthodoxy*; 1–421 text, (422)–(423) blank, (424) printer's
imprint.

Light-grey cloth stamped in gilt. Front: A / CHESTERTON /
CALENDAR / [*sundial ornament*]. Narrow ribbon border. Spine:
[*ornament*] / A / CHESTERTON / CALENDAR / [*ribbon ornament*] /
KEGAN PAUL / TRENCH, TRUBNER & CO. / [*ornament*] / Top
edges gilt, others uncut.

Published in January 1911, at 5s.

A. As above. BM 20 Jan. 11.

B. Dark-blue cloth. Front blind-stamped: [*ornament*] A [*ornament*] / CHESTERTON / CALENDAR / [*sundial ornament*]. Ruled
border. Spine stamped in gilt: [*rule*] / CHESTERTON / DAY
/ BY / DAY / KEGAN PAUL / [*rule*] / Top edges plain, others
uncut.

"The present publishers feel they are peculiarly indebted to Mr.
Chesterton himself for his kindness in allowing them to include
certain verses from poems which have not yet been printed *in
extenso* elsewhere." Prefatory Note, p. (v).

Some of the prose also appears here in book form for the first
time. The following is a record of such items:

VERSE Pp. 6–7. *The Wise Men.* From the *Daily News.* Collected in 1915 in *Poems* (37) with two additional verses.

P. 67. *The Seven Swords.* This is the first (and only?) appearance.
St. David in *The Queen of Seven Swords,* 1926, (65) is a much
altered version.

Pp. 91, 253, 320, 409, 411 and 420. Extracts from *Ballad of Alfred* which appeared later in the year, August 1911, as *The Ballad of the White Horse* (25).

P. 133. *The Silent People.* The closing lines of *The Secret People* which, with several textual changes, appeared in 1915 in *Poems* (37).

P. 193. *Ballad of the Sun*, p. 208. *Translation from Du Bellay*, p. 397. *The Truce of Christmas*, and p. 399 *The House of Christmas* were collected in 1915 in *Poems* (37).

PROSE. Passages on pp. 1, 116, 129, 217, 289, 316, 326, 327, 329, 348, 349, 363, 366 and 421 from the *Daily News*.

Pp. 114, 119, 158, 173, 275 and 290 from the *Illustrated London News*.

P. 345 from the *Observer*.

The source is not given of two poems which had already appeared in *The Wild Knight*, 1900: p. 153 *To Them that Mourn* (the first and the last two verses only) and p. 282 *The Skeleton*.

The variant title, *Chesterton Day by Day*, which appears on the spine of B, is used on both title-page and spine of the second edition, 1912.

The American edition, published by Dodd, Mead and Co., New York, 1911, is entitled *Wit and Wisdom of G. K. Chesterton* and omits the section *The Moveable Feasts*. It was advertised (in *The Appetite of Tyranny* (see 33)) as "Selected and arranged by his wife", but there is no statement to this effect in the book itself.

23. APPRECIATIONS [*in red*] AND / CRITICISMS OF THE WORKS / OF [*in black*] CHARLES DICKENS [*in red*] / BY / G. K. CHESTERTON / [*publisher's device*] / 1911 [*in black*] / LONDON: J. M. DENT & SONS, LTD. [*in red*] / NEW YORK: E. P. DUTTON & CO. [*in black*]

$8\frac{9}{16} \times 5\frac{1}{2}$. Five unsigned gatherings, then 4 to 7, two unsigned, and 10 to 14 in eights; 15 is two and 16 is eight leaves. Gathering 15 is folded round 16 and the signature of 16 is on the recto of the last leaf of that gathering (p. 241).

Pp. (2) + xxx + 244. Fly leaf blank and not included in the

pagination; (i) title-page, (ii) *All rights reserved*; iii–iv *Contents*; (v) *Illustrations*, (vi) blank; vii–xxx *Introduction*; 1–243 text, (244) blank.

The frontispiece and seven plates with protective tissues are not included in the collation.

Dark-green, finely-ribbed cloth. Publisher's device and ruled border blind-stamped on front. Spine stamped in gilt: CRITICISMS / AND / APPRECIATIONS / OF / CHARLES DICKENS' / WORKS / [*ornament*] / G. K. CHESTERTON / J. M. DENT & SONS · LD / Top edges gilt, others uncut. Light-green, narrow ribbon bookmark attached.

A. As above.   BM 24 Feb. 11.

B. Top edges green, others trimmed.

Published in February 1911, at 7s. 6d. 2,500 copies.

These critical essays originally appeared separately as introductions to the works of Dickens in the *Everyman Library*. (The introduction to *The Uncommercial Traveller*, which appeared in *Everyman* later in the year, is not included.) They are here collected with a long Introduction.

The title on the spine differs from that on the title-page and the heading to the Introduction repeats the inversion: CRITICISMS AND APPRECIATIONS.

The American edition, published by E. P. Dutton & Co., New York, 1911, has APPRECIATIONS AND CRITICISMS OF THE WORKS OF CHARLES DICKENS on title-page, front cover and spine, but CRITICISMS AND APPRECIATIONS above the Introduction (p. vii). Nine of the Introductions (Nos. 221, 224, and 227–233) were issued separately from Dickens' text and from one another, by E. P. Dutton & Co., New York, in 1907, to secure American copyright. Blue-grey paper wrappers lettered on front in this form: INTRODUCTION / TO THE / OLD CURIOSITY SHOP / BY / G. K. CHESTERTON / NEW YORK / E. P. DUTTON & COMPANY / 31 WEST TWENTY-THIRD STREET / 1907 / Stapled.

Re-issued by Dent in 1933 (1,000 copies), as CRITICISMS AND APPRECIATIONS, with a note: "First published in 1911 under the title 'Appreciations and Criticisms'. First published in this edition 1933."

24. THE INNOCENCE / OF / FATHER BROWN / BY /
G. K. CHESTERTON / WITH EIGHT FULL-PAGE PLATES BY /
SIDNEY SEYMOUR LUCAS / CASSELL AND COMPANY, LTD. /
LONDON, NEW YORK, TORONTO AND MELBOURNE / 1911
$7\frac{1}{2} \times 4\frac{3}{4}$. A four leaves, B–V in eights.

Pp. (viii) + 336. (i) Title-page, (ii) *All rights reserved*; (iii) dedication *To Waldo and Mildred D'Avigdor*, (iv) blank; (v) *Contents*, (vi) blank; (vii) *List of plates*, (viii) blank; 1–(336) text. Printer's imprint at foot of p. (336). The frontispiece, with protective tissue, and seven plates are on art paper and tipped in.

Bright-red cloth stamped in gilt. Front: THE INNOCENCE OF / FATHER BROWN / G. K. CHESTERTON / Blind ruled border. Spine: THE / INNOCENCE / OF / FATHER / BROWN / G. K. / CHESTERTON / CASSELL

Published in July 1911, at 6s. 5,000 copies.

Collected from *Cassell's Magazine* and the *Storyteller*.

The American edition, issued by the John Lane Co., N.Y., 1911, has illustrations by Will F. Foster.

25. THE BALLAD OF / THE WHITE HORSE / BY / G. K.
CHESTERTON / "I SAY, AS DO ALL CHRISTIAN MEN, THAT
IT IS A DIVINE / PURPOSE THAT RULES, AND NOT FATE." /
KING ALFRED'S ADDITION TO "BOETHIUS" / METHUEN
& CO. LTD. / 36 ESSEX STREET W.C. / LONDON
$6\frac{3}{4} \times 4\frac{1}{4}$. An unsigned gathering of eight leaves, b is two; 1 to 11 in eights; 12 is four leaves.

Pp. xx + 184. (i) Half-title, (ii) list of four books by the same author; (iii) title-page, (iv) *First Published in* 1911; v–viii *Prefatory Note*; ix *Contents*, (x) blank; (xi) Dedication, *To My Wife*, (xii) blank; xiii–xviii dedicatory poem; (xix) fly-title; (xx) blank; (1)–182 text; (183) blank, (184) printer's imprint.

Glazed olive-green cloth stamped in gilt. Front: THE BALLAD OF / THE WHITE HORSE / G. K. CHESTERTON / Ruled border. Spine: [*thick and thin rule*] / THE / BALLAD / OF THE / WHITE / HORSE / G. K. / CHESTERTON / [*crown and rose ornament*] / METHUEN / [*thin and thick rule*] / Top edges gilt, others uncut

Published August 31, 1911, at 5s. 1,500 copies. BM 31 Aug. 11.

The tenth edition, October 1928, was illustrated by Robert Austin, and of this, 100 numbered copies, printed on hand-made paper and signed by the author, were issued at £2 2s.

26. THE FUTURE OF RELIGION / MR. G. K. CHESTERTON'S / REPLY TO / MR. BERNARD SHAW. / (REPRINTED FOR THE HERETICS) / PRICE SIXPENCE

$7\frac{1}{2} \times 4\frac{1}{3}$. One gathering of twelve leaves.

Pp. 24. (1)–23 Text, (24) blank. There is no title-page.

Pale green paper wrappers. Front printed as above. Stapled.

Published late November, or December 1911.

Reprints from the *Cambridge Daily News* of November 18, 1911, a report headed "G. K. C. on G. B. S." of a lecture by G. K. C. to The Heretics on November 17, 1911, together with some preliminary and consequential material. The lecture followed one given to the same society by Bernard Shaw on May 29, 1911, and published in similar format as *The Religion of the Future*.

1912

27. MANALIVE / BY G. K. CHESTERTON / [*thin rule*] / [*ornament*] / [*thin rule*] / THOMAS NELSON AND SONS / LONDON, EDINBURGH, DUBLIN / LEEDS, AND NEW YORK / LEIPZIG: 35–37 KÖNIGSTRASSE. PARIS: 189, RUE SAINT-JACQUES [*double ruled border*]

$7\frac{3}{16} \times 4\frac{3}{4}$. [1]–12 in sixteens.

Pp. vi, 384. (i) Title-page, (ii) *First published in* 1912; (iii)–iv *Contents*; (v) fly-title, (vi) blank; (7)–383 text, (384) blank. Coloured frontispiece by Dudley Tennant tipped in.

Fine-ribbed, dark-blue cloth. Front blind-stamped MANALIVE / G. K. CHESTERTON in a panel with decorated border with publisher's initial, N, at foot. Spine lettered in gilt: MAN- / ALIVE / G. K. / CHESTERTON / [*blind decoration*] / NELSON / Green decorated endpapers.

Published in February 1912, in "Nelson's New Two-shilling Novels".

A. As above. BM 6 June 12.

B. Green cloth, plain endpapers.

The publisher's records were destroyed in the war and the number of copies printed is now unknown, but they state that the size of the editions in this series was "very large". When war broke out in 1914 it became difficult to obtain supplies of blue cloth and the remaining sheets of *Manalive* were bound in green cloth with plain endpapers. Thus, B is probably late 1914 or later. The American edition, New York, John Lane Company, 1912, has a frontispiece by Will F. Foster.

28. A MISCELLANY / OF MEN / BY / G. K. CHESTERTON / METHUEN & CO. LTD. / 36 ESSEX STREET W.C. / LONDON 6⅝ × 5. An unsigned gathering of four leaves, 1–16 in eights; 17 is six leaves.

Pp. viii + 268. (i), (ii) Blank; (iii) half-title, (iv) list of four books by the same author; (v) title-page, (vi) *First published in* 1912; (vii)–viii *Contents*; (1)–267 text, (268) printer's imprint. Following p. (268) is an eight-page catalogue, dated July 1912, in which this book is advertised as forthcoming under the title *Types of Men*.

Dark-blue matt cloth stamped in gilt. Front: A MISCELLANY OF MEN / G. K. CHESTERTON / Ruled border. Spine: A / MISCELLANY / OF MEN / [*trefoil ornament*] / G · K / CHESTERTON / [*arabesque design*] / METHUEN / Top edges gilt, fore-edges rough-trimmed, tail uncut.

Published October 10, 1912, at 5s. 2,000 copies. BM 11 Oct. 12.

Essays collected from the *Daily News*.

The American edition, New York, Dodd, Mead, 1912, has a *Preface* and an additional essay, *The Suffragist*.

1913

29. THE / VICTORIAN AGE / IN LITERATURE / BY / G. K. CHESTERTON / LONDON / WILLIAMS AND NORGATE [*lines 1–5 between the columns, 6–7 in the base of a portico border*] 6½ × 4. [A]–Q in eights.

Pp. v, 256. (i) Half-title, (ii) title of the series in portico border with NEW YORK / HENRY HOLT AND COMPANY in the base; (iii) title-page, (iv) printer's imprint; v *Contents*, vi *Editorial Note*; 7–251 text, (252) blank; 253–4 *Bibliographical Note*;

255–6 *Index*. Printer's imprint at foot of p. 256. An eight-page catalogue of the Home University Library following p. 256 is not included in the collation.

Light-green vertical-ribbed diaper cloth. Front blind-stamped with publisher's monogram in a small circle (*left*) and HOME / UNIVERSITY / LIBRARY in a small rectangle (*right*), both in a panel made by a rule joining the sides of a ruled border. Spine stamped in gilt: [*double rule*] / THE / VICTORIAN / AGE IN / LITERATURE / [*short rule*] / G. K. / CHESTERTON / [*double rule*] / [*single rule*] / WILLIAMS / & NORGATE / [*double rule*] / Top edges green.

Published *undated* as No. 70 in the Home University Library in February 1913, at 1s. (cloth) and 2s. 6d. (leather).

A. As above. BM 8 July 13.

B. Leather gilt.

C. Dark-green cloth.

The catalogue lists fifty-nine books in the Home University Library and advertises this book, under the title of *The Victorian Age*, as in preparation. Neither here nor anywhere else in the book is it given its number (70) in the series. Later advertisements give the number, and some add extracts from reviews.

An edition in larger format bound in red cloth, with a portrait frontispiece, was published in August 1925.

30. MAGIC / A FANTASTIC COMEDY / BY / G. K. CHESTERTON / LONDON / MARTIN SECKER / NUMBER FIVE JOHN STREET / ADELPHI

$6\frac{3}{4} \times 5\frac{1}{16}$. [A]–E in eights.

Pp. 80. (1) Half-title, (2) advertisement of *Thompson* by St. John Hankin and George Calderon; (3) title-page, (4) printer's imprint; (5) *The Characters*, (6) blank; (7) Note on the presentation of the play at the Little Theatre, London, on November 7, 1913, with a list of the cast, (8) blank; 9–72 text, printer's imprint at foot of p. 72; (73)–(80) advertisements.

A. Oatmeal wrappers printed in black. Front: MAGIC / BY [*silhouette of G. K. C. running down right-hand side from above line 1 to below line 6*] / A FANTASTIC COMEDY / IN A PRELUDE

AND / THREE ACTS / MR. G. K. CHESTERTON'S FIRST PLAY / PRICE ONE SHILLING NET / Ruled border. Spine, reading downwards: MAGIC : A FANTASTIC COMEDY G. K. CHESTERTON / Back: advertisement of SOME AUTUMN BOOKS. Insides of wrappers blank.

B. Blue cloth. Front and back blank. White paper label on spine printed in black reading downwards MAGIC / A FANTASTIC COMEDY / G. K. CHESTERTON / Line 2 is above line 3.

Published November 7, 1913, at 1s. (wrappers) and 2s. (cloth). BM 26 Nov. 13.

The sixth impression, 1914, is illustrated with photographs of the production. Some copies have a slip inserted announcing the Souvenir Edition presented by Kenelm Foss. (See 15.) (Both books of the Souvenir Edition, *George Bernard Shaw* and *Magic*, each bound in blue-grey boards with unbleached linen spine and paper label are enclosed in a blue-grey stiff paper cover with clasp.)

An edition of 150 copies printed on large Japon paper and signed by the author was published in September 1920 at 21s.

1914

31. THE FLYING INN / BY / G. K. CHESTERTON / METHUEN & CO. LTD. / 36 ESSEX STREET W.C. / LONDON

$7 \times 4\frac{3}{4}$. A four, B to U in eights.

Pp. viii + 304. (i) Half-title, (ii) list of six books by the same author; (iii) title-page, (iv) *First Published in 1914*; (v) dedication, *To Hugh Rivière*, (vi) blank; vii *Contents*, (viii) blank; 1–301 text, (302) printer's imprint; (303), (304) blank. Eight pages of advertisements of Methuen's Popular Novels, dated Autumn 1913, and 31 pages of a general catalogue, dated September 1913, are not included in the collation. The latter advertises this book as "in the Press" (p. 26).

Fine-grained red cloth blind-stamped on front: THE FLYING INN / G. K. CHESTERTON / Ruled border. Spine stamped in gilt: THE / FLYING / INN [*ornament*] G. K. / CHESTERTON / [*all within a classical portico*] METHUEN [*within a ruled frame*]. Tail rough-trimmed.

Published January 22, 1914, at 6s. 3,000 copies. BM 15 Jan. 14.

The songs in this book had already appeared in *The New Witness* (545) and were later published separately with one addition as *Wine, Water and Song* (38).

32. THE WISDOM OF / FATHER BROWN / BY / G. K. CHESTERTON / WITH A COLOUR FRONTISPIECE BY / SIDNEY SEYMOUR LUCAS / CASSELL AND COMPANY, LTD / LONDON, NEW YORK, TORONTO AND MELBOURNE / 1914

$7\frac{1}{2} \times 4\frac{7}{8}$. [A] four leaves, B to T in eights, U four.

Pp. (viii) + 312. (i) Half-title, (ii) blank; (iii) title-page, (iv) blank; (v) dedication, *To Lucian Oldershaw*, (vi) blank; (vii) *Contents*, (viii) blank; 1–(312) text. Printer's imprint at foot of p. (312).

Dark-blue cloth. Front blind-stamped: THE WISDOM OF / FATHER BROWN / G. K. CHESTERTON / Ruled border. Spine stamped in gilt: THE / WISDOM / OF / FATHER / BROWN / G. K. / CHESTERTON / CASSELL / Coloured frontispiece with protective tissue.

Published in October 1914, at 6s. 2,800 copies.

A. As described. BM 4 Nov. 14.

B. Light-blue cloth.

There were also a "Colonial Edition" of 1,300 copies at 3s. 6d., a "Canadian Edition" of 199 copies at 50 cents, and a cheap edition of 658 copies at 2s., making a total first impression of 4,957 copies.

Collected from the *Pall Mall Magazine*.

The Contents (p. vii) has a dropped numeral in the last line: "2" for "12".

33. THE / BARBARISM OF BERLIN / BY / G. K. CHESTERTON / [*leaf ornament*] / CASSELL AND COMPANY, LTD / LONDON, NEW YORK, TORONTO AND MELBOURNE

$6\frac{7}{16} \times 4\frac{9}{16}$. [A]–F in eights.

Pp. 96. (1) Half-title, (2) blank; (3) title-page, (4) *First Published 1914*; (5) *Contents*, (6) blank; 7–(95) text, (96) printer's imprint and F150. 1114.

Red paper wrappers lettered in black. Front: THE / BARBARISM / OF BERLIN / [*imperial German eagle within a circle*] / G. K. CHESTERTON / Spine, reading upwards: THE BARBARISM OF BERLIN G. K. CHESTERTON with 6D / NET at the foot, horizontally. Back: advertisements. Inside front and back wrappers blank.

Published in November 1914, at 6d. 15,000 copies. BM 3 Dec. 14.

This book appeared before publication as articles in the *Daily Mail* in October and November 1914.

The Appetite of Tyranny, published by Dodd, Mead and Co., New York, 1915, takes its title from section III of *The Barbarism of Berlin* and consists of this volume together with *Letters to an Old Garibaldian*.

34. LONDON / BY / G. K. CHESTERTON / WITH TEN PHOTO-GRAPHS BY / ALVIN LANGDON COBURN / [*ornament*] / LONDON: PRIVATELY PRINTED FOR / ALVIN LANGDON COBURN AND / EDMUND D. BROOKS & THEIR FRIENDS / 1914

$8\frac{1}{2} \times 5\frac{7}{8}$. A–E in eights.

Pp. 40. (1), (2) blank; (3) half-title, (4) blank; (5) title-page, (6) blank; 7–15 text, (16) blank; (17) *Plates*, (18) blank; 19 *List of illustrations*, (20) blank; (21)–(39) illustrations, consisting of ten photographs numbered I–X mounted on the rectos (pp. (21), (23) . . . (39)) with versos (pp. (22) (24) . . . (38)) blank; (40) printer's imprint. All edges uncut.

Grey paper boards, canvas spine. Front printed in black: LONDON / BY / G. K. CHESTERTON / WITH TEN PHOTO-GRAPHS BY / ALVIN LANGDON COBURN / [*ornament*] / Flat spine printed in black, reading upwards: LONDON /

The American edition has MINNEAPOLIS on the title-page between "friends" and "1914", and a photograph of Mr. and Mrs. Chesterton with Mr. Brooks as frontispiece.

This book also appeared in the United States without the photographs: LONDON / BY / G. K. CHESTERTON / PRIVATELY PRINTED / MINNEAPOLIS / 1914. Pp. 12. Brown paper wrappers. Stapled.

35. "EVERYMAN" BELGIAN RELIEF PAMPHLETS.—NO. 4 /
"EVERYMAN" [*so far in red*] / BELGIAN RELIEF AND [*black*] /
RECONSTRUCTION FUND [*black*] / [*double rule in red*] /
PRUSSIAN VERSUS [*black*] / BELGIAN CULTURE
[*black*] / [*double rule in red*] / BY [*black*] / G. K. CHESTERTON
[*red*] / [*black rule*] / ONE PENNY [*black*] / [*black rule*] / —ALL
DONATIONS IN MONEY SHOULD BE SENT TO—[*red*] / THE
TREASURER, 21 ROYAL TERRACE, EDINBURGH [*red*] [*all
after line 1, enclosed in a thick and thin border in black*]
$8\frac{3}{8} \times 5$. One gathering of six leaves. Stapled.

Pp. 12. (1) front wrapper, as above, (2) blank; (3)–8 text; (9)–
(10) advertisements; (11)–(12) blank.

Published by *Everyman* in 1914, at 1*d*.

Reprinted from *Everyman*.

1915

36. LETTERS TO AN / OLD GARIBALDIAN / BY / G. K.
CHESTERTON / METHUEN & CO. LTD. / 36 ESSEX STREET
W.C. / LONDON

$7 \times 4\frac{3}{4}$. [A]–C in eights.

Pp. 48. (1) Half-title, (2) blank; (3) title-page, (4) *First Published
in* 1915; (5) quotation from Swinburne, (6) blank; 7–48 text.
Printer's imprint on p. 48.

Light-blue paper wrappers lettered in dark blue. Front:
LETTERS TO AN / OLD GARIBALDIAN / BY / G. K. CHESTER-
TON / METHUEN & CO. LTD. LONDON / THREEPENCE NET /
Lines 1–5 enclosed in a double-ruled border with horizontal
double rules between lines 2 and 3 and between lines 4 and 5.
Back: advertisements.

Published January 7, 1915, at 3*d*. 4,000 copies. BM 31 Dec. 14.

Included in *The Appetite of Tyranny*, New York, 1914 (see 33).

37. POEMS / BY GILBERT KEITH / CHESTERTON / [*ornament*] /
BURNS & OATES, LTD. / 28 ORCHARD STREET / LONDON,
W. / 1915

$6\frac{5}{8} \times 4\frac{1}{2}$. A four leaves, B to K in eights, L four, M eight.

Pp. viii + 168. (i) Half-title, (ii) blank; (iii) title-page, (iv)
blank; v–vii *Contents*, viii *Author's Note*; (1)–156 text; (157)

colophon, (158) blank; (159)–(166) advertisements; (167), (168) blank. Portrait frontispiece on heavy paper with protective tissue not included in the pagination.

Light-red cloth stamped in gilt. Front: POEMS / G. K. CHESTERTON / [ornament]. Ornamental border. Spine: [ornamental rule] / POEMS / BY G. K. / CHESTER- / TON / [ornament] / BURNS & / OATES LTD. / [ornamental rule] / Top edges gilt, others uncut.

Published in April 1915, at 5s. 2,000 copies. BM 30 Apr. 15.

Collected from the *Acorn, Commonwealth, Daily Herald, Daily News, Eye-Witness, Nation, New Witness, Occasional Papers, Odd Volume, Pall Mall Magazine, Parents' Review, Speaker, A Volunteer Haversack* (201A), *The English Hymnal* (220), *The Man Who Was Thursday* (dedication) (11) and *The Napoleon of Notting Hill* (dedication) (7). Most of the Love Poems appear in print for the first time.

The poem *An Election Echo 1906*, p. 113, first appeared in the *Speaker* in 1900 (558). The mis-dating, 1906, is repeated in *Collected Poems* (69).

38. WINE, WATER / AND SONG / BY / G. K. CHESTERTON / METHUEN & CO. LTD. / 36 ESSEX STREET W.C. / LONDON
6⅝ × 4¼. [A] to D in eights.

Pp. 64. (1) Half-title, (2) list of seven books by the same author; (3) title-page, (4) *First published in 1915*; (5) *Note*, (6) blank; 7 *Contents*, (8) blank; 9–(64) text. Printer's imprint at foot of p. (64).

Orange wrappers with overlaps and orange end-papers. Front lettered in black: WINE / WATER / AND SONG / POEMS BY / G. K. CHESTERTON / [wreath ornament] / LONDON / METHUEN & CO. LTD / Border of one thick and two thin rules. At foot, below border, ONE SHILLING NET. Spine, reading downwards: WINE, WATER AND SONG BY G. K. CHESTER-TON / Back: advertisement of SOME DELIGHTFUL BOOKS BY G. K. CHESTERTON. Fore and tail edges uncut.

A. As above. BM 5 Aug. 15.
B. Parchment vellum.
Published August 6, 1915, at 1s. 2,000 copies.

The Note on p. (5) says that the songs in this book are taken from *The Flying Inn* with the exception of *The Good Rich Man* and *The Song of the Strange Ascetic*. In fact, the former song had appeared in *The Flying Inn* and only the latter now appears in book form for the first time. It had, however, appeared originally in the *New Witness* like the others. This mistake in the Note is corrected in later editions.

The 17th edition, 1943, is illustrated by Sillince, and has an Introduction by L. A. G. Strong.

38X. SEARCHLIGHTS NO. 22 / [*thick and thin rules*] / THE SO-CALLED BELGIUM BARGAIN / G. K. CHESTERTON / [*rule*] / [34 *lines of text*] / [*thick and thin rules*] / NATIONAL WAR AIMS COMMITTEE / DISTRIBUTED BY W. H. SMITH AND SON, LONDON: / BY JOHN MENZIES AND CO., LTD., EDINBURGH.

$8\frac{3}{8} \times 3\frac{3}{4}$. A folded leaf.

Pp. 4, unpaged. (1) as above, (2)–(4) text continued. Footnote on p. (4); *Reprinted from* The Illustrated London News.

Issued, *undated*, in 1915.

39. SPECIALLY WRITTEN FOR / "OUR DAY" / OCTOBER 21ST, 1915. / [*short double rule*] / A POEM / [*red cross*] / BY / G. K. CHESTERTON. / [*ornament*] / IN AID OF THE BRITISH RED CROSS AND ST. / JOHN OF JERUSALEM'S FUND FOR OUR SICK AND / WOUNDED SAILORS AND SOLDIERS AT THE FRONT

$7\frac{3}{4} \times 5$. A single folded leaf.

Pp. 4. (1) as above, (2)–(3) text of poem, "Under the Farm of all the winds . . ." (no title), (4) blank.

Published October 21, 1915. Price unknown.

Also published in the *Daily Telegraph* on the same day.

40. THE CRIMES / OF ENGLAND / BY / G. K. CHESTERTON / AUTHOR OF 'HERETICS', 'ORTHODOXY', / 'WHAT'S WRONG WITH THE WORLD', / ETC. / [*publisher's monogram*] / LONDON / CECIL PALMER & HAYWARD / OAKLEY HOUSE, BLOOMSBURY STREET

Frances,

Xmas. 1900.

—

Dearest: whatever others see
Herein, it is no mystery—
That I find all the world is good
Since you are all the world to me.

You will not blame my boastful hours,
It is not of such souls as yours
To spew the wrath of sorrow out
Upon the harmless grass & flowers

Do you fight on for all the press,
Wise as you are, you cannot guess
How I shall flame before God's Knights
The triumph of my own princess.

Almost this day of the strange star
We know the bonfire old & far
Whence all the stars as sparks are blown
Piled up to warm us after war

Inscription in a copy of *The Wild Knight* presented by
G. K. Chesterton to his fiancée, 1900

$7\frac{3}{8} \times 4\frac{5}{8}$. [A–H] in eights.

Pp. 128. (1) Half-title, (2) blank; (3) title-page, (4) *First Published* . . . 1915; printer's imprint; 5–7 *Contents*, (8) blank; 9–126 text; 127 *Note on the word "English"*, (128) blank.

A. Grey wrappers printed in black. Front: THE / CRIMES / OF / ENGLAND / BY G. K. / CHESTERTON / [*dot*] / ONE SHILLING / NET / [*publisher's monogram*] / LONDON: / CECIL PALMER & HAYWARD / Ruled border. Spine, running downwards: THE CRIMES OF ENGLAND: G. K. CHESTERTON / At foot, horizontally, 1/- / NET /

B. Crimson cloth. Front stamped in gilt: THE CRIMES OF ENGLAND / BY G. K. CHESTERTON / [*Tudor rose ornament*] / Publisher's monogram blind-stamped in bottom right-hand corner. Blind-ruled border. Spine stamped in gilt running downwards: THE CRIMES OF ENGLAND BY G. K. CHESTERTON

Published in November 1915, at 1s. (wrappers) and 2s. 6d. (cloth). BM 29 Nov. 15.

The second edition followed in December.

1916

41. DIVORCE / VERSUS / DEMOCRACY / BY / G. K. CHESTERTON / REPRINTED FROM "NASH'S MAGAZINE" / LOQUERE FILIIS ISRAEL UT PROFICISCANTUR [*set in three lines on both sides of an IHS design supported by two cherubs*] / LONDON / THE SOCIETY OF / SS. PETER & PAUL / PUBLISHERS TO THE CHURCH OF ENGLAND / 32 GEORGE ST., HANOVER SQUARE, / AND 302 REGENT ST., W. / 1916

$8\frac{7}{8} \times 5\frac{1}{2}$. One gathering of eight leaves.

Pp. 16. (1) Title-page, (2) blank; 3–4 *Preface* signed G. K. Chesterton; 5–(14) text; (15)–(16) advertisements.

Light-brown paper wrappers printed in dark blue. Front repeats, within an ornamental border, the title-page with line 6 omitted and with the addition, above the title: YORK BOOKS: XXI / CONTINUITY TRACTS / and, below the border on the left, PRICE 6D. Inside front wrapper has an advertisement of the

York Books, inside back wrapper an advertisement of the Glastonbury Books. Back: publisher's ornament. Sewn. Top edges rough-trimmed, fore edges uncut.

Published in January 1916, at 6d. BM 25 Mar. 16.

The text only from *Nash's Magazine*.

41A. TRUE TEMPERANCE MONOGRAPHS [*in a double-ruled frame*] / NO. 2 [*in bold type, breaking the lower lines of the frame*] / TEMPERANCE / AND / THE GREAT ALLIANCE / BY G. K. CHESTERTON. / [*ornament*] / THE TRUE TEMPERANCE ASSOCIATION, / CAXTON HOUSE, WESTMINSTER, S.W. / PRICE TWO PENCE.

$8\frac{1}{2} \times 5\frac{1}{2}$. One gathering of six leaves.

Pp. 12. (1) Front wrapper printed as above, (2) *Preface* [*unsigned*] stating the aims of the series; 3–10 text; (11) *List of Pamphlets and other Publications of the True Temperance Association*. Printer's imprint at foot; (12) blank [*back wrapper*].

White paper wrappers. Sewn.

Published, *undated*, by The True Temperance Association in 1916, at 2d. BM 4 Jul. 16.

1917

42. LORD KITCHENER / BY / G. K. CHESTERTON / LONDON / 1917

$9\frac{3}{8} \times 5\frac{1}{2}$. [(A)] two leaves, (B) and (C) eights. (B) is folded round (C), and the unsigned gathering [(A)] folded round both.

Pp. (iv) + 32. (i) Half-title, (ii) blank; (iii) title-page, (iv) blank; 1–(32) text. Imprint at foot of p. (32): *Printed in Great Britain by The Field and Queen (Horace Cox) Ltd., Breams Buildings, London E.C.4.*

White art paper wrappers printed in black. Front: LORD KITCHENER [*in horizontal scroll*] / [*photograph of Lord Kitchener in oval decorated border*] / BY / G· K· CHESTERTON [*in horizontal scroll*] / PHOTO BY ELLIOTT & FRY LTD., LONDON / Stapled.

Published in 1917.

43. A SHORT HISTORY / OF ENGLAND BY / G. K.
CHESTERTON / LONDON / CHATTO & WINDUS / MCMXVII

$7\frac{3}{8} \times 4\frac{7}{8}$. [A] four, B to Q in eights, R two leaves.

Pp. (viii) + 244. (i), (ii) Blank; (iii) half-title, (iv) blank; (v)
title-page; (vi) printer's imprint and at foot, *All rights reserved*;
(vii) *Contents,* (viii) blank; 1–241 text, (242) printer's imprint;
(243) publisher's device, (244) blank.

Light-red smooth cloth stamped in gilt. Front: design of St.
George and the Dragon in rectangle. Spine: A SHORT /
HISTORY / OF / ENGLAND / [*dot*] / G. K. / CHESTERTON /
CHATTO / & WINDUS / Top edges green. Tail rough trimmed.

Published October 18, 1917, at 5*s*. 2,500 copies. BM 18 Oct.
17.

Re-issued in October 1924 in Chatto and Windus' *St. Martin's
Library*. The title-page adds below "G. K. Chesterton":
"WITH A NEW FOREWORD BY THE AUTHOR." The additional
matter (pp. v–x) is headed: INTRODUCTION TO A NEW
EDITION.

44. UTOPIA OF USURERS / AND OTHER ESSAYS / BY GILBERT
K. CHESTERTON / [*publisher's monogram*] / BONI AND LIVER-
RIGHT / NEW YORK 1917

$7\frac{3}{8} \times 5\frac{7}{8}$. Fourteen unsigned gatherings of eight leaves and one
of four.

Pp. (xiv) + 218. (i)–(iv) Blank; (v) half-title, (vi) blank; (vii)
title-page; (viii) copyright statement; (ix)–(x) poem, *A Song of
Swords*; (xi)–(xii) *Contents*; (xiii) fly-title, (xiv) blank; 1–217
text, (218) blank.

Light-brown cloth stamped in gilt. Front: UTOPIA OF /
USURERS / BY GILBERT K. CHESTERTON /. Spine: UTOPIA /
OF / USURERS / [*rule*] / GILBERT / K. / CHESTERTON / BONI
AND / LIVERIGHT

Published New York, 1917.

Two poems, nine essays under the general title of *Utopia of
Usurers*, together with 17 other essays collected from the
Daily Herald.

1918

45. HOW TO HELP / ANNEXATION / BY / G. K.
CHESTERTON / LONDON: / HAYMAN, CHRISTY & LILLY,
LTD. / FARRINGDON ROAD, E.C.I. / 1918

$8\frac{1}{4}$ × $4\frac{1}{2}$. One gathering of eight leaves.

Pp. 16. (1) Title-page, (2)–16 text. Without covers. Sewn.

Published in 1918.

Reprinted from the *North American Review* for March 1918,
where it appeared under the heading: "Germany and Alsace-
Lorraine; how to help annexation".

1919

46. IRISH IMPRESSIONS / BY G. K. CHESTERTON [*leaf orna-
ment*] / [*publisher's device*] /. LONDON: 48 PALL MALL / W.
COLLINS SONS & CO. LTD. / GLASGOW MELBOURNE
AUCKLAND

$7\frac{1}{2}$ × $4\frac{3}{4}$. [A]–Q in eights.

Pp. (vi) + 250. (i) Half-title, (ii) advertisement of six books, in
panel; (iii) title-page, (iv) *Copyright* 1919; v *Contents*, (vi)
blank; (1)–243 text, (244) printer's imprint; (245)–(250) advertisements dated Autumn 1919.

Dark-green cloth printed in black. Front: IRISH IMPRESSIONS
/ G. K. CHESTERTON. Ruled border. Spine: IRISH / IM-
PRESSIONS / G. K. / CHESTERTON / COLLINS

Published November 4, 1919, at 7s. 6d. BM 15 Dec. 19.

The greater part of the text appeared in the *New Witness* in 1918.

1920

47. THE SUPERSTITION / OF DIVORCE / BY / G. K.
CHESTERTON / LONDON / CHATTO & WINDUS / 1920

$7\frac{1}{2}$ × $4\frac{7}{8}$. [A] four, [B]–K in eights, L four leaves.

Pp. (viii) + 152. (i) Half-title, (ii) blank; (iii) title-page, (iv)
Printer's imprint. *All rights reserved*; (v) *Introductory Note*, (vi)
blank; (vii) *Contents*, (viii) blank; (1) fly-title, (2) blank;
3–(152) text; printer's imprint at foot of p. (152).

Blue-black cloth lettered in pink. Front: THE SUPERSTITION /
OF DIVORCE / G. K. CHESTERTON Spine: THE / SUPER- /
STITION / OF / DIVORCE / G. K. / CHESTERTON / CHATTO
& / WINDUS / Fore and tail edges rough trimmed.

Published January 29, 1920, at 5s. 5,000 copies. BM 23 Jan. 20.

"The earlier part of this book came out in the form of five
articles which appeared in the *New Witness* at the crisis of the
recent controversy in the Press on the subject of divorce . . ."
Introductory Note. The articles had actually appeared nearly two
years before, in the issues of the *New Witness* (545) for March 22
and 29 and April 5, 12 and 19, 1918. They here fill the first third
of the book; the remaining matter appears for the first time.

48. CHARLES DICKENS / FIFTY YEARS AFTER / BY / GILBERT K. CHESTERTON / PRIVATELY PRINTED BY CLEMENT SHORTER / JUNE, 1920 [ruled border]

$10\frac{1}{4} \times 8$. One gathering of six leaves.

Pp. (ii) + 10. (i), (ii) blank; 1–7 text, (8) at foot, *Of this little
book 25 copies only have been privately printed by Clement Shorter,
with the permission of the author. The article first appeared in "The
Observer", June 6th., 1920.* (9), (10) blank.

Stiff blue wrappers lettered in black. Sewn, blue cord. There is
no title-page; the above particulars are taken from the front
wrapper.

Issued on the 50th anniversary (June 9, 1920) of the death of
Dickens.

49. OLD KING COLE / [double rule] / OLD KING COLE WAS A MERRY OLD SOUL, / AND A MERRY OLD SOUL WAS HE / HE CALLED FOR HIS PIPE, / HE CALLED FOR HIS BOWL, / AND HE CALLED FOR HIS FIDDLERS THREE

$8\frac{1}{4} \times 5\frac{1}{4}$. A single leaf, folded, unpaged.

(1) As above, (2)–(3) versions of the poem in the manner of
Tennyson, Yeats, Whitman and Browning. G. K. C. (4) blank.

Issued 1920, probably in the summer. Price unknown.

Reprinted in the *New Witness* (545) December 10, 1920, with
the following note: "The above parodies were originally

written for the Beaconsfield Convalescent Home and were on sale at a Bazaar to raise much-needed funds." See *Collected Poems* (69), Variations of an Air: Composed on Having to Appear in a Pageant as Old King Cole.

50. THE / USES OF DIVERSITY / A BOOK OF ESSAYS / BY / G. K. CHESTERTON / METHUEN & CO. LTD. / 36 ESSEX STREET W.C. / LONDON

$6\frac{3}{4} \times 4$. An unsigned gathering of four leaves, A to M in eights. Pp. viii + 192. (i) Half-title, (ii) list of six books by the same author; (iii) title-page, (iv) *First Published in* 1920; v–vi *Contents*; (vii) fly-title, (viii) blank; 1–191 text, (192) printer's imprint. An eight-page catalogue which follows is not included in the collation.

Light-blue grained cloth. Front blind-stamped: THE USES OF DIVERSITY/G·K·CHESTERTON / Ruled border. Spine stamped in gilt: THE / USES OF / DIVERSITY / [*trefoil ornament*] / G · K / CHESTERTON / METHUEN / Tail edges uncut.

Published October 21, 1920, at 6s. 2,500 copies. BM 21 Oct. 20.

Essays collected from the *Illustrated London News* and the *New Witness*.

51. THE NEW JERUSALEM / BY / G. K. CHESTERTON / HODDER AND STOUGHTON / LIMITED LONDON

$8\frac{7}{16} \times 5\frac{5}{16}$. An unsigned gathering of six leaves, A–T in eights. Pp. (2) + x + 304. A blank leaf, unnumbered; (i) half-title, (ii) blank; (iii) title-page, (iv) blank; v–vii *Preface*, (viii) blank; ix–x *Contents*; (1)–304 text.

Light-blue grained cloth. Front: blind-stamped double-ruled border. Spine stamped in gilt: [*double rule*] / THE NEW / JERUSALEM] [*ornament*] / G. K. / CHESTERTON / [*double rule*] / HODDER & STOUGHTON] [*double rule*] / Back: blind-stamped double-ruled border.

Published, *undated*, November 19, 1920, at 12s. 6d. 5,000 copies. BM 9 Dec. 20.

"Notes . . . now reproduced in a book as they were published in the newspaper."—Preface. The newspaper was the *Daily Telegraph*.

"The only exception refers to the last chapter on Zionism. . . .
A difference of opinion, which divided the writer of the book
from the politics of the newspaper, prevented the complete
publication of that chapter in that place."—*Preface*.

The newspaper publication ceased part-way through the last
chapter, "Zionism", at the words, ". . . the worst of all cures is
to deny the disease" (p. 276).

1922

52. EUGENICS AND / OTHER EVILS / by / g. k. chesterton / cassell and company, limited / london,
new york, toronto & melbourne / 1922 [*all within a
thick and thin ruled border*]

8 × 5⅛. [A–]L in eights; L* is two leaves.

Pp. (viii) + 188. (i) Half-title, (ii) blank; (iii) title-page, (iv)
blank; (v)–(vi) *To the Reader*; (vii) *Contents*, (viii) blank; 1–184
text; 185–188 *Index*. Printer's imprint and F40.122 at foot of
p. 188.

A. Dark-red ribbed cloth. Front lettered in black: eugenics /
and other evils / g. k. chesterton / Blind-ruled border.
Spine stamped in gilt: [*rule*] / eugenics / and other /
evils] [*short rule*] / g. k. / chesterton / cassell / [*rule*] /
Top edges light red. Fore and tail edges uncut.

B. Brown fine-grained cloth. Top edges brown, others uncut.

C. Light-brown smooth cloth. Top edges plain, others uncut.

D. Dark-red smooth cloth. No ruled border, no rules on spine.
Top edges plain, others cut. BM 7 Mar. 22.

Published in February 1922, at 6s. 4,000 copies.

53. WHAT I SAW IN AMERICA / by / g. k. chesterton /
hodder and stoughton / limited london /
mcmxxii [*all within a ruled border*]

8⁷⁄₁₆ × 5⁵⁄₁₆. An unsigned gathering of four leaves, A to T in
eights; U is two.

Pp. (2) + vi + 308. A blank leaf not included in the pagination;
(i) half-title, (ii) advertisement of *The New Jerusalem* in a panel;
(iii) title-page, (iv) printer's imprint; v–vi *Contents*; (1)–308 text.

Dark-green grained cloth. Front: blind-stamped double-ruled border. Spine stamped in gilt: [*double rule*] / WHAT I SAW IN AMERICA / [*ornament*] / G. K. / CHESTERTON / [*double rule*] / HODDER & STOUGHTON / [*double rule*] / Back: blind-stamped double-ruled border.

Published September 1, 1922, at 12s. 6d. 2,000 copies. BM 11 Sep. 22.

Collected from the *New Witness*.

54. **THE BALLAD OF ST. BARBARA** / AND OTHER VERSES / BY / GILBERT KEITH CHESTERTON / LONDON / CECIL PALMER / OAKLEY HOUSE BLOOMSBURY STREET W.C.I.

$8\frac{7}{16} \times 5\frac{7}{16}$. [A]–F in eights.

Pp. x + 86. (i), (ii) Blank; (iii) half-title, (iv) blank; (v) title-page, (vi) *First Edition* 1922 *Copyright* [*device*]: vii–viii dedicatory poem *To F.C. In Memoriam Palestine*, '19; ix–x *Contents*; 1–83 text, (84) printer's imprint; (85), (86) blank.

Decorated paper boards with black cloth spine. Front and back printed with a chequered pattern in yellow, brown and black. Spine stamped in gilt: THE / BALLAD / OF ST. / BARBARA / G. K. / CHESTERTON / CECIL / PALMER / Top edges yellow, others uncut.

Published in October 1922, at 7s. 6d. BM 24 Oct. 22.

Some of the poems, including *Songs of Education*, are collected from the *New Witness*.

55. **THE MAN** / **WHO KNEW TOO MUCH** / AND OTHER STORIES / BY / G. K. CHESTERTON / [*ornament*] / CASSELL AND COMPANY, LTD / LONDON, NEW YORK, TORONTO AND MELBOURNE

$7\frac{3}{8} \times 4\frac{1}{2}$. [A]–T in eights.

Pp. (x) + 310. (i), (ii) Blank; (iii) half-title, (iv) list of three books by the same author; (v) title-page, (vi) *First published in 1922*; (vii) dedication, *To a Mob of Nephews and Nieces at Fernley, Maidenhead*, (viii) blank; (ix) *Contents*, (x) blank; 1–(308) text; (309), (310) blank. Printer's imprint and F40.1022 at foot of p. (308).

Dark-green cloth stamped in dark blue. Front: THE MAN WHO / KNEW TOO MUCH / G. K. CHESTERTON / Ruled border. Spine: THE MAN / WHO KNEW / TOO MUCH / G. K. CHESTERTON / CASSELL / Tail edges uncut.

Published in November 1922, at 7s. 6d. 4,000 copies. BM 22 Dec. 22. The second edition of 2,000 copies followed in the same month.

The American edition, N.Y., Harpers, 1922, "with illustrations by W. Hatherell, R.I.", has only one illustration, the frontispiece. It omits the last three stories and restores the title of *The Fool of the Family* to *The Temple of Silence*, as in the *Storyteller*.

Collected from *Cassell's Magazine* and the *Storyteller*.

The Five of Swords from this volume was chosen by G. K. C. to represent him in *My Best Story. An anthology of stories chosen by their own authors*, Faber, 1929. It also appears in the *World's Classics* anthology, *Crime and Detection* (Second Series), 1930.

1923

56. FANCIES VERSUS / FADS / BY / G. K. CHESTERTON / METHUEN & CO. LTD. / 36 ESSEX STREET W.C. / LONDON
$6\frac{5}{8} \times 4\frac{1}{16}$. 1–16 in eights.

Pp. x + 246. (1) Half-title, (ii) list of ten books by the same author; (iii) title-page, (iv) *First Published in* 1923. *Printed in Great Britain*; v–viii *Introduction*; ix–x *Contents*; 1–(238) text; (239)–(246) advertisements [pages numbered 1–8]. Printer's imprint on p. (238).

Mauve smooth-grained cloth. Front blind-stamped: FANCIES VERSUS FADS / G · K · CHESTERTON / Ruled border. Spine stamped in gilt: FANCIES / VERSUS / FADS / [trefoil ornament] / G · K / CHESTERTON / METHUEN / Fore and tail edges rough-trimmed.

Published September 6, 1923, at 6s. 4,300 copies. BM 7 Sep. 23.

The first and last essays, *The Romance of Rhyme* and *Milton and Merry England*, first appeared in the *London Mercury*; the others in the *New Witness* and the *Illustrated London News*.

In the American edition, N.Y., Dodd, Mead, 1923, *The Revolt of the Spoilt Child* is changed to *Why Reforms Go Wrong*.

**57. ST. FRANCIS OF / ASSISI / BY / G. K. CHESTERTON /
H & S / HODDER AND STOUGHTON LTD. / LONDON
TORONTO** [*all within a double ruled border with rounded corners*]
$6\frac{3}{4} \times 4\frac{1}{4}$. [A] to M in eights.

Pp. vi, 192. (i) Half-title to *The People's Library*, (ii) list of six
books in the series; (iii) title-page, (iv) *General Preface*. At foot:
*Made and Printed in Great Britain. R. Clay & Sons, Ltd., Printers,
Bungay*; v *Contents*, (vi) blank; 7–185 text, (186)–(192) blank.
Blue endpapers.

Light-blue grained cloth. Front blind-stamped with a circular
device. Spine stamped in black: [*rule*] / PEOPLE'S / LIBRARY /
[*rule*] / ST. FRANCIS / OF ASSISI / G. K. / CHESTERTON /
[*rule*] / HODDER & / STOUGHTON / [*rule*]

Published *undated*, October 26, 1923, at 2s. 6d.   2,000 copies.

A. As above. BM 20 Nov. 23.

B. White end papers.

C. Later issues have the following variations: pp. (vi), 188.
White endpapers. The last two leaves of gathering M are the
back endpapers (M 7, (pp. [189]–[190]), M 8, (pp. [191]–[192])).
p. (ii). List of books in the series more than six. p. (iii). Title-
page. Last two lines: HODDERANDSTOUGHTON/PUBLISHERS
LONDON / p. (iv) Imprint at foot: *Printed in Great Britain for
Hodder and Stoughton, Limited, by Richard Clay & Sons, Limited,
Bungay, Suffolk*. Contents page is unnumbered. p. (vi) *First
published October* 1923.

Leather edition, September 1924, at 7s. 6d.

Illustrated edition with frontispiece and six coloured illustrations
from paintings by F. Cayley Robinson, October 1926, at 6s.

The twenty-first edition, in Hodder and Stoughton's *Black
Jacket Books*, 1939, includes the coloured illustrations.

1924

**58. THE END OF THE / ROMAN ROAD / A PAGEANT /
OF WAYFARERS. / BY / G. K. CHESTERTON. / ILLUSTRATED
BY T. H. ROBINSON. / PREFACE BY A. ST. JOHN ADCOCK. /
("OUT AND AWAY" SERIES) / LONDON: / THE CLASSIC
PRESS, / 18, TOOKS COURT, E.C.4. / 1924.**

$6\frac{1}{8} \times 4\frac{1}{4}$. [A]–H in fours.

Pp. 64. (1), (2) Blank; (3) half-title, (4) classical ornament; (5) title-page, (6) printer's imprint; 7–13 *Preface*, (14) blank; 15–60 text; (61)–(64) blank. Coloured frontispiece not included in the collation.

Light-blue cloth. Front stamped in gilt: THE END / OF THE / ROMAN ROAD. / BY G. K. CHESTERTON. / Fore and tail edges uncut. Grey-green marbled endpapers.

Published in March 1924, at 5s.   BM 13 June 24.

An essay written "just after the Great War".—*Preface*.

1925

59. THE SUPERSTITIONS / OF THE / SCEPTIC / GILBERT K. CHESTERTON / WITH A CORRESPONDENCE BETWEEN THE / AUTHOR AND MR. G. G. COULTON / [*publisher's mono-gram*] / CAMBRIDGE / W. HEFFER & SONS LTD. / 1925

$7\frac{5}{8} \times 4\frac{1}{2}$. [A] four leaves, B–D in eights.

Pp. (vi) + 50. (i) Half-title, (ii) *London Agents; Simpkin, Marshall, Hamilton, Kent and Co., Ltd.*; (iii) title-page, (iv) *Printed in Great Britain*; (v) *Preface* signed *Austin H. Johnson*, (vi) blank; 1–50 text; printer's imprint at foot of p. 50.

Cream paper wrappers printed in green. Front: THE SUPER-STITIONS / OF THE / SCEPTIC / GILBERT K. CHESTERTON / WITH A CORRESPONDENCE BETWEEN THE / AUTHOR AND MR. G. G. COULTON / [*publisher's monogram*] / [*short rule*] / NO. ONE / I.D.K. CLUB BOOKLETS / [*short rule*] / PRICE ONE SHILLING AND SIXPENCE NET. / Thin-ruled double border. Spine, reading upwards: THE SUPERSTITIONS OF THE SCEPTIC G. K. CHESTERTON / Insides of wrappers and back wrapper blank.

Published March 4, 1925, at 1s. 6d.   1,500 copies.   BM 7 Mar. 25.

The text is printed from a shorthand verbatim report of a lecture given by G. K. C. to the I.D.K. Club, Cambridge, and to it is added a correspondence between the author and Mr. G. G. Coulton which appeared in the *Cambridge Review*.

The discussion was continued by G. K. C. in the *Dublin Review* (520) and by Mr. Coulton in the *Review of the Churches*, Vol. II, No. 3 (New Series), July 1925 (*The Mediaeval Dance*).

60. TALES OF THE LONG BOW / BY / G. K. CHESTERTON / [*publisher's device*] / CASSELL AND COMPANY, LTD / LONDON, NEW YORK, TORONTO AND MELBOURNE

$7\frac{3}{8} \times 4\frac{3}{4}$. [A]–T in eights.

Pp. (viii) + 312. (i), (ii) Blank; (iii) half-title, (iv) list of three books by the same author, in a panel; (v) title-page, (vi) *First published* 1925 *Printed in Great Britain*; (vii) *Contents*, (viii) blank; (1)–(310) text; (311), (312) blank. Printer's imprint and *F*75.525 at foot of p. (310).

Light-green smooth cloth stamped in dark green. Front: TALES / OF THE LONG BOW / G. K. CHESTERTON / [*small paper label with publisher's device and* CASSELL *in brown*] / Ruled border. Spine: TALES / OF THE / LONG BOW / G. K. / CHESTERTON / CASSELL / Tail rough trimmed.

Published in June 1925, at 7s. 6d. 7,500 copies. BM 8 July 25

Collected from the *Storyteller*.

61. THE / EVERLASTING MAN / BY / G. K. CHESTERTON / HODDER AND STOUGHTON / LIMITED LONDON

$8\frac{1}{16} \times 5\frac{1}{2}$. An unsigned gathering of four leaves, A to T in eights, U six.

Pp. (viii) + 316. (i) Half-title, (ii) blank; (iii) title-page, (iv) printer's imprint; (v) *Prefatory Note*, (vi) blank; (vii) *Contents*, (viii) blank; (1)–316 text.

Dark-red cloth. Front and back blind-stamped ruled border. Spine stamped in gilt: [*rule*] / THE / EVERLASTING / MAN / [*ornament*] / G. K. / CHESTERTON / HODDER & STOUGHTON / [*rule*]

Published, *undated*, September 30, 1925, at 12s. 6d. 3,000 copies. BM 1 Dec. 25.

In the American edition, N.Y., Dodd, Mead, 1925, Appendix I differs slightly from the text of the English edition.

62. WILLIAM COBBETT / BY / G. K. CHESTERTON / [*publisher's monogram*] / HODDER AND STOUGHTON / LIMITED LONDON [*ruled border*]

$7\frac{5}{16} \times 4\frac{3}{4}$. An unsigned gathering of four leaves, A to R in eights, S four.

Pp. (viii) + 280. Blank leaf, (i) half-title, (ii) *Works by G. K. Chesterton* in panel; (iii) title-page, (iv) printer's imprint; v *Contents*, (vi) blank; (1)–277 text, (278)–(280) blank.

Bright-blue grained cloth. Front stamped in gilt: COBBETT [*in top right-hand corner*] / G. K. CHESTERTON [*in facsimile of the author's autograph. Bottom right-hand corner*] / Blind-ruled border. Spine: [*ornamental bar*] / COBBETT [*ornamental bar*] / G. K. / CHESTERTON / HODDER AND / STOUGHTON / [*ornamental bar*]

Published November 20, 1925, at 6s. 4,000 copies. BM 1 Dec. 25.

The list of *Intimate Biographies* by G. K. C. on p. (ii) includes *Savonarola* and *Napoleon* as "In Preparation". They never appeared.

The address by G. K. C. to the Royal Society of Literature on Cobbett to which he refers on p. (1) was published in *Essays by Divers Hands*, New Series, Vol. III (312).

1926

63. THE INCREDULITY / OF FATHER BROWN / BY G. K. CHESTERTON [*two trefoil ornaments*] / [*publisher's device*] / CASSELL AND COMPANY, LTD / LONDON, NEW YORK, TORONTO AND MELBOURNE

$7\frac{7}{16} \times 4\frac{5}{8}$. [A]–S in eights.

Pp. (viii) + 296. (i) Half-title, (ii) blank; (iii) title-page, (iv) *First published* 1926 *Printed in Great Britain*; (v) dedication, *To Patricia Burke*, (vi) blank; (vii) *Contents*, (viii) *Note*; 1–(296) text. Printer's imprint and F75.426 at foot of p. (296).

Black grained cloth stamped in red. Front: THE INCREDULITY / OF FATHER BROWN / [*dot*] / G. K. CHESTERTON [*in a panel with ruled border, with an outer border with wavy top and bottom and ruled sides*] / Wavy border within a blind-ruled border. Spine: THE / INCREDULITY / OF / FATHER / BROWN / [*dot*] / G. K. / CHESTERTON / [*publisher's device blind-stamped with red ruled frame*] / CASSELL / Wavy border top and bottom with ruled sides. Tail edges rough-trimmed.

Published in June 1926, at 7s. 6d. 7,500 copies. BM 12 July 26.

Collected from *Cassell's Magazine* and *Nash's Pall Mall Magazine*.

64. THE OUTLINE OF / SANITY / BY / G. K. CHESTERTON / [*publisher's device*] / METHUEN & CO. LTD. / 36 ESSEX STREET W.C. / LONDON

$6\frac{5}{8} \times 4$. An unsigned gathering of four leaves, A to P in eights.

Pp. viii + 232 + 8. (i) Half-title, (ii) list of twelve books by the same author; (iii) title-page, (iv) *First published in* 1926 *Printed in Great Britain*; v–vi *Contents*; vii *Note*, (viii) blank; 1–230 text; (231) blank, (232) printer's imprint. The remaining four leaves of the last gathering (P) are occupied by advertisements paginated (1)–8 and dated 10.26.

Green smooth-grained cloth. Front blind-stamped: THE OUTLINE OF SANITY / G · K · CHESTERTON / Ruled border. Spine stamped in gilt: THE / OUTLINE / OF SANITY / [*trefoil ornament*] / G · K / CHESTERTON / METHUEN /

Published December 2, 1926, at 6s. 4,000 copies. BM 2 Dec. 26.

A revised version, with additional matter, of a series of articles in *G. K.'s Weekly*, Vol. I, No. 16–Vol. II, No. 37.

65. THE QUEEN OF / SEVEN SWORDS / BY / G. K. CHESTERTON / SHEED & WARD / 31 PATERNOSTER ROW, LONDON, E.C.4

$7\frac{1}{4} \times 4\frac{5}{8}$. [A] and B eight leaves, C two, folded round D which is eight.

Pp. 52. (1) Half-title, (2) blank; (3) title-page, (4) *Published . . . December, 1926* and printer's imprint; 5 *Contents*, (6) blank; 7–(50) text; (51), (52) blank.

Purple paper boards with orange linen spine. Front: an orange label printed in blue: THE QUEEN OF / SEVEN SWORDS / BY G. K. CHESTERTON / within a decorated border. Spine and back blank. The orange of the label is lighter than that of the spine.

A. As above. BM 7 Mar. 27.

B. Mustard-coloured boards with orange linen spine.

C. Tan-coloured imitation leather, yellow linen spine.

D. Mottled red and black imitation leather, stamped in gilt. Top edges gilt, others untrimmed. Red marbled end-papers.

E. Light-blue buckram. Front stamped in gilt with facsimile autograph of G. K. Chesterton. Spine stamped in gilt, running downwards: THE QUEEN OF SEVEN SWORDS with a *fleur de lys* ornament before and after each word (six in all).

Published in December 1926, at 2s. 6d. (boards) and 4s. 6d. (buckram).

The punctuation is defective in all issues but least so in D.

Two of the poems, *Regina Angelorum* and *The Towers of Time* had first appeared in *G. K.'s Weekly.* The volume is not included in *Collected Poems* (69), published in the following year.

1927

66. THE CATHOLIC CHURCH / AND CONVERSION / BY / G. K. / CHESTERTON / LONDON / BURNS, OATES & WASHBOURNE, LTD. / PUBLISHERS TO THE HOLY SEE / 1926

$7\frac{1}{4} \times 4\frac{5}{8}$. No signatures. Six gatherings of eight leaves and one of ten.

Pp. 116. (1) *The Calvert Series / Hilaire Belloc, General Editor / The Catholic Church and / Conversion*, (2) List of the *Calvert Series*; (3) title-page, (4) *Printed in the United States*; 5–9 *Editor's Note*, (10) blank; (11) *Contents*, (12) blank; (13)–115 text, (116) blank.

Navy-blue smooth cloth stamped in gilt. Front: THE / CALVERT / SERIES [*within a shield*] / Blind-ruled border. Spine stamped in gilt: [*double rule*] / THE / CATHOLIC / CHURCH / AND / CONVERSION / G. K. CHESTERTON / BURNS OATES & / WASHBOURNE / [*double rule*] /

Published, ante-dated, in January 1927, at 4s. 540 copies. BM 21 Dec. 26.

First English edition. The publishers bought 540 sets of sheets from Macmillans of New York in December 1926. They imported further sets as follows: 1,030 sets in March 1927; 260 sets in March 1928 and 260 sets in February 1929.

67. THE LEAGUE OF NATIONAL LIFE / [rule] / SOCIAL REFORM / VERSUS / BIRTH CONTROL / G. K. CHESTERTON / [rule] / SIMPKIN, MARSHALL, HAMILTON, KENT & CO. / LTD. / 17, AVE MARIA LANE, LONDON, E.C.4

$7\frac{1}{4} \times 4\frac{7}{8}$. One gathering of six leaves.

Pp. 12. (1) Title-page, (2) blank; (3)–12 text.

Dun paper wrappers. Front printed in black as title-page, but with the rules (lines 2 and 7) omitted and PRICE 3D. NET in place of the second rule and with a border of two thin rules enclosing the whole. Inside front wrapper The League of National Life authorises publication but ". . . the author alone is responsible for its statements and arguments". Inside back wrapper has a list of officials of The League of National Life. Back blank. Stapled.

Published, *undated*, February 1927, at 3d. BM 31 Aug. 27.

The text is an abstract from two articles in *Lansbury's Labour Weekly* (Dec. 25, 1926 and Jan. 22, 1927).

68. THE RETURN / OF DON QUIXOTE / BY / G. K. CHESTERTON / CHATTO & WINDUS / 97 AND 99 ST. MARTIN'S LANE / LONDON

$7\frac{3}{8} \times 4\frac{3}{4}$. An unsigned gathering of four leaves, A to T in eights, U four.

Pp. viii + 312. (i) Half-title, (ii) blank; (iii) title-page, (iv) *First Published 1927 Printed in Great Britain; All Rights Reserved*; (v) dedication, *To W. R. Titterton*, (vi) blank; vii–viii *Contents*; 1–(312) text. Printer's imprint at foot of p. (312).

Light-blue grained cloth. Front and back: blind-stamped double-ruled borders. Spine stamped in gilt: [*double thick and thin rules*] / THE / RETURN OF / DON / QUIXOTE / [*ornamental rule*] / G. K. / CHESTERTON / [*double thick and thin rules*] / [*thick and thin rules*] / CHATTO & WINDUS / [*thick and thin rules*] / Top edges blue. Tail edges uncut.

Published May 6, 1927, at 7s. 6d. 7,500 copies.

A. As above. BM 6 May 27. Some copies have four pages of advertisements.

B. Dark-blue cloth lettered in black. The advertisements begin with *The Return of Don Quixote*.

The greater part of *The Return of Don Quixote* was serialised in *G. K.'s Weekly* before publication (Dec. 12, 1925 to Nov. 11, 1926). The reduction in size of the paper brought the serial to an end in the middle of Chapter XIV. In the issue for November 20, 1926, the remainder of the story is summarised.

A copy deposited in the Library of Congress has on the title-page: DODD, MEAD & COMPANY / NEW YORK 1926 / It is shorter than the English edition, has many textual variations and was probably a trial copy. The ordinary American edition was issued by Dodd, Mead in 1927.

69. THE COLLECTED / POEMS / OF G. K. CHESTERTON / [*publisher's ornament*] / CECIL PALMER / 49 CHANDOS STREET / W.C.2

$8\frac{5}{8} \times 5\frac{3}{8}$. A to T, V, and X, Y, in eights; Z four leaves, ZZ eight.

Pp. (x) + 366. (i), (ii) Blank; (iii) half-title, (iv) blank; (v) title-page, (vi) *First Edition 1927 Copyright Printed in Great Britain*; (vii) *Contents and Acknowledgment*, (viii) blank; (ix) *Book One. New Poems* (1927), (x) blank; 1–356 text; (357), (358) blank; 359–364 *Index*; 365 blank, 366 printer's imprint.

Light-blue cloth. Front blind-stamped with a thick and thin ruled border. Spine stamped in gilt: [*thick and thin rules*] / THE / COLLECTED POEMS / OF / GILBERT KEITH / CHESTERTON / [*ornament*] / CECIL / PALMER / [*thin and thick rules*] / Top edges light blue.

A. As above. BM 2 July 27.

B. The title-page is a cancel and reads:
THE COLLECTED / POEMS / OF G. K. CHESTERTON / LONDON: / BURNS, OATES & WASHBOURNE, LTD. Verso: *First Edition 1927 Copyright. Printed in Great Britain for Cecil Palmer by W. H. Smith & Son, Scarborough.* Binding a slightly lighter shade of blue than that of A. Front: blind-stamped single-ruled border. Spine stamped in gilt: [*double rule*] / THE / COLLECTED POEMS / OF / GILBERT KEITH / CHESTERTON / BURNS

OATES & / WASHBOURNE] [*double rule*] / Top edges plain. Fore and tail edges uncut. BM 11 July 27.

Published in June 1927, at 10s. 6d.

The poems in Book One, collected from the *New Witness* and *G. K.'s Weekly*, appear in book form for the first time. All earlier volumes of poetry are included, except *Greybeards at Play* and *The Queen of Seven Swords*.

A limited edition of 250 copies numbered, and signed by G. K. Chesterton, was issued in November 1927 at two guineas. Pp. (2) + xvi + 358. No index. Decorated boards with an all-over zigzag design in black on pink. Parchment spine stamped in gilt: THE / COLLECTED POEMS / OF / GILBERT KEITH / CHESTERTON / [*ornament*] / CECIL / PALMER. Top edges gilt, others uncut. Certificate of limitation and signature on p. (v). Cardboard slip-case.

The third edition was published by Methuen on September 14, 1933. 3,000 copies. Certain omissions, additions and alterations made by G. K. C. himself for this edition are here noted:—

BOOK ONE. *New Poems* (1927) becomes *New Poems* (1932). *Variations on an Air* becomes *Variations of an Air*. These parodies had been published separately as *Old King Cole* (49). The last two poems in Book One, *A Song of Self-Esteem* and *A Song of Moderation*, are omitted and a new poem, *Jealousy*, is added.

BOOK TWO. The date, 1923, is corrected to 1922. The dedicatory poem *To F.C. In Memoriam Palestine* '19, which was omitted from the first edition of *Collected Poems*, is restored with this title: *Preface To | The Ballad of St. Barbara | To F.C. | In Memoriam Palestine*, 1919. *For Four Guilds* becomes *For Five Guilds* and a fifth poem, *The Shipwrights*, is added. All five poems are listed in the *Index of Titles*, but the general title, *For Four Guilds*, remains unchanged. *The Convert* is transferred from *Book Two* to *Book Six*, where it is printed as the last poem in the book.

BOOK THREE. The misdating, *Poems* (1913), is corrected to *Poems* (*Collected*, 1915) and a *Prefatory Note*, signed G. K. C. added (p. 108). *The Kingdom of Heaven* and *A World* are omitted. *Fragment from Dante* (p. 144) was called *The Beatific Vision* in the first edition, as in the original *Poems*. The change was probably made to avoid confusion with a poem with the same title in *The Wild Knight*.

BOOK FOUR. *Wine, Water and Song* (1915) becomes *Wine, Water and Song* (*First Published in "The Flying Inn"* 1914). *The Song of the Strange Ascetic* in this collection is not from *The Flying Inn* (see 38).

BOOK SIX. *The Wild Knight* (1900) becomes *The Wild Knight* (*First Published* 1900), but the text is that of the fourth edition (1914), and includes the Note to the Second Edition which is omitted from the first edition of *Collected Poems*. *An Apology* (p. 319), the first poem in *The Wild Knight* (1900), where it had no title, was omitted from the first edition of *Collected Poems* and is now restored. *The Neglected Child, To a Turk* and *The Aristocrat*, which were the "additional poems" in the fourth edition of *The Wild Knight* (1914) and were so included in the first edition of *Collected Poems*, are now transferred to Book Three.

70. [*wood engraving*] / GLORIA IN / PROFUNDIS / BY G. K. CHESTERTON / WOOD ENGRAVINGS BY ERIC GILL

$7\frac{1}{4} \times 4\frac{3}{4}$. A half-sheet folded as four leaves, the first and last leaves blank with the wrappers folded round them.

Pp. (4). (1) wood engraving, (2)–(3) text; (4) list of *The Ariel Poems*.

Bright yellow matt paper wrappers with overlaps. Sewn. Front printed in black as above. Back: THIS IS NUMBER 5 OF / THE ARIEL POEMS / PUBLISHED BY FABER & GWYER LIMITED / AT 24 RUSSELL SQUARE, LONDON, W.C.I / PRINTED AT THE CURWEN PRESS, PLAISTOW

A. As above. Issued in a buff envelope.

B. De Luxe Edition. Limited to 350 copies printed on Zanders' hand-made paper and signed by Eric Gill. Yellow paper boards printed on front as A. Back blank.

Published, *undated*, August 25, 1927, at 1s. (A) and 5s. (B). BM 6 Sep. 27.

There is no record of the number of copies issued of A. It went out of print in 1953. B was out of print in 1944.

71. THE SECRET OF / FATHER BROWN / BY / G. K.
CHESTERTON / [*publisher's device*] / CASSELL AND COMPANY,
LTD / LONDON, TORONTO, MELBOURNE AND SYDNEY

$7\frac{1}{4} \times 4\frac{5}{8}$. [A]–T in eights.

Pp. (viii) + 312. (i) Half-title, (ii) blank; (iii) title-page, (iv)
First Published in 1927 *Printed in Great Britain*; (v) dedication, *To
Father John O'Connor / of St. Cuthbert's, Bradford / Whose Truth is
Stranger than Fiction / With a Gratitude Greater than / the World*
(vi) blank; (vii) *Contents*, (viii) blank; 1–(310) text; (311), (312)
blank. Printer's imprint and 807.27 at foot of p. (310).

Black grained cloth. Front: blind-stamped ruled border. Spine
stamped in gilt: [*rule*] / THE / SECRET OF / FATHER / BROWN
/ G. K. / CHESTERTON / CASSELL / [*rule*] / Tail edges uncut.

Published in September 1927, at 7s. 6d. 8,000 copies. BM 11
Oct. 27.

Collected from *Cassell's Magazine* and the *Storyteller*.

72. UNIVERSITY OF LONDON, UNIVERSITY COLLEGE / CUL-
TURE AND THE / COMING PERIL / BY / GILBERT K.
CHESTERTON / BEING THE SEVENTH OF A SERIES OF /
CENTENARY ADDRESSES / SIR GREGORY FOSTER /
(PROVOST OF THE COLLEGE) / IN THE CHAIR / DELIVERED
IN THE GREAT HALL ON TUESDAY, JUNE 28, 1927 / LON-
DON / UNIVERSITY OF LONDON PRESS, LTD. / 10 & 11
WARWICK LANE, E.C.4 / 1927

$8\frac{1}{2} \times 5\frac{1}{2}$. One gathering of ten leaves.

Pp. 20. (1) Half-title, (2) list of lectures; (3) title-page, (4)
printer's imprint; 5–19 text, (20) blank.

Light-green linen paper wrappers printed in dark green. Front:
UNIVERSITY OF LONDON, UNIVERSITY COLLEGE / CUL-
TURE AND THE / COMING PERIL / [*wavy line*] / AN ADDRESS
DELIVERED IN THE GREAT HALL / BY GILBERT K.
CHESTERTON, ON / TUESDAY, JUNE 28TH 1927 / [*wavy
line*] / SIR GREGORY FOSTER / IN THE CHAIR / [*wavy line*] /
BEING THE SEVENTH OF A SERIES OF CENTENARY AD-
DRESSES / LONDON: UNIVERSITY OF LONDON PRESS,
LTD., / 10 & 11 WARWICK LANE, E.C.4 / [*wavy line*] /
PRICE ONE SHILLING NET / Back blank. Sewn.

Published in October 1927, at 1s. 1,000 copies. BM 31 Oct. 27.

Unsold copies were bound up in cloth in 1928 with the eleven other addresses and published as *Centenary Addresses* at 12s. 6d. (see 356).

73. THE JUDGEMENT OF / DR. JOHNSON / A COMEDY / IN THREE ACTS / BY / G. K. CHESTERTON / FOREWORD BY / C. C. MARTINDALE, S. J. / SHEED & WARD / 31 PATERNOSTER ROW / LONDON, E.C.4

$7\frac{5}{16} \times 4\frac{7}{8}$. [A] to F in eights.

Pp. x, 96. (i) Half-title, (ii) blank; (iii) title-page, (iv) *First published* 1927 *Made in Great Britain*; v–vii *Foreword*; viii *Note* signed *G.K.C*; ix *Characters*, (x) blank; 11–91 text. Printer's imprint at foot of p. 91, (92)–(96) blank.

A. Pictorial white paper wrappers with overlaps, printed in black and brown. Front: THE JUDGEMENT / OF / DR. JOHNSON [*this line in brown*] / A / COMEDY / [*illustration*] [*so far within a thin black ruled border*] / BY [*four small ornaments*] / G. K. CHESTERTON. [*The whole within a brown ruled border.*] / Spine: DOCTOR / JOHNSON / G. K. / CHESTER- / TON / PRICE / 2/6 / NET / SHEED / & / WARD. Back: Advertisement of The Readers' Theatre.

The front wrapper is folded round the first leaf of a section of two blank leaves which are unpaged and not included in the collation. The back wrapper is folded round the last leaf of gathering F (pp. (95), (96)).

B. Smooth brown cloth stamped in gilt. Front: THE JUDGEMENT / OF / DR. JOHNSON / [*rule*] / G. K. CHESTERTON / THE READERS' THEATRE / Blind-stamped ornamental border with ornamental line below line 5 and another above line 6. Spine and back blank. The last two leaves of F (pp. (93)–(96)) are the back endpapers.

C. As B, but spine stamped in gilt: [*double rule*] / DR. / JOHN- / SON / [*short rule*] / CHESTER- / TON / SHEED / AND / WARD / [*double rule*] / BM 27 Oct. 27.

D. Cloth-backed brown-paper boards. Front and back plain. Spine: smooth yellow cloth stamped in brown: [*double rule*] / THE / JUDGEMENT / OF / DR. JOHNSON / [*short rule*] / G. K. /

CHESTERTON / SHEED / AND / WARD / [*double rule*] / Top edges brown.

Published in October 1927 as No. IV in the Readers' Theatre series at 2s. 6d. (wrappers) and 3s. 6d. (cloth).

Produced at the Arts Theatre Club, London, January 20, 1932.

74. ROBERT LOUIS/STEVENSON/BY/G. K. CHESTERTON / [*publisher's monogram*] / HODDER AND STOUGHTON / LIMITED LONDON [*ruled border*]

$7\frac{5}{16} \times 4\frac{3}{4}$. [A]–Q in eights, R is two leaves.

Pp. x, 260.(i),(ii) Blank; (iii) half-title, (iv) list of works by G. K. Chesterton, in panel; (v) title-page, (vi) printer's imprint; vii–viii *Contents*; (9)–259 text, (260) blank.

Light-blue grained cloth. Front stamped in gilt: STEVENSON [*top right-hand corner*] / G. K. CHESTERTON [*in facsimile of the author's autograph. Bottom right-hand corner*] / Blind-ruled border. Spine stamped in gilt: [*ornamental bar*] / STEVENSON / [*ornamental bar*] / G. K. / CHESTERTON / HODDER AND / STOUGHTON / [*ornamental bar*] /

Published, *undated*, November 8, 1927, at 6s. 2,800 copies.

The biographies of Savonarola and Napoleon are still announced (p. iv) as "In Preparation".

1928

75. GENERALLY SPEAKING / A BOOK OF ESSAYS / BY / G. K. CHESTERTON] [*publisher's device*] / METHUEN & CO. LTD. / 36 ESSEX STREET W.C. / LONDON

$6\frac{3}{4} \times 4\frac{1}{8}$. An unsigned gathering of two leaves, a single leaf tipped in, 1 to 15 in eights, 16 is a single leaf, 17 is four leaves.

Pp. vi + 250. (i) Half-title, (ii) list of 13 books by the same author; (iii) title-page, (iv) *First Published in* 1928; v *Contents*, (vi) Note of acknowledgement; 1–(250) text. Printer's imprint at foot of p. (250).

Smooth blue cloth. Front blind-stamped: GENERALLY SPEAKING / G · K · CHESTERTON / Ruled border. Spine stamped in gilt: [*double rule*] / GENERALLY / SPEAKING / [*trefoil*

ornament] / G. K. / CHESTERTON / METHUEN / [*double rule*] /
Top edges gilt. Tail rough-trimmed.

Published October 18, 1928, at 6s. 4,000 copies. BM 17 Oct. 28.

Essays collected from the *Illustrated London News*.

76. THIS IS NUMBER ONE OF THE / WOBURN BOOKS, BEING
THE / SWORD OF WOOD, A STORY BY / G. K. CHES-
TERTON: PUBLISHED / AT LONDON IN 1928 BY / ELKIN
MATHEWS & MAROT [*all within an ornamental border in the top
left-hand corner. In bottom right-hand corner, publisher's monogram
within a similar decorated border*]

$7\frac{9}{16} \times 5\frac{1}{2}$. [A]–D in fours.

Pp. (ii) + 30. (i), (ii) blank; (1) title-page, (2) *Five hundred and
thirty numbered copies of this story have been set by hand in Imprint
Shadow, and printed by Robert MacLehose & Co. Ltd., at the
University Press, Glasgow, of which Nos. 1–500 only are for sale
and Nos. 501–530 for presentation. This is copy No. . . . (signature*
of G. K. Chesterton); 3–(26) text, (27)–(30) blank.

Pale-pink paper boards decorated and lettered in navy blue.
Front: THE / SWORD OF WOOD / BY / G. K. CHESTERTON /
Back: THE WOBURN BOOKS / Pale-pink endpapers, decorated
in navy blue. All edges uncut.

Published in October 1928, at 6s. BM 5 Nov. 28. Copy numbered 506.

This limited, signed edition was the only separate publication in
book form. *The Sword of Wood* was reprinted from the *Pall
Mall Magazine*, November 1913, and collected in *Stories,
Essays and Poems*, 1935 (865).

1929

77. THE POET AND / THE LUNATICS / EPISODES IN
THE LIFE OF GABRIEL GALE / BY / G. K. CHESTERTON /
[*publisher's device*] / CASSELL AND COMPANY, LTD / LONDON,
TORONTO, MELBOURNE AND SYDNEY

$7\frac{5}{16} \times 4\frac{13}{16}$. [A]–R in eights.

Pp. (vi) + 282. (i) Half-title, (ii) blank; (iii) title-page, (iv) *First
published 1929 Printed in Great Britain*; (v) *Contents*, (vi) blank;
1–(282) text. Printer's imprint and F60.629 at foot of p. (282).

The leaf E2 (pp. 61–62) is a cancel.

Black grained cloth. Front: blind-stamped ruled border. Spine stamped in gilt: [*rule*] / THE POET / AND THE / LUNATICS / G. K. / CHESTERTON / CASSELL / [*rule*] /

Published in July 1929, at 7s. 6d. 6,000 copies. BM 2 Aug. 29. Collected from *Nash's Magazine* and the *Storyteller*.

78. UBI ECCLESIA / BY G. K. CHESTERTON / [*illustration*] / DRAWINGS BY DIANA MURPHY

$7\frac{1}{4} \times 4\frac{5}{8}$. A half-sheet folded as four leaves, the first and last leaves blank with the wrappers folded round them.

Pp. (4). (1) Coloured illustration, (2) blank; (3)–(4) text.

Bright yellow matt paper wrappers with overlaps. Sewn. No title-page. Front printed in black as above. Back in black, THIS IS NO 21 OF / THE ARIEL POEMS / PUBLISHED BY FABER & FABER LIMITED / AT 24 RUSSELL SQUARE, LON-DON, W.C.I / PRINTED AT THE CURWEN PRESS, PLAISTOW

A. As above. BM 28 Nov. 29.

B. Limited edition. $8\frac{1}{2} \times 5\frac{3}{8}$. Sixteen unnumbered pages. (1), (2) blank; (3) *This large-paper edition, printed on English hand-made paper, is limited to four hundred copies. This is Number* ... / [*signature*, G. K. CHESTERTON], (4) blank; (5) illustration, as on front wrapper of A, (6) blank; (7) title-page: G. K. CHESTER-TON / UBI ECCLESIA / WITH DRAWINGS BY / DIANA MURPHY / LONDON: / FABER & FABER LTD / 1929 / (8) printer's imprint; (9) coloured illustration, as on p. (1) of A, (10) blank; (11) text, (12) blank; (13) text, (14) blank; (15) THIS IS NO. 21 OF / THE ARIEL POEMS / PUBLISHED IN LONDON BY FABER & FABER / LIMITED, AT 24 RUSSELL SQUARE, W.C.I / (16) blank.

Yellow paper boards stamped in gilt. Front: G. K. CHESTERTON / [*two stars*] / [*one star*] / UBI ECCLESIA / Back blank. Fore and tail edges uncut. BM 28 Nov. 29.

Published October 9, 1929, A (wrappers, *undated*) at 1s. and B (limited, signed) at 7s. 6d.

There is no record of the number of copies issued of A. B went out of print in 1948.

79. G. K. CHESTERTON / THE THING / IT IS NOT GIVEN FOR GOODS OR GEAR BUT FOR [*this line set within the blade of a sword pointing upwards and reading upwards*] / S & W 1929 [*this line set on both sides of the blade at the foot of the page*]

7½ × 5. [A] to Q in eights.

Pp. 256. (1) Half-title, (2) blank; (3) title-page, (4) publisher's imprint; 5–6 *Contents*; 7–10 *Introduction*; 11–255 text, (256) printer's imprint.

Light-blue cloth stamped in dark blue. Front: Circular monogram, GKC, in top left-hand corner. Spine: [*double rule*] / THE / THING / [*single rule*] / G. K. / CHESTERTON / [*double rule*] / [*double rule*] / SHEED / AND / WARD / [*double rule*] /

Published in October 1929, at 7s. 6d. BM 1 Nov. 29.

Thirty-five essays collected from the *Criterion, G.K.'s Weekly, Nash's Magazine, Outline, Referee, T.P.'s Weekly* and *Universe* with an Introduction.

In the Contents (p. 6) the last two essays are wrongly numbered 41 and 42, for 35 and 36.

The Devil's Devices or Control versus Service, by Douglas Pepler, with woodcuts by Eric Gill, Hampshire House Workshops, Hammersmith, 1915, has, facing the title-page, a picture of a sword inscribed: *It is not given for goods or gear but for the Thing. To G.K.C., Eric Gill and J.E. from the Author Douglas Pepler.*

80. G. K. C. AS M.C. / BEING A COLLECTION OF THIRTY- / SEVEN INTRODUCTIONS / BY / G. K. CHESTERTON / SELECTED AND EDITED / BY / J. P DE FONSEKA / [*publisher's device*] / METHUEN & CO. LTD. / 36 ESSEX STREET W.C. / LONDON

7⅜ × 4⅞. [a] four leaves, b and 1–16 in eights, 17 two, 17* is eight.

Pp. xxiv + 276. (i) Half-title, (ii) blank; (iii) title-page, (iv) *First Published in* 1929 *Printed in Great Britain*; v–viii dedicatory letter to E. V. Lucas signed *G. K. Chesterton*; ix–xx *Preface*; xxi–xxii *Contents*; (xxiii) fly-title, (xxiv) blank; 1–272 text; 273 *Bibliographical Note*, (274) *Acknowledgement*; (275) blank, (276) printer's imprint. Frontispiece: *Bibliophilus Maximus*

G. K. C. drawn from life by J. H. Dowd, on art paper, not included in the collation.

Smooth purple cloth stamped in gilt on the spine: [*double rule*] / G. K. C. / AS / M.C. / [*leaf ornament*] / THIRTY-SEVEN / INTRODUCTIONS / METHUEN / [*double rule*] / Front and back plain. Fore and tail edges uncut.

A. As above. BM 30 Oct. 29.

B. Grey-blue cloth lettered in dark blue.

Published October 31, 1929, at 7s. 6d. 2,500 copies.

A selection of introductions contributed by G. K. C. to books published between 1903 and 1929. The last item, *Apologia*, is a reprint of the opening article in the (advance) specimen number of *G.K.'s Weekly*, November 8, 1924. The *Bibliographical Note* on p. 273 is a list of introductions by G. K. C. not included in *G. K. C. as M.C.* It is incomplete.

81. THOMAS CARLYLE. 1795–1881. / [*twelve lines of text signed* G. K. CHESTERTON] / PRINTED FOR THE NATIONAL PORTRAIT GALLERY, LONDON, BY / B. MATTHEWS (PHOTO PRINTERS) LTD., BRADFORD, ENGLAND

A post-card, 5½ × 3½. Reg. No. 968.

Issued by the National Portrait Gallery, 1929. Price 2d.

This specially written "miniature biography" is printed on the verso of a photographic post-card which has on the recto a reproduction of THOMAS CARLYLE. PAINTING BY SIR JOHN E. MILLAIS, BT., P.R.A.

82. ROBERT BROWNING, 1812–1889 / [*eleven lines of text, signed* G. K. CHESTERTON] / PRINTED BY B. MATTHEWS (PHOTO PRINTERS) LTD., / BRADFORD, ENGLAND

A post-card, 5½ × 3½. Reg. No. 1269.

Issued by the National Portrait Gallery, 1929. Price 2d.

This specially written "miniature biography" is printed on the verso of a photographic post-card which has on the recto a reproduction of a chalk drawing of ROBERT BROWNING (1859) by Field Talfourd.

The text also appears on National Portrait Gallery Post-Card Reg. No. 1001. ROBERT BROWNING. PAINTING BY G. F. WATTS, R.A., issued in 1929.

1930

83. FOUR / FAULTLESS FELONS / BY / G. K. CHESTERTON / [publisher's device] / CASSELL AND COMPANY, LTD / LONDON, TORONTO, MELBOURNE AND SYDNEY

$7\frac{5}{16} \times 4\frac{5}{8}$. [A]–T in eights.

Pp. (2) + vi + 312. First leaf blank and unpaged; (i) half-title, (ii) list of seven books by the same author, in a panel; (iii) title-page, (iv) *First published* 1930 *Printed in Great Britain*; v–vi *Contents*; (1)–(310) text; (311), (312) blank. Printer's imprint, dated 7.30 at foot of p. (310).

Black grained cloth. Front: blind-ruled border. Spine stamped in gilt: [rule] / FOUR / FAULTLESS / FELONS / G. K. / CHESTERTON / CASSELL / [rule]

Published in August 1930, at 7s. 6d. 6,000 copies. BM 8 Oct. 30.

Collected from *Cassell's Magazine* and the *Storyteller*.

84. THE GRAVE OF ARTHUR / BY G. K. CHESTERTON / [illustration] / DRAWINGS BY / CELIA FIENNES

$7\frac{1}{4} \times 4\frac{5}{8}$. A half-sheet folded as four leaves, the first and last leaves blank with the wrappers folded round them.

Pp. (4). (1) coloured illustration, (2)–(3) text, (4) blank.

Mauve paper wrappers with overlaps. Front printed in black as above. Back, in black: THIS IS NO. 25 OF / THE ARIEL POEMS / PUBLISHED BY FABER & FABER LIMITED / AT 24 RUSSELL SQUARE, LONDON, W.C.1 / PRINTED AT THE CURWEN PRESS, PLAISTOW / Sewn.

A. As above. BM 16 Oct. 30.

B. Limited edition. $8\frac{1}{2} \times 5\frac{1}{2}$. One gathering of eight leaves. Pp. (16). (1) *This large paper edition, printed on English handmade paper, is limited to three hundred and fifty copies. This is Number . . .* (*Signature of G. K. Chesterton*), (2) blank; (3) illustration, (4) blank; (5) title-page: THE GRAVE OF ARTHUR / BY / G. K. CHESTERTON / WITH DRAWINGS BY / CELIA FIENNES /

LONDON / FABER & FABER LTD / 1930 (6) printer's imprint; (7) coloured illustration, (8) blank; (9) text, (10) blank; (11) text concluded, (12) blank; (13) *This is No. 25 of the Ariel Poems Published in London by Faber & Faber Limited, at 24 Russell Square W.C.1*, (14)–(16) blank.

Mauve paper boards stamped on front in gilt: G. K. CHESTER-TON / [*three stars*] / THE GRAVE OF ARTHUR / Uncut. BM 16 Oct. 30.

Published September 1930, A (*undated*) at 1s., B at 7s. 6d.

85. THE RESURRECTION OF / ROME / BY / G. K. CHESTERTON / HODDER AND STOUGHTON / LIMITED LONDON / ST. PAUL'S HOUSE / WARWICK SQUARE / E.C. / 4

$8\frac{5}{8} \times 5\frac{5}{8}$. ($A_R$) to W_R in eights, X_R is two and *W_R four leaves.

Pp. 348. (1) Half-title, (2) *Works by G. K. Chesterton*; (3) title-page, (4) dedication, *To the Memory of Charles Scott Moncrieff who fought for England and hoped so much for Italy and died like a Roman soldier in Rome*; (5) *Contents*, (6) blank; (7)–346 text; (347), (348) blank. Printer's imprint at foot of p. 346.

Bright-red smooth cloth. Front stamped ROME in gilt and black. Thick black rules at head and tail. Spine stamped in gilt: THE / RESURREC- / TION · OF / ROME / BY — G. K / CHESTER- / TON: / [*publisher's monogram*] / HODDER AND / STOUGHTON Top edges blue-black.

Published, *undated*, October 2, 1930, at 12s. 6d.   3,000 copies. BM 27 Oct. 30.

A cheap edition, with illustrations, was issued in Sept. 1934, at 5s. The American edition, N.Y., Dodd, Mead, 1930 omits two appendices.

86. COME TO THINK OF IT . . . / A BOOK OF ESSAYS / BY / G. K. CHESTERTON / [*publisher's device*] / METHUEN & CO. LTD. / 36 ESSEX STREET W.C. / LONDON

$6\frac{11}{16} \times 4\frac{1}{8}$. An unsigned gathering of eight leaves, 1 to 14 in eights, 15 two leaves wrapped round 16 which is eight.

Pp. xvi + 244. (i) Half-title, (ii) list of eleven books *By the same author* / *uniform with this volume*; (iii) title-page, (iv) *First Published in* 1930 *Printed in Great Britain*; (v) dedication *To /Captain Bruce S. Ingram, M.C., O.B.E.* / *Editor of the* Illustrated London News / *For suffering me week after week* / *for* / *Twenty-five Years* / *On that Paper*, (vi) blank; vii–viii *Contents*; ix–xiii *Introduction*, (xiv) blank; (xv) fly-title, (xvi) blank; 1–243 text, (244) printer's imprint. Eight pages of advertisements, dated 3.30, are not included in the collation.

Smooth royal-blue cloth. Front blind-stamped: COME TO THINK OF IT / G · K · CHESTERTON / Ruled border. Spine stamped in gilt: [*double rule*] / COME / TO THINK / OF IT / G · K / CHESTERTON / METHUEN / [*double rule*] / Top edges gilt. Tail rough-trimmed.

Published October 2, 1930, at 6s. 4,000 copies. BM 1 Oct. 30.

Essays collected from the *Illustrated London News*. Selected and arranged by J. P. de Fonseka.

87. THE TURKEY AND THE / TURK, / G. K. CHESTERTON / ARRANGED AND PICTURED / BY THOMAS DERRICK. / PRINTED AND PUBLISHED / ST DOMINIC'S PRESS / DITCHLING / [*device*]

11¼ × 8⅝. Fourteen unsigned gatherings of four leaves and one of two.

Pp. (116). (1)–(4) Blank; (5) title-page, (6), (7), blank, (8) illustration of the Turk astride the Turkey and below, *This is No. . . . of one hundred copies* / *printed on Batchelor hand-made* / *paper on a hand press, July* 1930 / *Author* (signature of G. K. Chesterton) / *Artist* (signature of Thomas Derrick); (9) THE / TURKEY / AND THE TURK / BY / G. K CHESTERTON / ARRANGED AND PICTURED BY / THOMAS DERRICK. [*All within an illustration of a proscenium with below, a conductor and three members of the orchestra*], (10) illustration of a Christmas tree in a tub; (11)–(109) text and illustrations, (110)–(112) blank; (113) colophon: a hand holding an open book with the letters A, H and P disposed around it (the device of the Association of Hand Printers), (114)–(116) blank. (See illustration facing p. 144.)

A. Morocco-backed, fine-grained light-green cloth. Front

stamped in gilt with the illustration on p. (8) in reverse. Spine: black morocco stamped in gilt: THE TURKEY AND THE TURK. CHESTERTON. [*reading upwards*] and at foot, horizontally, the St. Dominic's Press device. Gilt fillet at the junction of the morocco with the cloth front and back. All edges uncut.

B. Morocco-backed white paper boards with an all-over pattern in black front and back. Spine: black morocco stamped in gilt: THE / TURKEY / AND THE / TURK / [*short rule*] / G. K. CHESTERTON. / [*St. Dominic's Press device*] / Pp. (108). (1)–(3) blank, (4)–(105) as A (8)–(109); (106)–(108) blank. The title-page and the colophon are omitted. BM 30 Jan. 31.

C. Plain grey canvas lettered as B.

Published in an edition limited to 100 copies signed by author and artist in November 1930 at £5 5s.

The text is reprinted from the Christmas number of *G.K.'s Weekly*, Vol. II, No. 38, December 5, 1925, where it appeared with illustrations by G. K. C.

A was the "normal" binding. It was issued in a yellow dust jacket with a reproduction in black of the illustration on p. (9). I know of no copy of B other than that in the British Museum. C was possibly bound by an amateur binder at Ditchling. Several copies have the illustrations hand coloured by Mr. Edgar Holloway.

Very few bound copies were issued; some sets of sheets were sold off unbound, and most of the edition was ultimately burnt. Some copies were bound privately: the copy in the collection of Miss Dorothy Collins was bound by Mr. Anthony Gardner, who also bound at least two other copies that are now in U.S.A.

88. AT THE SIGN / OF THE WORLD'S END / BY / G. K. CHESTERTON / A WAR-TIME EDITORIAL FROM A / MSS [*sic*] INSCRIBED "G.B.S. VERSUS / THE FREE PRESS" IN WHICH THE / WRITER FLAYS HARMSWORTH AND / ENGLAND'S "PROFESSIONAL" / POLITICIANS / [*device*] / THE HARVEST PRESS / 1930

$9\frac{1}{4} \times 6\frac{1}{8}$. A half-sheet folded as four leaves.

Pp. (8). (1), (2) Blank; (3) title-page, (4)–(6) text; (7), (8) blank. Printer's and publisher's imprints at foot of p. (6).

Light-green stiff paper wrappers. The front has a white paper label lettered in black: AT THE SIGN / OF THE WORLD'S END / BY / G. K. CHESTERTON

Published in 1930 by The Harvest Press, Palo Alto, in an edition limited to 25 copies, hand-set in 14-point Bulmer Roman printed on Old Stratford Book by James D. Hart and Hartley Jackson.

This "war-time editorial" is from *The New Witness*, Vol. XI, No. 277, February 22, 1918.

1931

89. ALL IS GRIST / A BOOK OF ESSAYS / BY / G. K. CHESTERTON / [*publisher's device*] / METHUEN & CO. LTD. / 36 ESSEX STREET W.C. / LONDON

$6\frac{5}{8} \times 4$. An unsigned gathering of four leaves, 1–14 in eights. Pp. viii + 216 + 8. (i) Half-title, (ii) list of 12 books by the same author; (iii) title-page, (iv) *First Published in* 1931 *Printed in Great Britain*; v–vi [*misprinted "v"*] Contents; (vii) fly-title, (viii) blank; 1–(216) text. Printer's imprint at foot of p. (216). The remaining four leaves of gathering 14 have advertisements paginated 1–8 and dated 3.31.

Smooth dark-green cloth. Front blind-stamped: ALL IS GRIST / G · K · CHESTERTON / Ruled border. Spine stamped in gilt: [*double rule*] / ALL IS / GRIST / [*three-leaf ornament*] / G. K. / CHESTERTON / METHUEN / [*double rule*] / Top edges gilt. Tail rough-trimmed.

Published October 22, 1931, at 6s. 4,000 copies. BM 21 Oct. 31.

Essays collected from the *Illustrated London News*.

1932

90. CHAUCER / BY / G. K. CHESTERTON / LONDON / FABER & FABER LIMITED / 24 RUSSELL SQUARE

$8 \times 5\frac{1}{4}$. [A]–T in eights.

Pp. 304. (1), (2) Blank; (3) half-title, (4) blank; (5) title-page, (6) publisher's and printer's imprints, *All Rights Reserved*; 7 Contents, (8) blank; 9–12 *Introduction*; 13–293 text, (294) blank; 295–302 *Index*; (303), (304) blank.

Bright-green, fine-grained cloth. Spine stamped in gilt: CHAUCER / [ornament] / G. K. / CHESTERTON / FABER / AND FABER / Front and back plain.

The pictorial dust-jacket, by Rex Whistler, has a representation of G. K. C. in the foreground.

Published April 11, 1932, at 12s. 6d. BM 24 Mar. 32.

There is no record of the size of the first edition. Cheap editions in the *Rose and Crown* series were issued in 1935 and 1940 at 5s. and 6s. respectively.

A second edition (3,660 copies) at the original price of 12s. 6d. was published by Faber and Faber on September 3, 1948.

91. SIDELIGHTS / ON NEW LONDON AND / NEWER YORK / AND OTHER ESSAYS / BY / G. K. CHESTERTON / LONDON / SHEED & WARD / MCMXXXII

7⅛ × 4¾. [A]–P in eights.

Pp. 240. (1), (2) Blank; (3) half-title, (4) blank; (5) title-page, (6) printer's and publisher's imprints; 7–8 *Contents*; 9–235 text, (236)–(240) blank.

Orange cloth. Spine stamped in green: SIDE- / LIGHTS / G.K.C. / [rule] / [skyscraper design] / [rule] / S & W / Front and back plain. Top edges orange.

Published in May 1932, at 6s. BM 17 May 32.

Essays collected from the *Bookman*, *Fortnightly Review*, *G.K.'s Weekly*, *Nash's Magazine*, *Shakespeare Review*, *Spectator* and *Week-End Review* with an Introduction: A First Word.

92. CHRISTENDOM / IN / DUBLIN / BY / G. K. CHESTERTON / LONDON / SHEED & WARD / MCMXXXII

7⅛ × 4⅝. [A] four leaves, B–E in eights.

Pp. 72. (1) Half-title, (2) blank; (3) title-page, (4) *Printed in the Irish Free State by Cahill & Co. Ltd. Dublin for Sheed & Ward 31 Paternoster Row London E.C.4 First Published November 1932*; (5) *Contents*, (6) blank; 7–72 text. Printer's imprint at foot of p. 72.

Light-green smooth cloth. Spine stamped in dark green: G.K.C. / [rule] / CHRISTENDOM IN DUBLIN [reading upwards] / S & W / Front and back plain.

Published in November 1932, at 2s. 6d. BM 28 Nov. 32.

From *Studies* and the *Universe*.

1933

93. 'ALL I SURVEY' / A BOOK OF ESSAYS / BY / G. K.
CHESTERTON / [*publisher's device*] / METHUEN & CO. LTD. /
36 ESSEX STREET W.C. / LONDON

$6\frac{9}{16} \times 3\frac{7}{8}$. An unsigned gathering of two leaves, an unsigned
single leaf, 1 to 14 in eights, 15 is four leaves, with 16, a single
leaf inserted between the first and second leaves of the gathering.

Pp. vi + 234. (i) Half-title, (ii) list of eighteen books by the same
author; (iii) title-page, (iv) *First published in* 1933 *Printed in
Great Britain*; v–vi *Contents*; 1–233 text, (234) printer's imprint.
Eight pages of advertisements, dated 9.32, are not included in
the collation.

Blue-green cloth. Front blind-stamped: ALL I SURVEY /
G . K . CHESTERTON / Ruled border. Spine stamped in gilt:
[*double rule*] / ALL I / SURVEY / [*trefoil ornament*] / G. K. /
CHESTERTON / METHUEN / [*double rule*] / Top edges gilt,
others uncut.

Published March 23, 1933, at 6s. 4,000 copies. BM 23 Mar. 33.

Essays collected from the *Illustrated London News*.

94. ST. THOMAS AQUINAS / BY / G. K. CHESTERTON /
[*device*] / LONDON / HODDER & STOUGHTON LIMITED

$6\frac{3}{4} \times 4\frac{5}{16}$. [A]–P in eights.

Pp. xii, 240. (i) Half-title, (ii) list of 41 books *Uniform with this
volume*; (iii) title-page, (iv) *First printed . . . September* 1933
Printer's imprint at foot; (v) dedication *To Dorothy Collins
without whose help the author would have been more than normally
helpless*, (vi) blank; vii *Contents*, (viii) blank; ix–xii *Introductory
Note*; 13–237 text, (238)–(240) blank.

Bright-blue grained cloth. Front blind-stamped with a circular
device as on title-page. Spine lettered in black: ST THOMAS /
AQUINAS / G. K. / CHESTERTON / [*circular device blind-stamped*]
/ [*publisher's monogram*] / HODDER & / STOUGHTON

Published September 21, 1933, at 2s. 6d.   10,000 copies.   BM 19 Oct. 33.

Apart from minor details, this book is uniform with *St. Francis of Assisi* (57), but *The People's Library* series is not mentioned.

1934

95. AVOWALS AND DENIALS / A BOOK OF ESSAYS / BY / G. K. CHESTERTON / [*publisher's device*] / METHUEN & CO. LTD. LONDON / 36 ESSEX STREET W.C.I

$6\frac{5}{8} \times 4$. An unsigned gathering of two leaves, a single leaf unsigned, 1 to 13 in eights, 14 is one leaf, 15 four.

Pp. vi + 224. (i) Half-title, (ii) list of books by the same author; (iii) title-page, (iv) *First published in* 1934 *Printed in Great Britain*; v–vi *Contents* and *Note*; 1–218 text. Printer's imprint at foot of p. 218. Eight pages of advertisements not included in the collation.

Smooth red cloth. Front blind-stamped: AVOWALS AND DENIALS / G · K · CHESTERTON / Ruled border. Spine stamped in gilt: [*double rule*] / AVOWALS / AND / DENIALS / [*trefoil ornament*] / G. K. / CHESTERTON / METHUEN / [*double rule*] / Top edges gilt, tail uncut.

Published November 8, 1934, at 6s.   4,000 copies.   BM 8 Nov. 34.

Essays collected from the *Illustrated London News*.

1935

96. THE SCANDAL OF / FATHER BROWN / BY / G. K. CHESTERTON / [*device*] / CASSELL / AND COMPANY, LIMITED / LONDON, TORONTO, MELBOURNE / AND SYDNEY

$7\frac{1}{4} \times 4\frac{3}{4}$. [A]–P in eights.

Pp. (viii) + 248. (i), (ii) Blank; (iii) half-title, (iv) list of 8 books by the same author; (v) title-page, (vi) *First published 1935*, printer's imprint and F60.235; (vii) *Contents*, (viii) blank; 1–248 text.

Smooth dark-blue cloth. Spine stamped in gilt: [*rule*] / THE / SCANDAL / OF / FATHER / BROWN / G. K. / CHESTERTON / CASSELL / [*rule*] / Front and back plain.

Published in March 1935, at 7s. 6d. 6,000 copies. BM 10 Apr. 35.
Collected from the *Storyteller*.

97. THE WELL AND THE / SHALLOWS / by / g. k.
chesterton / london / sheed and ward / 1935

7¾ × 5. [A]–S in eights.

Pp. x + 278. (i) Half-title, (ii) blank; (iii) title-page, (iv)
printer's and publisher's imprints and *First Published September*,
1935; v–vii *Introductory Note*, (viii) blank; ix–x *Contents*; 1–277
text, (278) blank.

Light-blue cloth. Front and back plain. Spine lettered in gilt:
THE WELL / AND THE / SHALLOWS / [*short rule*] / g. k. /
chesterton / sheed & ward / Top edges blue.

Published in September 1935, at 6s. BM 4 Oct. 35.

Essays and papers collected from the *Catholic Herald*, *Daily
Mail*, *Fortnightly Review*, *G.K.'s Weekly*, *London Mercury*,
Universe and the *Liverpool Cathedral Souvenir Programme* (393).

98. THE WAY OF / THE CROSS [*in brown*] / an interpreta-
tion by / frank brangwyn, r.a. / with a commentary
by / gilbert keith chesterton [*in black*] / [*a cross, in
brown*] / hodder and stoughton / limited. publishers.
london [*in black*]

14⅛ × 10½. No signatures. Two gatherings of eight leaves, one
of four, and one of six, are followed by seven gatherings of four
leaves.

Pp. 108. (1), (2) Blank; (3) half-title, (4) blank; (5) title-page,
(6) printer's imprint; (7) *Contents*, (8) blank; (9) *A Commentary
by G. K. Chesterton*, (10) blank; 11–51 text of the Commentary
on rectos only, all versos blank and unpaged, (53)–(108) fourteen
plates interpreting the Stations of the Cross mounted on the
rectos with each plate preceded by a page bearing the title of the
Station. All versos blank. There is no pagination after page 51.
Certificate of limitation on the verso of the first free end-paper:
*This Edition de Luxe is limited to Two Hundred and Fifty copies,
signed by Mr. Brangwyn and Mr. Chesterton, and numbered, of
which this is No. . . . . .* [Signatures of Frank Brangwyn and G. K.
Chesterton.]

Full cream vellum. Front stamped in gilt: THE WAY OF / THE CROSS / Spine and back plain. Top edges gilt, others uncut. Issued in a cardboard slip case.

Published, *undated*, December 5, 1935, at £7. 7s. BM 3 Mar. 36.

An ordinary edition of 2,500 copies at 12s. 6d. followed on March 12, 1936. 11⅛ × 8¼. Black cloth lettered in white. Front: THE WAY OF / THE CROSS / Spine: THE / WAY OF / THE / CROSS.

99. [*device*] / G. K. CHESTERTON / EXPLAINS THE / ENGLISH / "THE ENGLISH SPIRIT IS REALLY A SHY BIRD" / [*device*] / THE BRITISH COUNCIL / SHELL-MEX HOUSE. THE STRAND. LONDON W C 2 [*printed in red and all within a ruled border of two thick and four thin lines*]

$8\frac{9}{16}$ × $5\frac{5}{8}$. One gathering of six leaves, the first and last of which are unpaged and have the overlaps of the wrappers folded round them. Stapled.

Pp. (2) + 8 + (2). 1–8 text. Page 1 is headed "*Explaining the English*", *by G. K. Chesterton*. There is no title-page; the details above are collated from the front wrapper.

Light-blue paper wrappers with overlaps. Front printed in red as above. Back plain.

Published, according to the British Council, in 1935. BM 13 June 36.

Written specially for the British Council, and distributed by that body. No charge was made.

Collected in *A Handful of Authors* (110).

1936

100. AS I WAS SAYING / A BOOK OF ESSAYS / BY / G. K. CHESTERTON / [*publisher's device*] / METHUEN & CO. LTD. LONDON / 36 ESSEX STREET W.C.

$7\frac{11}{16}$ × $4\frac{1}{8}$. An unsigned gathering of four leaves, 1 to 14 in eights, 15 is four.

Pp. (2) + vi + 232. A blank leaf, unpaged; (i) half-title, (ii) list of twenty books by the same author; (iii) title-page, (iv) *First published in* 1936 *Printed in Great Britain*; v–vi *Contents*; 1–(228) text; (229) blank; (230) printer's imprint; (231), (232) blank.

Blue-black smooth cloth. Front blind-stamped: AS I WAS SAYING / G · K · CHESTERTON / Ruled border. Spine stamped in gilt: [*double rule*] / AS / I WAS / SAYING / [*trefoil ornament*] / G. K. / CHESTERTON / METHUEN / [*double rule*] / Top edges gilt, tail uncut.

Published June 11, 1936, at 6s. 2,500 copies. BM 11 June 36.

Essays collected from the *Illustrated London News*.

101. AUTOBIOGRAPHY / BY / G. K. CHESTERTON / WITH 9 ILLUSTRATIONS / HUTCHINSON & CO. / (PUBLISHERS) LTD. / LONDON

$8\frac{7}{16} \times 5\frac{1}{4}$. [A] to X in eights, Y is six leaves.

Pp. 348. (1) Half-title, (2) *Books by G. K. Chesterton*; (3) title-page, (4) *Made and Printed in Great Britain at The Mayflower Press Plymouth. William Brendon & Son, Ltd.* 1936; 5 *Contents*, (6) blank; 7 *List of Illustrations*, (8) blank; 9–343 text, (344) blank; 345–(348) *Index*.

Smooth black cloth. Spine stamped in gilt: [*thick and thin rule*] / G. K. / CHESTERTON / AUTOBIOGRAPHY / HUTCHINSON / [*thin and thick rule*] / Front and back plain. Nine plates.

Published November 5, 1936, at 10s. 6d.

A. As described. BM 5 Nov. 36.

B. Imprint on title-page: LONDON / BURNS OATES & WASHBOURNE LTD and on p. (4): *Printed in Great Britain for Burns Oates & Washbourne Ltd.* 1936 and on spine: BURNS OATES.

Both A and B have the same errors in the list of *Books by G. K. Chesterton* on p. (2): *The Napoleon of Notting-Hill, The Queen of the Seven Swords* and *The Well of the Shadows*.

A limited edition of 250 numbered copies on large paper and bound in green calf-backed cloth was issued by Hutchinson in December 1936 at 21s. BM 11 Jan. 37.

The American edition, N.Y., Sheed and Ward, 1936, is entitled *The Autobiography of G. K. Chesterton*. It has ten plates, of which four do not appear in the English edition.

102. THE LEGEND OF / THE SWORD / BY / G. K.
CHESTERTON / THE BOLTON PRESS / 1936

$7\frac{1}{8} \times 4\frac{5}{8}$. A single leaf folded.

Pp. 4. (1) Title-page as above, (2)–4 text.

Printed by the School of Printing and Book ·Production, City
of Dublin Municipal Technical Schools, 1936.

The text originally appeared as a "Top" (unsigned) in *G.K.'s
Weekly*, Vol. VIII, No. 183, September 15, 1928.

Collected in *The Coloured Lands* (105).

103. A BEACONSFIELD BALLAD

$10\frac{1}{4} \times 8$. A single leaf. Recto: A BEACONSFIELD BALLAD. /
[ornament] / [four eight-line verses] / G.K.C. [*All within a thin
double-ruled frame*]. Verso blank.

Issued (n.d.) probably in the 1930s. See 530.

1937

104. THE PARADOXES OF / MR. POND / BY / G. K.
CHESTERTON / [*publisher's device*] / CASSELL AND COMPANY
LTD / LONDON, TORONTO, MELBOURNE AND SYDNEY

$7\frac{5}{16} \times 4\frac{11}{16}$. [A] to O in eights, P is four leaves, Q eight.

Pp. (vi) + 258. (i) Half-title, (ii) list of nine *Other books by G. K.
Chesterton*; (iii) title-page, (iv) printer's imprint and F.1236;
(v) *Contents*, (vi) blank; (1)–257 text, (258) blank.

Smooth black cloth. Spine printed in pink: THE / PARADOXES
/ OF / MR POND / G. K. / CHESTERTON / CASSELL / Front and
back plain.

Published, *undated*, in March 1937, at 7s. 6d. 5,000 copies. BM
3 Apr. 37.

Collected from the *Storyteller*.

1938

105. THE COLOURED / LANDS / BY / G. K. CHESTERTON /
ILLUSTRATED BY / THE AUTHOR / LONDON / SHEED &
WARD / MCMXXXVIII

$9\frac{5}{8} \times 7\frac{1}{8}$. [A] and B eights, C two leaves and C* four; D to K in eights, L four, M to P in eights. C is folded round C* and the six leaves are of art paper, as also is gathering L. Five additional leaves of art paper carrying illustrations are included in the pagination but not in the collation: pp. (17)/18 (recto blank); (23)/24 (recto blank); 27/28; 105/(106) (verso blank); 207/(208) (verso blank).

Pp. viii, 238. (i) Half-title, (ii) blank; (iii) title-page, (iv) printer's imprint and, *First Published November*, 1938; v–vii *Contents*, (viii) *Acknowledgements*; 9–16 *Introduction* by Maisie Ward; (17) blank, 18 coloured illustration; 19–238 text and illustrations.

Paper boards with cloth spine. Front and back have an all-over pattern in black and white on yellow. Spine yellow, stamped in black: [*double rule*] / THE / COLOURED / LANDS / [*rule*] / G. K. / CHESTERTON / [*double rule*] / [*double rule*] / SHEED / AND / WARD / [*double rule*] / The light-brown dust jacket, lettered in red and black, has on the front a reproduction of a crayon drawing by GKC in red, yellow, green and black, which does not appear in the book.

Published in November 1938.
A. As described. 7s. 6d.   BM 22 Nov. 38.
B. De luxe edition. White vellum with gilt lettering.

A collection of verse, prose and drawings, many hitherto unpublished, including some *juvenilia*, composed between 1891 (when G. K. C. was 17) and 1934.

Some of the material is collected from the *Eye-Witness*, *New Witness* and *G.K.'s Weekly*. *The Coloured Lands* (p. 19) had appeared in *Number Three Joy Street* (332), *Ballade of the Grotesque* in *One Hundred and One Ballades* (373), *Bob-up-and-Down* in *The Silver Ship* (383) and *The Legend of the Sword* had had separate publication in 1936 (102).

1940

106. THE / END OF THE ARMISTICE / BY / G. K. CHESTERTON / LONDON / SHEED & WARD / 1940

7¼ × 4¾. [A]–O in eights.

Pp. 224. (1) Half-title, (2) blank; (3) title-page, (4) printer's imprint and *First Published February* 1940 *by Sheed and Ward*,

Ltd. From 31 *Paternoster Row London, E.C.*4.; 5–10 *Compiler's Note* signed, *F. J. Sheed*; 11–12 *Contents*; (13)–224 text.

Red matt cloth. Spine stamped in gilt: THE END / OF THE / ARMISTICE / G. K. / CHESTERTON / SHEED & WARD / Front and back plain.

Published in February 1940, at 6s. BM 8 Feb. 40.

Essays collected from *G.K.'s Weekly*. "I have sorted out and arranged these essays . . . as Chesterton's analysis of the whole problem of Germany in Europe."—Compiler's note.

1941

107. "I SAY / A DEMOCRACY / MEANS . . ." / BY / G. K. CHESTERTON / PRIVATELY PRINTED / NEW YORK

$8\frac{7}{8} \times 5\frac{5}{8}$. One gathering of four leaves, unpaged. Stapled.

Pp. (8). (1),(2) Blank; (3) title-page,(4) facsimile reproduction of letter in G. K. C.'s hand headed *Private Members and the Cabinet*; (5) the same, in print, (6) facsimile, continued; (7) printed version, continued, (8) *Limited Edition to* 125 *Copies. / Printed with the permission of Miss Dorothy Collins, Executor of / the Estate of G. K. Chesterton. / This is Copy No. . . . / All rights, especially that of translation, reserved.*

Stiff blue paper wrappers. Front printed in black within a thick and thin ruled frame: "I SAY / A DEMOCRACY / MEANS . . ." / BY / G. K. CHESTERTON.

Issued, *undated*, in 1941.

The text is part of a letter to *The Nation* dated January 26, 1911. The full text and that of preceding and subsequent letters is given in *Gilbert Keith Chesterton* (782).

1950

108. THE COMMON MAN / BY / G. K. CHESTERTON / LONDON / SHEED AND WARD / 1950

$7\frac{7}{8} \times 5$. [A] to I in sixteens.

Pp. vi + 282. (i) Half-title, (ii) blank; (iii) title-page, (iv) *First Published* 1950 *by Sheed and Ward, Ltd.* 110/111 *Fleet Street, London, E.C.*4. Reservation of rights. Printer's imprint at foot; v–vi *Contents*; 1–279 text, (280)–(282) blank.

Bright-blue matt cloth. Spine stamped in gilt: THE / COMMON / MAN / G. K. / CHESTERTON / SHEED / & / WARD / Published September 29, 1950, at 12s. 6d. 5,000 copies. BM 16 Sep. 50.

Essays, articles and introductions written between 1901 and 1936 collected from: *America, Architectural Design and Reconstruction, Daily Graphic, Daily Herald, Daily News, Fortnightly Review, G.K.'s Weekly, Good Words, Illustrated London News, London Mercury, New Quarterly, New York American, New York Herald, New York Times, New Witness, Observer, Radio Times, T.P.'s Weekly*, and *Universe*; and from the following books: *The Song of Roland* (293), *The Adventures of Peregrine Pickle* (409), *A Tale of Two Cities* (394), *Six Centuries of English Literature* (391), *Giotto. The Legend of St. Francis* (371), *If I Were a Preacher* (362), *If it had Happened Otherwise* (379), *The Hound of Heaven* (407).

1952

109. THE SURPRISE / BY / G. K. CHESTERTON / WITH A PREFACE BY / DOROTHY L. SAYERS / SHEED AND WARD / LONDON AND NEW YORK

$7\frac{1}{4} \times 4\frac{3}{4}$. [1]–4 in eights.

Pp. 64. (1) Half-title, (2) blank; (3) title-page, (4) *First Published 1952* and publisher's imprint. *Copyright* Printer's imprint; 5–9 *Preface*, (10) *Characters* and at foot, *This play was written in 1932 for production by Miss Patricia R. Burke, but it was put aside before revision and has never been acted. Dorothy Collins*; 11–63 text, (64) blank.

Light-green paper boards. Front lettered in dark green: THE SURPRISE / A PLAY / G.K.CHESTERTON / Spine and back blank. Published October 17, 1952, at 5s. 3,000 copies. BM 27 Sep. 52.

Produced by Hull University Dramatic Society on June 5, 1953.

1953

110. A HANDFUL OF AUTHORS / ESSAYS ON BOOKS AND WRITERS / BY / G. K. CHESTERTON / EDITED BY / DOROTHY COLLINS / SHEED AND WARD / LONDON AND NEW YORK

$7\frac{3}{4} \times 5$. [A]–G in sixteens.

Pp. viii + 216. (i) Half-title, (ii) blank; (iii) title-page, (iv) *First
Published* 1953 *by Sheed and Ward Ltd.* 110/111 *Fleet Street
London, E.C.4 and Sheed and Ward, Inc.* 840 *Broadway New
York,* 3 *Printed in Great Britain by Purnell and Sons, Ltd. Paulton
(Somerset) and London;* v–vii *Contents* with sources and dates of
essays, (viii) blank; 1–214 text; (215), (216) blank.

Dark-brown matt cloth. Spine stamped in gold (reading upwards): s & w [*dot*] A HANDFUL OF AUTHORS [*dot*] CHESTER-
TON / Front and back plain.

Published October 23, 1953, at 10s. 6d.   5,000 copies.   BM
26 Sep. 53.

A selection of G. K. C.'s writings on books and authors contributed to newspapers, periodicals and books between 1901
and 1935, now first collected. Part of the last essay, *A Shy Bird,*
had separate publication in 1935 as a British Council pamphlet,
G. K. Chesterton Explains the English (99).

1955

111. THE GLASS WALKING-STICK / AND / OTHER ESSAYS
/ FROM / THE ILLUSTRATED LONDON NEWS / 1905–1936 /
BY / G. K. CHESTERTON / EDITED BY / DOROTHY COLLINS
/ WITH A PREFACE BY / ARTHUR BRYANT / [*publisher's device*]
/ METHUEN & CO. LTD. LONDON / 36 ESSEX STREET,
STRAND, WC2

$7\frac{1}{4} \times 4\frac{1}{2}$. [A] to G, [H] and I–K in eights, L is four leaves
folded round L_2 which is eight; M is eight.

Pp. x + 190. (i) Half-title, (ii) blank; (iii) title-page, (iv) *First
published in* 1955. Printer's imprint; (v)–vi *Contents Showing
year of publication in the Illustrated London News;* (vii)–x *Preface;*
1–190 text.

Royal-blue grained cloth stamped in gilt. Front: facsimile
autograph of G. K. Chesterton. Spine: THE / GLASS /
WALKING-/ STICK / [*rule*] / G. K. / CHESTERTON / METHUEN /
Back blank.

Published in July 1955, at 10s. 6d.   3,500 copies.   BM 11 July 55.

The dust-jacket varies from the title-page thus: *With an
Introduction by Sir Arthur Bryant.*

B

BOOKS AND PAMPHLETS CONTAINING CONTRIBUTIONS BY G. K. CHESTERTON

The place of publication is London, unless otherwise stated.

1902

201. THOMAS CARLYLE. By G. K. Chesterton and J. E. Hodder Williams. Hodder and Stoughton. *"The Bookman" Booklets*, No. 1. December.
Re-issued as No. 1 in *"The Bookman" Biographies* in November 1903.
Only four booklets appeared in *"The Bookman" Booklets*. These were re-issued in November 1903 as *"The Bookman" Biographies* and four others added. Two of these also appeared in 1906 in the *Little Books for Bookmen* series. Each booklet, with one exception, contained two or more contributions by two or more authors, and numerous illustrations, reprinted from *The Bookman*. The exception is *Thomas Carlyle*, which has only one article (pp. 1–36) which had appeared over G. K. C.'s name in *The Bookman* for May 1902, followed by a biographical note and a note on some portraits of Carlyle. The title-page gives G. K. Chesterton and J. E. Hodder Williams as joint authors: it would appear that the latter supplied the two notes.

201A. A VOLUNTEER HAVERSACK. Edited by Archibald Stodart Walker. Printed for the Brigade. Edinburgh. Contains: *A Marriage Song*, pp. 181–2. (37.)

1903

202. ROBERT LOUIS STEVENSON. By W. Robertson Nicoll and G. K. Chesterton. Hodder and Stoughton. *"The Bookman" Booklets*, No. 2. Contains: *The Characteristics of Robert Louis Stevenson*, pp. 9–34.
Re-issued as No. 2 in *"The Bookman" Biographies*, November.
Re-issued in *Little Books for Bookmen*, 1906.

203. LEO TOLSTOY. By G. K. Chesterton, G. H. Perris and Edward Garnett. Hodder and Stoughton. March. *"The Bookman"* Booklets, No. 3. Contains: *Tolstoy*, pp. 1–6.
Re-issued as No. 4 in *"The Bookman"* Biographies, November 1903.

204. CHARLES DICKENS. By G. K. Chesterton and F. G. Kitton. Hodder and Stoughton. May. *"The Bookman"* Booklets, No. 4. Contains: *Charles Dickens*, pp. (1)–17.
Re-issued as No. 3 in *"The Bookman"* Biographies, November 1903.

205. BOSWELL'S *LIFE OF JOHNSON*. Abridged and edited by G. Nugent Banks and Hinchcliffe Higgins. Isbister. September. *Introduction* (80).
Re-issued by Pitman in 1905 in two volumes.

206. TENNYSON. By G. K. Chesterton and Dr. Richard Garnett, C.B. Hodder and Stoughton. November. *"The Bookman"* Biographies, No. 6. Contains: *Tennyson*, pp. 1–12.
Front cover reads: ALFRED TENNYSON.
Re-issued in *Little Books for Bookmen*, 1906.

207. THACKERAY. By G. K. Chesterton and Lewis Melville. Hodder and Stoughton. November. *"The Bookman"* Biographies, No. 8. Contains: *Thackeray*, pp. 1–11.

208. THE VENTURE. An Annual of Art and Literature. Edited by W. S. Maugham and Laurence Housman. Contains: *The Philosophy of Islands*, pp. 2–9.

1904

209. THE AUTOCRAT OF THE BREAKFAST-TABLE. By Oliver Wendell Holmes. Blackie's *Red Letter Library*. January. *Introduction* (80).

210. THE PILGRIM'S PROGRESS. By John Bunyan. Cassell's *National Library*. New Series. No. 22. April. *Introduction*, pp. (5)–14. Reprinted in Cassell's *Little Classics*, 1909.

211. SARTOR RESARTUS. By Thomas Carlyle. With an
      Introduction by G. K. Chesterton. Cassell's *National Library*.
      October. *Introduction*, pp. (5)–8.

212. THE RELIGIOUS DOUBTS OF DEMOCRACY.
      Edited by George Haw. Macmillan. Contains: *Christianity and
      Rationalism, Why I Believe in Christianity, Miracles and Modern
      Civilisation, The Eternal Heroism of the Slums.*
      A pamphlet reprinting a controversy in *The Clarion* between
      G. K. C., Robert Blatchford and others. (See 510, 511, 517.)

213. ENGLAND: A NATION. Being the Papers of the Patriots'
      Club. Edited by Lucian Oldershaw. London and Edinburgh.
      R. Brimley Johnson. Contains: *The Patriotic Idea*, pp. 1–43.

214. WAYFARERS' LOVE. Contributions from Living Poets.
      Edited by the Duchess of Sutherland. Archibald Constable.
      October. Contains: *Secrecy*, p. 64. Not collected. There was
      also an edition of 100 copies on large paper bound in vellum,
      numbered and signed by the Editor.

215. MR. CROWLEY AND THE CREEDS AND THE
      CREED OF MR. CHESTERTON. Privately printed
      [1904].
      Reprints G. K. C.'s review of *The Sword of Song* by Aleister
      Crowley from the *Daily News* of September 24, 1904, under
      the heading *Mr. Crowley and the Creeds* with a Reply, *The
      Creed of Mr. Chesterton* and a *Post-script* by Aleister Crowley.

1905

216. CREATURES THAT ONCE WERE MEN. By Maxim
      Gorky. Translated from the Russian by J. K. M. Shirazi.
      With Introductory [*sic*] by G. K. Chesterton. Alston Rivers.
      February. *Introductory*, pp. v–xi.

217. A BEGGAR'S WALLET. Containing contributions in
      Prose, Verse and Pictorial Illustration, gathered from certain
      Workers in Art and Letters by Archibald Stodart Walker.
      Edinburgh. Dobson Molle. 1905. Contains a sonnet: *Free
      Love*, p. 190.

1906

218. LITERARY LONDON. By Elsie M. Lang. T. Werner
Laurie. (n.d.) November. *Introduction*, pp. vii–xiii (80).

219. ESSAYS: LITERARY AND CRITICAL. By Matthew
Arnold. Dent. *Everyman Library*. *Introduction*, pp. ix–xiv (80).

220. THE ENGLISH HYMNAL. Oxford University Press.
Contains: No. 562, *O God of Earth and Altar* (collected in 37).
Also included in *Songs of Praise* (1925), *The Westminster
Hymnal* (New and revised edition, 1940) and *Congregational
Praise* (1951).

220A. PREACHERS FROM THE PEW. Lectures delivered at
St. Paul's Church, Covent Garden, under the Auspices of the
London Branch of the Christian Social Union. Edited by the
Rev. W. Henry Hunt. W. H. Lord & Co. (n.d.). The con-
tents consist of ". . . a series of talks from the Pulpit by men
usually in the Pew". Contains two talks by G. K. Chesterton:
Vox Populi, Vox Dei, and *The Citizen, the Gentleman, and the
Savage*. These were delivered on March 16th and March 30th,
1905. See extracts from Frances Chesterton's diary quoted in
782, p. 160.

1907

221. THE OLD CURIOSITY SHOP. By Charles Dickens.
Dent. *Everyman Library*. February. *Introduction*, pp. vii–xvi
(23).

222. FROM WORKHOUSE TO WESTMINSTER: the
Life Story of Will Crooks, M.P. By George Haw. With an
Introduction by G. K. Chesterton. Cassell. March. *Intro-
duction*, pp. xiii–xx.

223. THE BOOK OF JOB. With an Introduction by G. K.
Chesterton. S. Wellwood. May. *Introduction*, pp. v–xxiii (80).
A new edition, illustrated in colour by C. M. Tongue, with
the same Introduction, was published by Cecil Palmer and
Hayward in 1916.

224. BLEAK HOUSE. By Charles Dickens. J. M. Dent. *Everyman Library*. September. *Introduction*, pp. vii–xiv (23).

225. CHRISTMAS BOOKS. By Charles Dickens. J. M. Dent. *Everyman Library*. September. *Introduction*, pp. vii–xiv (23).

226. DAVID COPPERFIELD. By Charles Dickens. J. M. Dent. *Everyman Library*. September. *Introduction*, pp. vii–xv (23).

227. DOMBEY AND SON. By Charles Dickens. J. M. Dent. *Everyman Library*. September. *Introduction*, pp. vii–xvi (23).

228. GREAT EXPECTATIONS. By Charles Dickens. J. M. Dent. *Everyman Library*. September. *Introduction*, pp. vii–xiii (23).

229. MARTIN CHUZZLEWIT. By Charles Dickens. J. M. Dent. *Everyman Library*. September. *Introduction*, pp. vii–xiv (23).

230. NICHOLAS NICKLEBY. By Charles Dickens. J. M. Dent. *Everyman Library*. September. *Introduction*, pp. vii–xiv (23).

231. OLIVER TWIST. By Charles Dickens. J. M. Dent. *Everyman Library*. September. *Introduction*, pp. vii–xiv (23).

232. SKETCHES BY BOZ. By Charles Dickens. J. M. Dent. *Everyman Library*. September. *Introduction*, pp. vii–xiv (23).

233. THE PICKWICK PAPERS. By Charles Dickens. J. M. Dent. *Everyman Library*. September. *Introduction*, pp. vii–xv (23).

234. ENGLISH HUMORISTS OF TO-DAY. By J. A. Hammerton. Hodder and Stoughton. Contains: *The Advantages of Having One Leg*, pp. 262–266, "chosen with his permission (from) one of his Saturday essays in the *Daily News*" (25/8/06). Also a caricature of G. K. C. by Max Beerbohm from *The Idler* and an assessment of his achievement to date by the Editor.

1908

235. A CHILD'S HISTORY OF ENGLAND. By Charles
      Dickens. J. M. Dent. *Everyman Library*. February. *Introduction*,
      pp. vii–xii (23).

236. AMERICAN NOTES AND PICTURES FROM
      ITALY. By Charles Dickens. J. M. Dent. *Everyman Library*.
      February. *Introduction* to *American Notes*, pp. vii–xiv, and to
      Pictures from Italy, pp. xv–xvi (23).

237. HARD TIMES. By Charles Dickens. J. M. Dent. *Everyman
      Library*. February. *Introduction*, pp. vii–xiii (23).

238. LITTLE DORRIT. By Charles Dickens. J. M. Dent.
      Everyman Library. February. *Introduction*, pp. vii–xiii (23).

239. OUR MUTUAL FRIEND. By Charles Dickens. J. M. Dent.
      Everyman Library. February. *Introduction*, pp. vii–xiv (23).

240. POEMS. By John Ruskin. With an essay on the Author by
      G. K. Chesterton. Routledge. *Muses' Library*. July. Con-
      tains: *John Ruskin*, pp. v–xvi (110).

241. THE COTTAGE HOMES OF ENGLAND. By W. W.
      Crotch. Industrial Publishing Co. Third Edition. The *Intro-
      duction* appears for the first time in this edition. (80.)

241A. POETS OF OUR DAY. Edited by N. G. Royde-Smith.
      Methuen. Contains: *Translation from Du Bellay* (547, 37).

1909

242. REPORT from the Select Committee of the House of Lords
      and the House of Commons on the Stage Plays (Censorship).
      His Majesty's Stationery Office. Contains: *Evidence* by Mr.
      G. K. Chesterton, pp. 346–348. Quoted in *The Oxford Book
      of English Talk*, Edited by James Sutherland. O.U.P. 1953.

243. A VISION OF LIFE: POEMS by Darrell Figgis. With
      an Introduction by Gilbert K. Chesterton. John Lane, The
      Bodley Head. June. *Introduction*, pp. vii–xiii.

To Father O'Connor. — GK Chesterton

The scratching pen, the aching tooth,
The Plea for Higher Unity,
The aged buck, the earnest youth,
The Missing Link, the Busy Bee
The Superman, the Third Degree,
Are things that I should greatly like
To take a sling quite suddenly
As far as Heaven from Heckmondwike

As far as Hood is from Fitzooth
As far as seraphs from a flea
As far as Campbell from the truth,
Or old Bohemia from the sea
Or Shakespeare from Sir Herbert Tree
Or Nathan from an Arab Sheik
Or most of us from £.S.D —
As far as Heaven from Heckmondwike

As far as actresses from youth,
As far, as far as lunch from tea,
As far as Horton from Maynooth
As far as Paris from Paree
As far as Hawske is from a gee
Or I am from an old high bike,
As far as Stead from Sanity
As far as Heaven from Heckmondwike.
— Envoy.

Prince, Cardinal that is to be,
Cardinals do not go on strike
I'm far from wishing it (D.V.)
As far as Heaven from Heckmondwike

Inscription in a copy of *The Ballad of the White Horse* presented to
Father O'Connor, 1911

244. THE MEADOWS OF PLAY. By Margaret Arndt. Elkin Mathews. November. *Introduction* (80).

245. THE WONDERFUL YEAR, 1909. The *Daily News*. Contains: a poem, *The Hope of the Year* (pp. ix–x) and a frontispiece portrait of G. K. C.

246. THACKERAY. Edited by G. K. Chesterton. George Bell and Sons. *Masters of Literature* series. Contains: *Introduction*, pp. ix–xxxii, and editorial notes throughout.

247. EDWIN DROOD and MASTER HUMPHREYS' CLOCK. By Charles Dickens. J. M. Dent. *Everyman Library*. *Introduction* to *Edwin Drood*, pp. vii–xiv, and to *Master Humphrey's Clock*, pp. xiv–xx (23).

248. PAST AND PRESENT. By Thomas Carlyle. With an Introduction by G. K. Chesterton. Oxford University Press. *World's Classics*. *Introduction*, pp. (v)–xii.

249. BARNABY RUDGE. By Charles Dickens. J. M. Dent. *Everyman Library*. *Introduction*, pp. vii–xiv (23).

250. A TALE OF TWO CITIES. By Charles Dickens. J. M. Dent. *Everyman Library*. *Introduction*, pp. vii–xiii (23).

250A. THE SECOND PROBLEMS BOOK. Prizes and Proximes from the *Westminster Gazette*, 1908–1909. Edited by N. G. Royde-Smith. Sidgwick & Jackson. (Cover reads: The Second Westminster Problems Book.) Contains: *Sorrow* (From the French of Charles Guérin), pp. 5–6.

1910

251. CHRISTMAS STORIES. By Charles Dickens. J. M. Dent. *Everyman Library*. February. *Introduction*, pp. vii–xi (23).

252. REPRINTED PIECES. By Charles Dickens. J. M. Dent. *Everyman Library*. *Introduction*, pp. vii–xi (23).

253. PROCEEDINGS of the Nationalities and Subject Races
Congress. P. S. King. Contains: text of a speech, *What to do
with the Backward Races*.

254. EYES OF YOUTH. A book of verse by various writers.
Herbert and Daniel. (n.d.) December. *Foreword*, pp. vii–x.
There were also ten copies bound in vellum for presentation.

1911

255. SAMUEL JOHNSON. By Alice Meynell and G. K. Chesterton. Herbert and Daniel. *Regent Library.* August. The *Introduction*, pp. (vii)–xx, is signed by G. K. Chesterton only. (80.)

256. THE UNCOMMERCIAL TRAVELLER. By Charles
Dickens. J. M. Dent. *Everyman Library*. September. *Introduction*, pp. vii–ix.
This Introduction is not collected in *Appreciations and Criticisms of the Works of Charles Dickens* (23).

257. THE BOOK OF SNOBS. By William Makepeace
Thackeray. With an Introduction by Gilbert K. Chesterton.
Blackie's *Red Letter Library*. December. *Introduction*, pp. iii–x
(80).

1912

258. THE ENGLISH AGRICULTURAL LABOURER. By
The Rev. A. H. Baverstock. With an Introduction by G. K.
Chesterton. The Vineyard Press. A. C. Fifield. February.
Introduction, pp. iii–vii.

259. AESOP'S FABLES. A new translation by V. S. Vernon
Jones. With an Introduction by G. K. Chesterton and
Illustrations by Arthur Rackham. Heinemann. October.
Introduction, pp. v–xi (80). Also issued in a large-paper edition
limited to 1,450 numbered copies signed by Arthur Rackham.

260. FAMOUS PAINTINGS. Selected from the World's Great
Galleries and reproduced in colour. With an Introduction by
G. K. Chesterton and Descriptive Notes. Cassell and Co.
(n.d.) Two volumes. *Introduction*, Vol. I, pp. (iii)–vii.

261. TITANIC DISASTER FUND. Souvenir programme of a matinée at the Royal Opera House, Covent Garden, May 14, 1912. Contains: *A Ballade of Theatricals*. (Not collected.)

262. A CHRISTMAS CAROL AND OTHER TALES. By Charles Dickens. The Waverley Book Company. Two volumes. *Introduction*. Vol. I, pp. v–viii.

1913

263. REX *v.* CHESTERTON. Central Criminal Court. May 27–June 7, 1913. Law Report.
Evidence by G. K. Chesterton, p. 513.

264. REPORT FROM THE SELECT COMMITTEE on Marconi's Wireless Telegraph Co., Ltd., Agreement. Together with the Proceedings, Minutes of Evidence and Appendices. H.M.S.O. Two volumes.
Evidence by G. K. Chesterton.

1914

265. A CLUSTER OF GRAPES. Being the First Book of an Anthology of Twentieth Century Poetry collected by Galloway Kyle. Erskine Macdonald. Contains: *Sonnet with the Compliments of the Season, When I Came Back to Fleet Street,* and *The Truce of Christmas* (37).

266. TRIAL OF JOHN JASPER, Lay Precentor of Cloisterham Cathedral in the County of Kent, for the Murder of Edwin Drood, Engineer. Heard by Mr. Justice Gilbert Keith Chesterton sitting with a Special Jury, in the King's Hall, Covent Garden, W.C., on Wednesday, the 7th January, 1914. Verbatim report of the proceedings from shorthand notes of J. W. T. Ley. Chapman and Hall.
Bernard Shaw was Foreman of the Jury and Cecil Chesterton also took part. The trial lasted nearly five hours.

267. CHRISTIANA AND HER CHILDREN. A Mystery Play. Adapted by Mrs. Duncan Pearce from Bunyan's *Pilgrim's Progress*. Tailh y Pererin. Longmans, Green. *Preface,* p. 9.

268. DO MIRACLES HAPPEN? By G. K. Chesterton, Joseph
      McCabe, Hilaire Belloc and others. Christian Common-
      wealth Co., Ltd.
      Report of a discussion at the Little Theatre on Monday after-
      noon, January 19, 1914. Speeches by G. K. C., pp. 1–6 and
      21–23.

269. KING ALBERT'S BOOK. Hodder and Stoughton. Con-
      tains: *The Largest Window in the World*, pp. 143–144.

270. SONGS AND SONNETS FOR ENGLAND IN WAR
      TIME. John Lane, The Bodley Head. Contains: *Alliterativism*,
      pp. 36–37. Reprinted from *The New Witness*, August 13,
      1914. Collected in 69.

1915

271. BOHEMIA'S CLAIM FOR FREEDOM. Edited by J.
      Prochazka with an Introduction by G. K. Chesterton.
      Published on behalf of the London Czech Committee by
      Chatto and Windus. July. *Introduction*, pp. 5–6.

272. LAUGHS AND WHIFTS OF SONG. By Theodore
      Maynard. Erskine Macdonald. Contains an introductory
      essay, *On Theodore Maynard's Poems*, pp. 9–12. Dedicated
      to Gilbert Keith Chesterton.

273. LEST WE FORGET: A War Anthology. Edited by H. B.
      Elliott. Jarrold and Sons. Contains: *The Wife of Flanders*.
      Reprinted from *The New Witness*, August 27, 1914. Collected
      in 37. (This volume also includes contributions by Frances
      Chesterton and Cecil Chesterton.)

273A. POEMS OF THE GREAT WAR. Published on behalf
      of the Prince of Wales's National Relief Fund. Chatto &
      Windus. Contains: *The Wife of Flanders*. See 273.

273B. HOW BELGIUM SAVED EUROPE. By Charles
      Sarolea, with a Preface by Count Goblet D'Alviella. Heine-
      mann. Contains: "Appendix II. *The Martyrdom of Belgium*.
      An Appeal by G. K. Chesterton" reprinted from the *Illus-
      trated London News*.

274. THE BLINDED SOLDIERS AND SAILORS GIFT
      BOOK. Edited by George Goodchild. Jarrolds. (n.d.)
      Contains: *Shakespeare and the Germans*, pp. 129–131.

                              1916

275. HILAIRE BELLOC: The Man and his Work. By C. C.
      Mandell and Edward Shanks. With an Introduction by G. K.
      Chesterton. Methuen. January. *Introduction*, pp. vii–xii (80).

276. HINDUISM: the World Ideal. By Harendranath Maitra.
      Palmer and Hayward. *Introduction*, pp. ix–xiii.

277. COTTAGE ECONOMY. By William Cobbett. With an
      Introduction by G. K. Chesterton. Douglas Pepler. At
      the Hampshire House Workshops. May. *Preface*, pp. vii–x.
      Re-issued by Peter Davies, 1926.

278. A SONG OF THE OPEN ROAD and other Verses. By
      Louis J. McQuilland. With a Proem in Verse by "G.K.C."
      Heath Cranton. (n.d.) August. Contains: *Proem: Ballade to an
      Irishman / To L. J. McQ*, pp. 7–8.

279. THE SOUL OF RUSSIA. Edited by Winifred Stephens.
      Macmillan. Contains: *The English Blunder About Russia*,
      pp. 4–7.

280. WAR CARTOONS. By Will Dyson. Hodder and
      Stoughton. (n.d.) Contains: *Might and Right*, one page (un-
      numbered) facing a cartoon.

281. RAEMAKERS' CARTOONS. "Land and Water." Two
      volumes. Contains: commentaries by G. K. C. to the follow-
      ing cartoons: Vol. I: *Satan's Partner*; *Europe, 1916*; *Miss
      Cavell*; *Seduction*; *The Great Surprise*; *Ferdinand the Chameleon*;
      The Dutch Journalist to his Belgian Confrère; *Easter, 1915*. Vol.
      II: *The Beginning of the Expiation*; *Gallipoli*; *Peace Reigns at
      Dinant*; *Five on a Bench*.

282. SONGS OF THE SPECIALS. By E. W. Fordham. With
      an Introduction by G. K. Chesterton. Illustrations by Hugh
      Rivière. Cecil Palmer and Hayward. *Introduction*, pp. 1–7.
      Note on p. 8: "It is a well-recognised fact that volumes such
      as this should include a 'Foreword'. Mr. Chesterton, though
      he has been good enough to write an Introduction, has a
      conscientious objection to Forewords. . . ."

283. THE BOOK OF ITALY. Edited by Raffaello Picolli. New
      York. Frederick A. Stokes Company. Contains: *Italy and the
      German Professors*, pp. 77–82.

1917

284. PRACTICAL PACIFISM AND ITS ADVERSARIES:
      "Is it peace, Jehu?" By Severin Nordentoft. With an Intro-
      duction by G. K. Chesterton. Allen and Unwin. March.
      Introduction, pp. 1–5.

285. CHARLOTTE BRONTË, 1816–1916. A Centenary
      Memorial. Prepared by the Brontë Society. T. Fisher Unwin
      Ltd. Contains: *Charlotte Brontë as a Romantic*, pp. 49–54.

286. R. E. VERNÈDE. LETTERS TO HIS WIFE. Collins.
      A tribute to Vernède by G. K. C. which had appeared in
      The Pauline is quoted in the Introduction, pp. xvi–xix.

287. LIBERTY. By Sir James Crichton-Browne, M.D., Major-
      General Long, Will Thorne, M.P., The Dean of Durham,
      G. K. Chesterton, and Professor H. E. Armstrong, F.R.S.
      Eveleigh Nash Company. Contains: *V. The False Motive of
      the Movement*, pp. 36–41.

1918

288. THE HOUSE OF LYNCH. By Leonard Merrick. Hodder
      and Stoughton. (n.d.) *Introduction*, pp. v–x.

289. AUSTRALIA AT WAR. A Winter Record made by Will
      Dyson on the Somme and at Ypres during the Campaigns of
      1916 and 1917. With an Introduction by G. K. Chesterton.

Cecil Palmer and Hayward. November. *Introduction* (2 pp., unnumbered).

290. PROVOCATIONS. By Sybil Bristowe. With an Introduction by G. K. Chesterton. Erskine Macdonald. December. *Introduction*, pp. 7–9.

1919

291. A HISTORY OF THE UNITED STATES. By Cecil Chesterton. With an Introduction by G. K. Chesterton. Chatto and Windus. January. *Introduction*, pp. vii–xiii (80).

292. THE SKELETON KEY. By Bernard Capes. Collins. April. *Introduction* (80).

293. THE SONG OF ROLAND. Done into English, in the original measure by Charles Scott Moncrieff. With an Introduction by G. K. Chesterton and a Note on Technique by George Saintsbury. Chapman and Hall. November. *Introduction*, pp. ix–xii (108).

294. THE SOUL OF IRELAND. By W. J. Lockington, S.J. Harding and More. *Introduction*, pp. (xi)–(xiv) (80).
There was also an edition limited to 200 copies.

295. DRESSING GOWNS AND GLUE. By Capt. L. de G. Sieveking, D.S.C. With Illustrations by John Nash. With an Introduction about the Verses by G. K. Chesterton And an Introduction about the Drawings by Max Beerbohm And something about all concerned by Cecil Palmer. Edited by Paul Nash. Cecil Palmer and Hayward. September. Contains: *About the Poems*, pp. 11–12.
The Introduction was reprinted in *Bats in the Belfry* (334).

296. THE READERS' CLASSICS. Edited by G. K. Chesterton, Holbrook Jackson and R. Brimley Johnson. Bath. Cedric Chivers Ltd.
This series was planned before 1914, but publication was delayed until 1919, when the following four books were issued:

I. *David Copperfield.* II. *Ivanhoe.* III. *Vanity Fair.* V. *Essays of Elia.* Many other classics were announced for inclusion in the series, but no more were issued. Each of the published volumes has a general introduction to the series: *The Readers' Classics. A Word About Their Aim and Purpose* by the Editors, and also a paragraph headed *Notes on the Series* by the Editors. "For each volume we have obtained two or three new appreciations by living writers; and have further collected the most suggestive comments hitherto published . . ." G. K. C. is included in the list of contributors of original appreciations, but he did not contribute original matter to any of the published volumes. In the *Comments* he is represented in Vol. I, *David Copperfield*, by extracts from his *Charles Dickens* (10) and from his Introduction to *David Copperfield* in the Everyman Library (226); in II, *Ivanhoe*, by a short extract from *Charles Dickens* (10), and in III, *Vanity Fair*, by an extract from his Introduction to *Thackeray* in Bell's *Masters of Literature* series (246).

297.   A MISCELLANY OF POETRY, 1919. Edited by W. Kean Seymour. Cecil Palmer and Hayward. Contains: *Elegy in a Country Churchyard* and *The Ballad of St. Barbara* reprinted from *The New Witness*. Collected in 54.

1920

298.   LIFE IN OLD CAMBRIDGE. Illustrations of English History. By M. E. Monckton Jones. With a Preface by G. K. Chesterton. Cambridge. W. Heffer and Sons. March. *Preface*, pp. xiii–xviii (80).

299.   REPORT of the First Anglo-Catholic Congress, London, 1920. Society for the Promotion of Christian Knowledge. Contains: report of a speech, *The Church and Social Problems*, pp. 194–197.

300.   IS IT A NEW WORLD? A series of Articles and Letters contributed by Correspondents to the *Daily Telegraph*, August–September 1920. Hodder and Stoughton. Contains: *Starting Afresh*, pp. 219–227 (518).

1921

301. THE LITTLE WINGS. Poems and Essays. By Vivienne Dayrell (Vivienne Dayrell-Browning) with an Introduction [*sic*] by G. K. Chesterton. Oxford. Blackwell. January. *Introduction* (headed *Preface by G. K. Chesterton*), 4 pp. (unnumbered).

302. A BOOK OF DRAWINGS. By H. M. Bateman. With an Introduction by G. K. Chesterton. Methuen. *Introduction*, pp. v–vii (80).

302A. "WHAT I THINK." A Symposium on Books and Other Things by Famous Writers of To-day. Edited by H. Greenhough Smith. Newnes. (n.d.) Contains: *The Book I Most Enjoyed Writing* and *The Book I Shall Never Write*.

1922

303. POST-INDUSTRIALISM. By A. J. Penty. With a Preface by G. K. Chesterton. Allen and Unwin. (n.d.) May. "*Mr. Chesterton's Preface*," pp. 7–10.

304. A CHRISTMAS CAROL in Prose. Being a Ghost Story of Christmas by Charles Dickens. With four Illustrations in Colour and four Woodcuts by John Leech. A facsimile of the original edition. With an Introduction by G. K. Chesterton and a Preface by B. W. Matz. Cecil Palmer. Published in aid of the funds of the National Book Trade Provident Society. *Introduction*, pp. vii–xi (80).

305. LOVE AND FREINDSHIP and other early works now first printed from the original MS by Jane Austen. With a Preface by G. K. Chesterton. Chatto and Windus. November. *Preface*, pp. ix–xv (80).
Also an edition de luxe of 260 numbered copies.

306. THE RETURN OF CHRISTENDOM. By a Group of Churchmen. With an Introduction by Bishop Gore and an Epilogue by G. K. Chesterton. Allen and Unwin. *Epilogue*, pp. 245–251.
Reprinted in *Catholicism, Capitalism or Communism*, 1926 (333).

1923

307. THE INVALIDS. A Chronicle by J. C. Squire. 125 copies
      numbered and signed by J. C. Squire. Privately printed. Con-
      tains *Lines on a Cricket Match*, p. 33. The chronicle describes a
      match at Knotty Green, near Beaconsfield, played on Sep-
      tember 30, 1921, with G. K. C. as host. Knotty Green de-
      feated J. C. Squire's team, the Invalids, and G. K. C. composed
      the poem in celebration (811).

308. CHILD MEDIUMS. Being an exposure of an evil which is
      working the ruin of the bodies and souls of our children, by
      Irene Hernaman. With an Introduction by Gilbert K.
      Chesterton. Ditchling, Sussex. St. Dominic's Press. April.
      Introduction, pp. 1–7.

309. YEA AND NAY. A Series of Lectures and Counter-Lectures
      given at the London School of Economics in aid of the
      Hospitals of London. Brentano's. Contains: *V. Is Modern
      Journalism Worth the Price We Pay For It?* Lecture by C. A.
      McCurdy; Counter-Lecture by G. K. Chesterton, pp. 89–110.

310. THE OUTLINE OF LITERATURE. Edited by John
      Drinkwater. Newnes. Contains: *Dickens and Thackeray*,
      Vol. II., Chapter XXX, pp. 464–480.

311. THE MUSTARD TREE. By O. R. Vassall-Phillips. With
      an Introduction by G. K. Chesterton, A Preface by Mgr.
      Benson and an Epilogue by Hilaire Belloc. Burns and Oates.
      Second Edition, 1923. The *Introduction* by G. K. C. appears
      for the first time in this edition, pp. ix–xiv.

312. ESSAYS BY DIVERS HANDS. The Royal Society of
      Literature. New Series. Vol. III. Edited by Frederick S. Boas.
      Humphrey Milford. Contains: *Essay V. William Cobbett*,
      pp. 89–97.

313. NATIONAL CATHOLIC CONGRESS. Official Con-
      gress Guide and Programme. Birmingham. August. Contains:
      Anti-Catholic History, pp. 119–121.

314. THE MAKING OF RURAL EUROPE. By Helen Douglas Irvine, M.A. George Allen and Unwin. *Introduction*, pp. 7–10.

315. THE GUIDING BOOK. Edited by Ann Kindersley. Hodder and Stoughton. (n.d.) November. Contains: *Palestine*, pp. 142–146.

316. THE CATHOLIC WHO'S WHO AND YEAR BOOK 1924. Burns and Oates. December. *Preface*.

1924

317. PURPLE HOURS. By Philip Macer-Wright. With a Foreword by G. K. Chesterton. Gay and Hancock Ltd. April. *Foreword*, pp. vii–xii.

318. GEORGE MACDONALD AND HIS WIFE. By Greville Macdonald. With an Introduction by G. K. Chesterton. George Allen and Unwin. May. *Introduction*, pp. 9–15 (80).

319. THE UN-DIVINE COMEDY. By Zygmunt Krasinski. George G. Harrap and Co. Warsaw. Ksiaznica Polska. (n.d.) *Preface*, pp. v–xiii.

320. NUMBER TWO JOY STREET. A medley of prose and verse for boys and girls. Oxford. Blackwell. (n.d.) September. Contains: *The Dragon at Hide and Seek*, pp. 38–49. Reprinted in *Wish to Goodness* (357), 1928.

321. WILL MEN BE LIKE GODS? Humanitarianism or Human Happiness? By Owen Francis Dudley. Introduction by G. K. Chesterton. Longmans, Green. October. *Introduction*, pp. (iii)–viii (80).

322. THE NEW WORLD OF THE THEATRE, 1923–1924. By J. T. Grein. With a Preface by G. K. Chesterton. Martin Hopkinson. November. *Preface*, pp. vii–xi.

323. THE BOOK OF THE QUEEN'S DOLL'S HOUSE.
VOLUME TWO. THE BOOK OF THE QUEEN'S
DOLL'S HOUSE LIBRARY. Edited by E. V. Lucas.
Methuen. Contains: *The Ballade of Three Horns*, pp. 55–61.

324. ROSEMARY. Collected & Compiled by F. de Burgh and
Walter Stoneman. The "Not Forgotten" Association. Sampson Low. (n.d.) Contains: *On Optimism*, pp. 7–10.

325. THE CATHOLIC WHO'S WHO AND YEAR
BOOK, 1925. Burns and Oates. *Preface*, pp. xi–xiv (80).

326. THE BOOK OF THE MICROCOSM. Edited by
Dorothy Una Ratcliffe. Privately printed. Contains: *The
Apology of Bottom the Weaver*, pp. 26–29 (69).

326A. THE GRANTA AND ITS CONTRIBUTORS—
1889–1914. Compiled by F. A. Rice, with an Introduction
by A. A. Milne. Constable. Contains: *Ballade of the Renaissance of Wonder* (528) and a drawing (615A).

1925

327. ABISHAG. By Alexandre Arnoux. Translated by Joyce
Davis. With a Preface by G. K. Chesterton. Thornton Butter-
worth. March. *Preface*, pp. 7–12 (80).

328. MY CIRCUS LIFE. Being the Life and Adventures and the
World Travels and Experiences of an Artist and Circus
Proprietor now aged 79 years. The last of the Mohicans
emanated from "The Cradle of the Circus World", Astley's
Amphitheatre, Westminster Bridge Road, London. James
Lloyd. Introduction by G. K. Chesterton. Noel Douglas.
July. *Introduction*, pp. v–vii.

329. GOD AND INTELLIGENCE IN MODERN
PHILOSOPHY. A Critical Study in the light of the
Philosophy of Saint Thomas. By Fulton J. Sheen. With an
Introduction by G. K. Chesterton. Longmans, Green.
October. *Introduction*, pp. vii–ix.

330. THE WRONG LETTER. By Walter S. Masterman.
      With a Preface by G. K. Chesterton. Methuen. *Preface*, pp.
      v–viii (80).

331. MODERNISM AND THE CHRISTIAN CHURCH.
      By Francis Woodlock, S.J. With a Preface by G. K. Chester-
      ton. Longmans, Green. *Preface*, pp. iii–vi.

332. NUMBER THREE JOY STREET. A medley of prose
      and verse for boys and girls. Oxford. Basil Blackwell. (n.d.)
      Contains: *The Coloured Lands* (105).

1926

333. CATHOLICISM,   CAPITALISM   OR   COM-
      MUNISM. By Rev. J. C. Harrington. . . . With an Epilogue
      by Gilbert K. Chesterton. St. Paul, U.S.A. The E. M.
      Lohmann Company. January. *Epilogue*, pp. 443–5.
      A reprint of the *Epilogue* to *The Return of Christendom*, 1922
      (306).

334. BATS IN THE BELFRY. By L. de Giberne Sieveking.
      Routledge. *Introduction*.
      A reprint of the *Introduction* to *Dressing Gowns and Glue* (295).

335. CHOSEN POEMS. By Douglas Ainslie. With a Preface by
      G. K. Chesterton. The Hogarth Press. March. *Preface*, pp.
      9–14.
      Later reprinted as the *Introduction* to *Conquest of Pleasure*, by
      Douglas Ainslie (Grant Duff), New York, 1944 (411).

336. SOME DICKENS WOMEN. By Edwin Charles. With a
      Foreword by G. K. Chesterton. T. Werner Laurie. July.
      Foreword, pp. v–vii (80).

337. THE TOYS OF PEACE and other Papers. By "Saki"
      (H. H. Munro). With an Introduction by G. K. Chesterton
      and a Memoir. Collected Edition. John Lane, The Bodley
      Head. August. *Introduction*, pp. xi–xiv.

338. GILBERT AND SULLIVAN. A Critical Appreciation of the Savoy Operas. By A. H. Godwin. With an Introduction by G. K. Chesterton. J. M. Dent. September. *Introduction*, pp. vii–xv (80).

339. THE HISTORY OF RASSELAS, Prince of Abissinia. By Doctor Johnson. With an Introduction by G. K. Chesterton. J. M. Dent. October. *Introduction*, pp. vii–x (80).

340. THE SHIP OF DESTINY. By G. Laurence Groom. Preface by G. K. Chesterton. Leeds. The Swan Press. *Preface*, pp. 6–8. Edition limited to 250 numbered copies.

341. TWELVE MODERN APOSTLES AND THEIR CREEDS. With an Introduction by Dean Inge. New York. Duffield and Co. Contains: *Why I am a Catholic* (550).

342. ESSAYS BY DIVERS HANDS. VOL. VI. Edited by G. K. Chesterton. The Royal Society of Literature. Humphrey Milford. *Introduction*, pp. v–xiii (80).

343. THE MAN WHO WAS THURSDAY. A Play in Three Acts. Adapted fro mthe novel of G. K. Chesterton by Mrs. Cecil Chesterton and Ralph Neale. With a Foreword by G. K. Chesterton. Ernest Benn. *Foreword*, pp. 3–(5).

344. LEAFLETS FOR LEAGUERS NO. I. The League. (n.d.) Contains: *The Purpose of the League.*

345. THE FLYING CARPET. Designed by Cynthia Asquith. Partridge & Co. (n.d.) Contains: *To Enid who acted the Cat in Private Pantomime*, pp. 57–59.

346. THE STOCK EXCHANGE ANNUAL, 1926–7. Contains: *Some Doubts on Advertisement.*

346A. LEAFLETS FOR LEAGUERS No. 3. The League (n.d.). Contains: *The League*, p. 6.

1927

347. THE LIFE OF CHARLES DICKENS. By John Forster. J. M. Dent. *Everyman Library*. February. Two volumes. Contains an *Introduction* in the first volume, pp. ix–xiii (80).

348. THE CHANGE: Essays on the Land. By G. C. Heseltine. With a Foreword by G. K. Chesterton. Sheed and Ward. March. *Foreword* (headed *Introduction*), pp. 9–14 (80).

349. GRANDMAMMA'S BOOK OF RHYMES FOR CHILDREN. Written by Mrs. Elizabeth Turner. Introduced by G. K. Chesterton. Decorated by Maud Reed Cooper. Humphrey Milford. August. *Introduction*, pp. iii–vii (80).

350. THE DEFENCE OF THE WEST. By Henri Massis. Translated by F. S. Flint. With a Preface by G. K. Chesterton. Faber and Gwyer. November. *Preface*, pp. v–x.

351. LIBERTY AND PROPERTY. By H. E. Humphries. The League. (n.d.) *Preface*, p. 4.

351A. ABOUT JEAN STIRLING MACKINLAY. Christian the Printer. (n.d.) *Foreword*.

1928

352. DO WE AGREE? A Debate between G. K. Chesterton and Bernard Shaw with Hilaire Belloc in the Chair. Cecil Palmer. July.

353. WHERE ARE THE DEAD? Cassell and Co. Contains: *The Rout of Reason*, pp. 24–29. Reprinted from the *Daily News*, June 4, 1928 (517).

354. THE GOLDEN ARROW. By Mary Webb. Jonathan Cape. Collected Edition. November. *Introduction*, pp. vii–xi (80).

355. DRINKING SONGS AND OTHER SONGS. By W. R. Titterton. Cecil Palmer. *Introduction*, pp. vii–ix (526. *First pages from a New Book*.) (80).

356. CENTENARY ADDRESSES. Bound Together in One
Volume. With a Preface by Dr. R. W. Chambers. Uni-
versity of London Press. Contains: *Culture and the Coming
Peril* (72).

357. WISH TO GOODNESS. By Laurence Housman. Oxford.
Basil Blackwell. (n.d.) Contains: *The Dragon at Hide and Seek*,
pp. 21–32, reprinted from *Number Two Joy Street* (320), 1924.

357A. THE EUROPEAN SCRAPBOOK. The Year's Golden
Harvest of Thought and Achievement. New York. W. H.
Wise & Co. Contains: *The Americanisation of England*, an
abstract of an address by G. K. Chesterton at the Delphian
Coterie dinner, London, and three articles from the *Illustrated
London News*: *Thomas Hardy, The Voice of America, The
Real War Makers*.

1929

358. THE SECRET OF THE CURÉ D'ARS. By Henri
Ghéon. Translated by F. J. Sheed. With a note on the Saint
by G. K. Chesterton. Sheed and Ward. February. Contains:
The Challenge of the Curé D'Ars, pp. 211–216 (80).

359. THE ENCYCLOPAEDIA BRITANNICA. 14th Edi-
tion. 1929. Contains: Vol. 7, pp. 331–335, *Charles Dickens*;
Vol. 11, pp. 883–885, *Humour*.

360. THE LEGION BOOK. Edited by Capt. H. Cotton
Minchin. Cassell. Contains: *To St. Michael in Time of Peace*,
p. 145. Also a caricature of G. K. C. by Low.
There was also a large paper edition, privately printed and
limited to 600 copies, of which only 500 were for sale.

361. CATHOLIC EMANCIPATION, 1829–1929. Longmans, Green. Contains: *XIII. The Outlook*, pp. 267–81.

362. IF I WERE A PREACHER. Cassell. Contains: *A Sermon
Against Pride*. Reprinted from the *Daily Telegraph* (518).
Collected in 108.

Lepanto.

(Tripoli was taken on the anniversary of the Battle of Lepanto.)

White founts falling in the Courts of the sun,
And the Soldan of Byzantium is smiling as they run,
There is laughter like the fountains in the face of all men feared,
It stirs the forest darkness, the darkness of his beard,
It curls the blood-red crescent, the crescent of his lips,
For the inmost sea of all the earth is shaken with his ships.
They have dared the white republics up the capes of Italy,
They have dashed the Adriatic round the Lion of the Sea,
And the Pope has cast his arms abroad for agony & loss,
And called the Kings of Christendom for swords about the cross.
The cold queen of England is looking in the glass;
The shadow of the Valois is yawning at the Mass,
From evening isles fantastical rings faint the Spanish gun,
And the Sultan upon the Golden Horn is laughing in the sun.

Dim drums throbbing, in the hills half-heard,
Where only on a nameless throne a crownless prince has stirred
Where risen from a doubtful seat & half attainted stall,
The last knight of Europe takes weapons from the Wall
The last and lingering troubadour to whom the bird has sung
That once went singing southward when all the world was young
In that enormous silence, tiny and unafraid,
Comes up along a winding road the noise of the Crusade.

One of two extant MS. versions of *Lepanto*, 1911

363. THE FAME OF BLESSED THOMAS MORE. Being addresses delivered in his honour in Chelsea, July 1929, by Father Ronald Knox, Hilaire Belloc, G. K. Chesterton, Lord Justice Russell, Henry Browne, S.J., Reginald Blunt and Bede Jarrett, O.P. With an Introductory Essay by Professor R. W. Chambers. Sheed and Ward. October. Contains: *A Turning-Point in History*, pp. 61–64.

364. LETTERS ADDRESSED TO A. P. WATT AND HIS SONS, 1883–1929. A. P. Watt and Son. Contains two letters, pp. 44–47.

1930

365. THE TRIBUTE. Tendered by Artists, Authors and Advertisers of the Empire on the Anniversary of His Majesty's Recovery. Edited by D. Mackenzie. John Horn. Contains: *Advice to Literary Murderers*, pp. 161–163.

366. VANITY FAIR, A NOVEL WITHOUT A HERO. By William Makepeace Thackeray, with an introduction by G. K. Chesterton and illustrations by John Austen. Oxford. Printed for the Limited Editions Club by the Oxford University Press. Two volumes, boxed. Edition limited to 1,500 copies, signed by the artist. *Introduction* (110).

367. THE EIGHTEEN-EIGHTIES. Essays by Fellows of the Royal Society of Literature. Edited by Walter de la Mare. Cambridge University Press. Contains: *Gilbert and Sullivan*, pp. 136–158.

368. KING LEAR. By William Shakespeare. Illustrated by Yunge. San Francisco. David Magee. Edition limited to 240 copies: 30 special copies (of which 25 for sale) numbered I–XXX signed by G. K. Chesterton and containing an extra set of illustrations printed on Japanese paper signed by the artist; 210 copies (of which 200 for sale) printed on J. Barcham Green's handmade paper, numbered 31 to 240. *Introduction*, pp. vii–x.

1931

369. SPAIN: Its Story Briefly Told. By Catherine Moran. Philip Earle. July. *Introduction*, pp. i–iv.

370. THE BURNS WE LOVE. By A. A. Thomson. Herbert Jenkins. October. *Foreword*, pp. 5–10.

371. GIOTTO. THE LEGEND OF ST. FRANCIS: as depicted in the Assisi frescoes, and faithfully copied by E. M. Cowles. 28 plates (loose in portfolio). J. M. Dent. October. *Foreword*, pp. 7–14 (108).

372. THE MESSENGER OF THE SNOW. By Ferdynand Goetel. Translated from the Polish by M. C. Slomezanka and G. N. Murray, with a Preface by G. K. Chesterton. Elkin Mathews and Marrot. October. *Preface*, pp. v–x.

373. ONE HUNDRED AND ONE BALLADES. With Illustrations by John Nash. Cobden Sanderson. October. Contains: twelve ballades by G. K. C. reprinted from *The Eye Witness* and *The New Witness* (1912–13), pp. 26–42. Four of these had already appeared in *Poems* and in *Collected Poems*: *Ballade of an Anti-Puritan, Ballade of a Book Reviewer, Ballade of Suicide, Ballade of the First Rain*. The others appear here in book form for the first time. P. 107. *Last Ballade*. By Hilaire Belloc, G. K. Chesterton, Maurice Baring, J. S. Phillimore, T. Michael Pope and Cecil Chesterton.

374. MARGARET DOUGLAS. A Selection from her Writings. Together with appreciations of her life and work by Hilaire Belloc, G. K. Chesterton and others. Ditchling. St. Dominic's Press. November. Edition limited to 150 copies. Contains: a poem, *In Memoriam. M.D.*

375. THE FOTHERGILL OMNIBUS for which Eighteen Eminent Authors have written Short Stories upon One and the Same Plot. With Introductions by John Fothergill, R. G. Collingwood and Gerald Gould. Eyre and Spottiswoode. November. Contains: *The End of Wisdom*, pp. 105–121. There was also an edition of 250 copies printed on special paper, each copy numbered, and signed by the authors.

376. REVALUATIONS. Studies in Biography by Lascelles Abercrombie, Lord David Cecil, G. K. Chesterton and others. O.U.P. December. Contains: *Mary Queen of Scots*, pp. 1–25.
"With one exception, the biographical studies which follow were read by the authors at the City Literary Institute during the Lent term, 1931. The exception was the extemporary discourse on Mary Stuart by Mr. Chesterton who, declaring that he makes speeches but does not deliver lectures, agreed to read and approve before publication the verbatim transcript included here."—*Introduction*, by A. C. Ward.

377. THE FLOATING ADMIRAL. By certain members of the Detection Club (Dorothy L. Sayers, G. K. Chesterton, Canon Victor L. Whitechurch, G. D. H. and Margaret Cole, Henry Wade, etc.). Hodder and Stoughton. December. G. K. C. contributed the *Prologue*: "The Three Pipe Dreams," pp. 13–18.

378. AFOOT IN PORTUGAL. By John Gibbons. Newnes. (n.d.) *Foreword*, pp. 1–4.

378A. THE MERCURY BOOK OF VERSE. Being a Selection of Poems Published in the *London Mercury*, 1919–1930, with an Introduction by Sir Henry Newbolt. Macmillan. Contains: *Sonnets in Summer Heat*, pp. 78–79.

378B. IS THERE A RETURN TO RELIGION? A Debate. Yes: Gilbert K. Chesterton. No: E. Haldeman-Julius. Girard, Kansas. Haldeman-Julius Publications.

379. IF IT HAD HAPPENED OTHERWISE: Lapses into Imaginary History. Edited by J. C. Squire. Longmans, Green. February. Contains: *If Don John of Austria had married Mary Queen of Scots*, pp. 21–48. Reprinted from *The London Mercury*. Collected in 108.

1932

380. THE CATHOLIC LAND MOVEMENT. By Father Vincent McNabb, O.P., S.T.M., and Commander H. Shove, D.S.O., R.N. With a Foreword by G. K. Chesterton. Catholic Truth Society. April. *Foreword*, 3 pp. (unnumbered).

381. FLEET STREET. Edited by W. W. Cobbett and Sidney Dark. Eyre and Spottiswoode. Contains: *The Artistic Side*, pp. 379–383. Reprinted from *G.K.'s Weekly*, November 29, 1930 (526).

382. COSMOLOGY. By Daniel C. O'Grady. Ottawa. Graphic Publishers Ltd. *Preface*, 5 pp. (unnumbered).

383. THE SILVER SHIP. Edited by Lady Cynthia Asquith. Putnam. Contains: *Bob-Up-and-Down*. Reprinted from *G. K.'s Weekly*, December 12, 1931 (526) and collected in 105.

384. THE GREAT VICTORIANS. Edited by H. J. Massingham and Hugh Massingham. Ivor Nicholson and Watson. (n.d.) Contains: *Charles Dickens*, 1812–1870, pp. 161–171. (110. *The Great Gusto*.)

385. ESSAYS OF THE YEAR 1931–1932. The Argonaut Press. September. Contains: *The Essay*, pp. xi–xviii.

386. RECOLLECTIONS OF AN OCTOGENARIAN. By I. G. Homewood. With an Introduction by G. K. Chesterton. John Murray. December. *Introduction*, pp. ix–xii.

387. THE PENN COUNTRY OF BUCKINGHAMSHIRE. Evans Bros. December. *Introduction*, pp. 7–8. Also a limited edition, *de luxe*.

388. THE WEEK-END CALENDAR. Edited by Gerald Barry. Geoffrey Bles. December. Contains: *A Note on Notting Hill*, pp. 44–46. Reprinted from *The Week-End Review* (571).

389. ALL FALL DOWN! or The Nonsense-Fancier's Assistant. Compiled by Nicolas Bentley. Ivor Nicholson and Watson. (n.d.) December. ". . . It is the wish of my contributors to remain anonymous. For this reason I have withheld individual attribution of their efforts, but at the same time have disclosed their identity . . . " p. viii, How This Book Came to be Written. Contains: *All Through the Night*, pp. 65–68. Reprinted from *G.K.'s Weekly*, August 20, 1927 (526).

389A. JOHN HENRY NEWMAN. The Romantic, the Friend, the Leader. By Sister Mary Aloysi Kiener, S.N.D., Ph.D. Foreword by Reverend John Cavanagh, C.S.C., Ll.D. Introduction by G. K. Chesterton. Boston. Collegiate Press Corporation.

1933

390. SPECTATOR'S GALLERY. Essays from *The Spectator*, 1932. Edited by Peter Fleming and Derek Verschoyle. Jonathan Cape. Contains: *St. Thomas Aquinas*, pp. 279–283 (559).

391. SIX CENTURIES OF ENGLISH LITERATURE, 1370–1920. Passages Selected from the Chief Writers and Short Biographies. By Richard Ferrar Patterson. London and Glasgow. Blackie. April. *Vol. VI; Meredith to Rupert Brooke*. With Introductory *Essay* by G. K. Chesterton, pp. xv–xxvi (108).
   G. K. C. is himself represented by *Lepanto* (pp. 314–317). The "short biography" which prefaces the poem includes, among his works, "Catholic Essays (1929)." This refers, presumably, to *The Thing*.

392. THE ENGLISH WAY. Studies in English Sanctity from St. Bede to Newman. Edited by Maisie Ward. Sheed and Ward. June. Contains: *Alfred the Great*, pp. 56–64, *Thomas More*, pp. 209–217.

393. LIVERPOOL CATHEDRAL. Souvenir Programme. Solemn Blessing and Laying of the Foundation-Stone of the Liverpool Metropolitan Cathedral of Christ the King. Whit Monday, June 5. Contains: *The Church and Agorophobia*, p. 18 (97).

394. A TALE OF TWO CITIES. By Charles Dickens. Macmillan. December. *Introduction*, pp. vii–xvi (108).

395. THE SMITH OF SMITHS. Being the Life, Wit and Humour of Sydney Smith. By Hesketh Pearson. Hamish Hamilton. January. *Introduction*, pp. 11–14.

396. REBUILDING THE CHURCH IN ENGLAND. The Liverpool Cathedral Book. Burns, Oates and Washbourne (n.d.) Contains: *Epilogue. The Last Turn*, p. 168.

397. HAVE WE LOST GOD? This Vital Question has been put
      by W. R. Titterton to numerous people, including G. K.
      Chesterton. Grayson and Grayson. Contains: *The Revival I
      Want*, pp. 37–42.

398. THE POSTHUMOUS PAPERS OF THE PICKWICK
      CLUB. By Charles Dickens. With an Introduction by G. K.
      Chesterton and illustrations by John Austen. Oxford.
      Printed for the Limited Editions Club (New York) by the
      Oxford University Press. Two volumes. Edition limited to
      1,500 sets signed by the artist. *Introduction*, Vol. I, pp. (v)–xi.

399. PAULINE AND OLD PAULINE, 1884–1931. By
      Henry Arthur Sams. With a Foreword by John Bell, High
      Master of St. Paul's School. Privately printed at the Uni-
      versity Press Cambridge. Chapter V, *The Junior Debating
      Club* includes extracts from *The Debater* and two drawings: a
      reproduction of the title-page for June 1893 and *In Memoriam
      J.D.C.*

1934

400. G.K.'s. A Miscellany of the First 500 Issues of *G.K.'s Weekly*.
      Rich and Cowan Ltd. October. Contains: *Introduction*, and
      numerous contributions (prose, verse and illustrations) by
      G. K. C.   Reprinted from *G.K.'s Weekly*.

1935

401. A CENTURY OF DETECTIVE STORIES. Hutchin-
      son. (n.d.) April. *Introduction*, pp. (9)–(11). *The Secret Garden*
      (pp. 343–361) is reprinted from *The Innocence of Father
      Brown*.

402. THE PRINCESS ELIZABETH GIFT BOOK. Edited
      by Cynthia Asquith and Eileen Bigland. Hodder and
      Stoughton. (n.d.) October. Contains: a poem, *The Good
      Grocer*, pp. 34–35.

403. FRANCIS THOMPSON AND OTHER ESSAYS. By
      Fr. Vincent McNabb. Ditchling. Pepler and Sewell. Saint
      Dominic's Press. December. *Introduction*, pp. vii–x.

1936

404. FREEDOM. By Sir Ernest Benn, G. K. Chesterton, Bernard Shaw, and others. Based on a series of broadcast talks given in 1935. George Allen and Unwin. January. Contains: *Essay XII* (pp. 128–136). The text of this talk first appeared in *The Listener* (536) under the title *The Liberty that Matters* and set off a long, and unfinished, controversy with, among others, Dr. Coulton. See also *The Well and the Shallows* (97), pp. 258–277, for G. K. C.'s reply to some of the criticisms of the broadcast.

405. A PAPAL CHAMBERLAIN. The Personal Chronicles of Francis Augustus Macnutt. Edited by the Rev. John J. Donovan. London and New York. Longmans, Green. *Preface*, pp. vii–x.

406. THE MENACE TO CATHOLICISM IN GERMANY. Pamphlet issued by the British Non-Sectarian Anti-Nazi Council. *Introduction*, p. (1).

407. THE HOUND OF HEAVEN. By Francis Thompson. Boston, U.S.A., Bruce Humphries Inc. June 25. *Introduction* (108).

408. A. R. ORAGE: A MEMOIR. By Philip Mairet. J. M. Dent. August. *Introduction*, pp. v–viii.

409. THE ADVENTURES OF PEREGRINE PICKLE. By Tobias Smollett. With an introduction by G. K. Chesterton and illustrations by John Austen. Oxford. Printed for the Limited Editions Club at the University Press. Edition limited to 1,500 copies signed by the artist. Two volumes. *Introduction*, Vol. I, pp. v–x (108).

1942

409A. THE BETRAYAL. A Passion Drama in Three Acts with a Prologue. By Geoffrey Nevil Dowsett, O.M.I. With a Preface by G. K. Chesterton. New York. Samuel French. The introduction was written in 1934.

1943

410. GILBERT KEITH CHESTERTON. By Maisie Ward. New York. Sheed and Ward. Contains much unpublished material: prose, verse, letters, drawings (782).

1944

411. CONQUEST OF PLEASURE. By Douglas Ainslie (Grant Duff). New York. *Introduction.* This Introduction is a reprint of the Preface to *Chosen Poems* (335), 1926.

1946

411A. TO THE QUEEN'S TASTE. Consisting of the best stories published in the first four years of *Ellery Queen's Mystery Magazine.* Boston, U.S.A. Little, Brown & Co. Contains: *Dr. Hyde, Detective.* (Not collected.)

1952

412. RETURN TO CHESTERTON. By Maisie Ward. Sheed and Ward (811).
"This book is made up chiefly of unpublished letters, verses and *jeux d'esprit* of Chesterton's, over eighty in all . . ." Introduction.

1953

413. THE ENGLISH FIRST EDITIONS OF HILAIRE BELLOC. By Patrick Cahill. With an Open Letter to Hilaire Belloc by G. K. Chesterton. Published by the Compiler. The open letter (pp. 4–6) is reprinted from *The New Witness*, April 27, 1923 (545).

1956

414. TIME AND TIDE ANTHOLOGY. Introduction by Lady Rhondda. Edited by Anthony Lejeune. Deutsch. Contains: *Candida and a Candid Friend*, pp. 90–92. Reprinted from *Time and Tide.*

C

PERIODICALS CONTAINING CONTRIBUTIONS BY G. K. CHESTERTON

(See note, p. 14)

501. **ACADEMY**

1895. July 22. The Ruskin Reader. (An unsigned review.) "It is by this event that the beginning of my friend's career as a writer may be dated." E. C. Bentley, *Those Days* (773). But see the *Speaker* (558).

502. **ACORN**

1905. No. 1. The Sun. (37. Ballad of the Sun. A revised version.)

502A. **ALBANY REVIEW**

1907. April. A Fragment from a Ballad Epic of Alfred (25).

503. **ARCHITECTURAL DESIGN AND RECON-STRUCTION**

1932. Feb. Vandalism (108).

504. **BIBLIOPHILE**

1908. March. Vol. I, No. 1. W. E. Henley (110).

505. **BOOK FAIR**

1907. First Spring Number. John Ruskin. Reprinted in 240 and collected in 110.

506. **BOOK MONTHLY**

1904. Literary London and its Spirit of Place (110).

507. **BOOKMAN**

1899. Dec. Velasquez and Poussin. (An unsigned review.) ". . . But long before this it was apparent that the centre of gravity in my existence had shifted from what we will (for the sake of courtesy) call Art to what we will (for the sake of courtesy) call Literature. The agent in this change of intention was, in the first instance, my friend Ernest Hodder Williams.

BOOKMAN *(cont.)*

. . . He was attending Latin and English lectures at University College while I was attending, or not attending, to the art instructions of the Slade School. I joined him in following the English course. . . . Hodder Williams and I often talked about literature following on these literary lectures; and he conceived a fixed notion that I could write. . . . In consequence of this, and in connection with my art studies, he gave me some books on art to review for the *Bookman*, the famous organ of his firm and family. I need not say that, having entirely failed to learn how to draw and paint, I tossed off easily enough some criticisms of the weaker points of Rubens or the misdirected talents of Tintoretto. I had discovered the easiest of all professions; which I have pursued ever since." *Autobiography*, pp. 99–100 (101).

1900. June. Literary Pictures of the Year. I. Shakespeare, Tennyson, Dickens. July. II. The Three Classes of Literary Art (in collaboration with J. E. Hodder Williams). Aug. III. The Three Classes of Literary Art *(cont.)*. Dec. The Literary Portraits of G. F. Watts, R.A.

1902. May. Carlyle (201). Oct. Tennyson (206).

1903. Feb. Thackeray (207).

1929. Dec. Magic and Fantasy in Fiction (91).

1932. Oct. Books I have never Read. (Contribution to a symposium collected by Grant Uden.)

508.   CASSELL'S MAGAZINE

1911. Feb. The Invisible Man (24). March. The Eyes of Apollo (24). April. The Strange Justice (24. The Honour of Israel Gow). May. The Sins of Prince Saradine (24). June. The Flying Stars (24). July. The Three Tools of Death (24).

1921. Sept. The Hole in the Wall (55).

1925. April. The Mirror of Death (71. The Mirror of the Magistrate). May. The Man with Two Beards (71). July. The Chief Mourner of Marne (71). Aug. The Song of the Flying Fish (71). Nov. The Worst Crime in the World (71).

1926. March. The Actor and the Alibi (71). April. The Ghost of Gideon Wise (63).

1929. April. The Moderate Murderer (83). Sept. The Ecstatic Thief (83).

509. CATHOLIC HERALD
> 1946. Sept. 27. To the Jesuits (Spain, 1936).
> 1952. Dec. 5. A Vision of Edens. A long unpublished poem written at the age of 17 or 18, with eleven drawings. Dec. 26. Humanity. An early poem. (See 519.)

509A. CHRISTMAS SPIRIT. (Christmas Annual of Toc H.)
> 1920. The Fantastic. A poem by G. K. Chesterton, in facsimile handwriting.

510. CLARION
> 1895. April 20. Easter Sunday. "The first of his poetry to be given to the world." E. C. Bentley (773). Not so. See the *Speaker* (558).
> The *Clarion* Controversy.
> 1903. March 27. (Robert Blatchford refers to G. K. C.'s column in the *Daily News*.) July 31. (R. B. replies to criticisms made by G. K. C. in the *Daily News*.) Aug. 7. Mr. Blatchford and Free Will. (Letter from G. K. C.) 14. (Love or Hate. A Reply to G. K. Chesterton.) 28. Mr. Blatchford and Free Will. (Letter from G. K. C.) Sept. 4. (The Battle of the Danube. A reply to G. K. C. by R. B.) Nov. 13. (Clerical Logic by R. B. refers to G. K. C.'s articles in *Commonwealth*.) 20. Mr. Blatchford, Persecution and other things. (Letter from G. K. C.) Dec. 4. (A Few Arrears. R. B. replies to G. K. C. and opens the columns of the *Clarion* to critics.)
> 1904. July 22. Christianity and Rationalism. 29. We are all Agnostics until——. August 5. Mr. Blatchford's Religion. Dec. 23. The Inconsistency of Mr. Blatchford (Letter).
> See also the *Daily News* (517), *Commonwealth* (511) and *The Religious Doubts of Democracy* (212).

511. COMMONWEALTH
> 1902. Jan. The Mystery of Patriotism. Dec. The Nativity. (37 and 553.)
> 1903. July to Dec. The Dogmas of Free Thought I–VI. (See 510 and 212.) Dec. The Feast of the Snow (37 and 553).
> 1904. June. The Two Compromises. (An address to the

COMMONWEALTH (cont.)

Christian Social Union in St. Paul's Church House.) Nov. Aggressive Infidelity. (Speech at the Church Congress.)

1905. Jan. "Passionate peace is in the sky" (37. The Truce of Christmas). March to Dec. *The Ball and the Cross* (17). Dec. Society (Lecture to the C.S.U.).

1906. Feb., April, June and Nov. *The Ball and the Cross* (17).

1907. Aug. The New Theology and the Social Movement (Speech to the Saltley Christian Fellowship). Nov. Hymn for the Church Militant (37).

512. CORNHILL

1930. July. Gilbert and Sullivan (367).

513. CRITERION

1929. April. Is Humanism a Religion? (79).

514. DAILY GRAPHIC

1907. Sept. 12. Boy and Girl: the problem of their upbringing. (108. Two Stubborn Pieces of Iron.)

1909. The Real Dr. Johnson (108).

515. DAILY HERALD

1913. April 12. The Epitaph of Pierpont Morgan (108). May 3. The Tyranny of Bad Journalism (44). June 14. Revive the Court Jester (44). July 26. A Workman's History of England (44). Sept. 27. The Poetry of the Revolution (44). Oct. 11. A Song of Swords (37). Nov. 22. The French Revolution and the Irish (44). Dec. 6. *Utopia of Usurers* (44). I. Art and Advertisement. 13. II. Letters and the New Laureates. 20. III. Unbusinesslike Business. 27. IV. The War on Holidays.

1914. Jan. 3. V. The Church of the Servile State. 12. VI. Science and the Eugenists. 19. VII. The Evolution of the Prison. 24. VIII. The Lash for Labour. 31. IX. The Mask of Socialism. Feb. 7. The Art of Missing the Point (44). 13. Liberalism: a Sample (44). March 21. The Fatigue of Fleet Street (44). April 15. The New Name (44). May 30. The Empire of the Ignorant (44). Aug. 1. A Real Danger (44). 22. The Amnesty for Aggression (44). Sept. 26. The Tower of Babel (44).

516. DAILY MAIL

> 1914. Oct. 30. *The Barbarism of Berlin* (33): Introduction. The Facts of the Case. Nov. 2. I. The Fight for a Promise. 4. II. The Prussian Idea of Honour. 9. The Appetite of Tyranny.

517. DAILY NEWS

> G. K. C. contributed a weekly article and occasional reviews, many of the early ones unsigned, from Jan. 6, 1901, to Feb. 1, 1913. In the following list of contributions that were afterwards collected in book form, the serial number after each entry refers to the book. When the title was changed significantly, the new title is given after the serial number.
>
> 1901. March 14. The Mistake about Stevenson (4). July 16. The Soul of Charles II (4). 26. A Re-reading of Carlyle (4). Aug. 5. A Handbook on Tennyson (14). 10. The Position of Sir Walter Scott (4). 19. Browning and his Ideal (110). Sept. 2. Detectives in Fiction (110. Sherlock Holmes, I). 3. The Divine Parody of Don Quixote (110). 12. A Grammar of Shelley (110). 17. The Voyage of Ithabel (110. Historical Novels). 24. Elizabeth Barrett Browning (14). 26. Books for Boys (108). Oct. 18. The Life of Stevenson (110). 24. A Re-issue of Tolstoy (4). Dec. 2. The Optimism of Byron (4). 5. The Wild Governess (4. Charlotte Brontë).
>
> 1902. Feb. 14. The Decline of Satire (4. Pope and the Art of Satire). Nov. 27. The Frivolous Man (108). Dec. 9. A Minor Poet (14. The German Emperor).
>
> 1903. March 14. The Return of the Angels (510). April 4. Making the World Small (14). 11. The Inside (14). Nov. 14. Mr. Blatchford and my Neighbour (510). 21. The Unknown Animal (510). 28. Faith and the Fantastic (510).
>
> 1904. April 16. Some Policemen and a Moral (16). Sept. 24. Mr. Crowley and the Creeds (215).
>
> 1905. April 1. A Note on a Satirist (9. The Wit of Whistler). June 2. Mr. Masefield's Short Stories (110). July 1. A Memory of the Last Election (16. How I met the President). Sept. 16. The Twelve Men (16). Oct. 7. A Fragment of Fact (16. The Secret of a Train). Nov. 4. A Piece of Chalk (16). Dec. 25. The Wise Men (37).
>
> 1906. March 24. What I found in my Pocket (16). April 7. The Extraordinary Cabman (16). May 5. In the Place de la Bastille (16).

DAILY NEWS (cont.)

26. The Great Opportunist (110. Ibsen). June 16. A Tragedy of Twopence (16). Aug. 11. The Perfect Game (16). 25. Advantages of Having One Leg (236, 16). Nov. 3. An Accident (16). Dec. 1. The Wind and the Trees (16). 8. In Topsy-Turvy Land (16). 22. The Shop of Ghosts (16).

1907. Jan. 2. An Edition of Dumas (110. On Writing Badly). 12. The Prehistoric Railway Station (16). Feb. 2. The Toy Theatre (16). On Lying in Bed (16). March 4. A Song of De-feat (37). 9. A Glimpse of my Country (16). 23. On Absence of Mind (110. Sherlock Holmes, II). April 20. Reading the Riddle (108). 27. The Orthodox Barber (16). June 15. The End of the World (16). 29. The Lion (16). July 6. The Riddle of the Ivy (16). Nov. 9. The Diabolist (16). Dec. 14. The Dragon's Grandmother (16). 21. The Red Angel (16).

1908. Jan. 4. A Criminal Head (20). 25. A Somewhat Improb-able Story (16. Angry Street: a Bad Dream). April 18. The Tower (16). May 2. The Ballad of a Strange Town (16). 9. Humanity, an Interlude (16). 16. The Little Birds who won't Sing (16). June 6. The Travellers in State (16). Aug. 22. The Dickensian (16). 29. The Two Noises. (16). Oct. The Red Town (20). 31. The Giant (16). Nov. 7. The Long Bow (20). Dec. 5. How I Found the Superman (20). 19. After the Milton Celebration (110. The Taste for Milton).

1909. Jan. 16. The Three Temples (20. On Gargoyles). Feb. 13. Simmons and the Social Tie (20). 20. The Divine Detective (28). April 24. A Cab Ride across Country (16). May 22. A Great Man (16). June 12. The Case for Macaulay (110). 19. The Mystery of a Pageant (16). July 3. The Ultimate Lie (21A). 10. Cheese (20). 24. A Drama of Dolls (20). Aug. 7. The Wildness of Domesticity (18). 21. Liberty (28. The Free Man). 28. The Surrender of a Cockney (20). Oct. 9. The Three Kinds of Men (20). 16. The Nightmare (20). 30. Dukes (20). Nov. 13. The Futurists (20). 27. The Man and his News-paper (20). Dec. 4. Pseudonyms (28. The Nameless Man). 11. The Anarchist (20). 20. The Revolutionist (37). 25. The Modern Scrooge (20).

1910. Jan. 8. The Flat Freak (20). Feb. 26. The Telegraph Poles (20). March 5. The Field of Blood (20). April 16. The Wheel (20). 23. The Steward of the Chiltern Hundreds (20). 30. The

DAILY NEWS (cont.)

Appetite of Earth (20). May 21. A Stone (20. The New House). 28. The Wings of Stone (20). June 4. The Sentimentalist (20). 11. The Orientalism of the Empire (28. The Sultan). 25. The Furrows (20). July 16. The Real Disfranchisement (28. The Voter and the Two Voices). 23. The Wrath of Roses (20). 30. The Strangeness of Luxury (20). Aug. 13. The Triumph of the Donkey (20). 20. The Garden of the Sea (20). 27. Ethandune (20). Sept. 3. The Glory of Grey (19, 20). 10. The Chorus (20). 17. The Gold of Glastonbury (20). 24. The High Plains (20). Oct. 1. The Romance of the Marshes (20). Nov. 5. Romantic Rain (28. The Romantic in the Rain). Dec. 3. The Enchanted Island (28. The Enchanted Man). 17. Realities (28. The Real Journalist).

1911. Jan. 7. The Lie of the Photograph (28. The False Photograph). 14. The Thing (28). 28. Mr. Harrogate's House (28. The Hypothetical Householder). Feb. 18. The Insane Quiet (28. The Mad Official). April 15. The Sun of Easter (28. The Priest of Spring). 29. The Shy Town (28. The Poet and the Cheese). May 6. Thinking Backwards (28). 13. The Marching Towers (28. The Architect of Spears). June 10. Content. (28. The Contented Man). 17. With Apologies to King John (28. The Mediaeval Villain). July 1. The Two Fires. (28. The Wrong Incendiary). 15. The Case for Revolution (28. The Red Reactionary). 22. The Miser (28). Aug. 5. The True Romance (110. Cervantes). 12. The Wild Animal (28. The Elf of Japan). 26. The Kind of Man (28. The Other Kind of Man). Sept. 30. The Crisis (28. The Conscript and the Crisis). Oct. 21. The Solar Myth (28. The Sun Worshippers). Nov. 4. The Unicorn (108. Monsters and the Middle Ages). 18. The Slime of the Dragon (28. The New Theologian). 25. The Separatist (28). Dec. 9. The Unutterable (28. The Mystagogue). 30. The Mummers (28).

1912. March 2. The Spade Guinea (28. The Gardener and the Guinea). 23. The Scot (28). 30. The Fool (28). May 11. The Dullness of Cliques (28. The Sectarian of Society). 25. The Charter (28. The Chartered Libertine). June 8. The Doubt at the Root (28. The Man on Top). 15. The Aristocratic 'Arry (28). Oct. 31. The March of the Black Mountain (37).

1913. Feb. 1. The Unknown Livery. (The last article in a twelve

DAILY NEWS (*cont.*)
years' series. See *Gilbert Keith Chesterton* by Maisie Ward (782) p. 297. The *Song of Strange Drinks* to which she refers had appeared in *The New Witness* on Jan. 23, 1913.)
1928. June 4. The Rout of Reason (in *Where are the Dead?* series) (353).

518. DAILY TELEGRAPH
1915. Oct. 21. "Our Day" (39).
1920. Aug. 3, 5, 7, 10, 12, 14, 17, 19, 21, 24, 26, 28, 31. Sept. 2, 4, 7, 9, 10, 13, 15, 16. *The New Jerusalem* (51). Sept. 11. Starting Afresh (in *Is it a New World?* series) (300).
1928. Dec. 31. "If I Were a Preacher." A sermon against the sin of pride (362). Collected in 108. This, "the first of a series of contributions by distinguished authors under the general title: 'If I Were a Preacher'", provoked a lively controversy in which Dr. G. G. Coulton and Hilaire Belloc, among others, took part:—
1929. Jan. 3. (Letter from Dr. Coulton.) 4. The Psychology of Pride. A reply by G. K. Chesterton. 7. (Letter from Dr. Coulton.) 8. (Letter from Hilaire Belloc.) 9. A Rejoinder from Mr. Chesterton. 10. Dr. Coulton's Claims. Mr. Chesterton adds a Postscript. 12. (Challenge to Mr. Chesterton. Dr. Coulton's Offer.) 14. (Disputed Quotation. Letter from Hilaire Belloc. Letter from Dr. Coulton.) 16. (Dr. Coulton and his Critics. Letter from Dr. Coulton.) 17. (A Rejoinder to Dr. Coulton. Letter from Hilaire Belloc.) 21. (Mr. Belloc and Dr. Coulton. Letter from Hilaire Belloc.) Mr. Chesterton's Epilogue.

519. DEBATER
Journal of the Junior Debating Club. "Hence Loathèd Melancholy." Edited by the Secretary, J. D. C.
1891. Vol. 1, No. 1. March. Dragons: A Sketch. *Sunset and Dawn.* A poem. No. 2. April. Report of a paper on Old Ballads read by G. K. C. on Jan. 30, 1891, at "Mr. C.'s house." *Adveniat Regnum Tuum.* A poem. Vol. 2. No. 3. May. Royal Death Scenes. No. 4. June. *Danton.* A poem. No. 5. July. *Doubt.* A poem. No. 6. Aug. *William of Orange.* A poem. No. 7. Sept. On Shakespeare's Method of Opening his Plays. Being the

DEBATER (*cont.*)

First Paper read in the Junior Debating Club. The Chairman [G. K. C.]. No. 8. Oct. Poetry and Science. *Simon de Montfort*. A poem. No. 9. Nov. The Happiness of Genius. No. 10. Dec. The Prize Essay. "Boys' Literature." (This is preceded by a letter to the Editor from the examiners which awards the prize to essay No. 1 by the Chairman [G. K. C.] and says of the entries ". . . most of them are careless and unsystematic and nearly all barren of ideas, the prevailing tendency being towards cheap and somewhat priggish moralisation". In the margin of G. K. C.'s own copy is pencilled in his hand, "Very fair and quite right. Don't want to be buttered up". And beside the essay, "Worst thing I've ever done, I hope".) *Algernon Sydney*. A poem. J.D.C. Minutes. "After the minutes had been read and confirmed, the Secretary proposed a vote of congratulation to the Chairman for having a poem accepted by the *Speaker*. This was carried enthusiastically." (See 558.) 1892. No. 11. Jan. Humour in Fiction. *Theory*. A poem. No. 12. Feb. *Idolatry*. A poem. Vol. 3, No. 13. March. *Humanity*. A poem (509). No. 14. May. Report of a paper read by the Chairman [G. K. C.] on the New School of Poetry. The formation of the J.D.C. Sketching Club is also announced. "Mr. Bentley proposed Mr. Chesterton as Chairman, who was elected without opposition. . . . The Chairman read a paper on Japanese Art, in which he dealt mainly with the contrast afforded by its grotesque and impressional treatment to the usually decorative character of Oriental art. As few remarks were made upon this paper, the meeting shortly dispersed." No. 15. July. *Worship*. A poem. "As we go to press we hear the pleasant news that our Chairman, Mr. Chesterton, has gained the Milton Prize for English verse at St. Paul's School, the subject for treatment being St. Francis Xavier, the apostle of the Indies." . . . "After a vote of congratulation had been awarded to Mr. Chesterton for his gaining of the Milton Prize . . . a Debate on Collaboration in Literature was held, the Chairman stating 'That collaboration in writing is not productive of good results'. . . ." No. 16. Sept. The Chairman read a paper on "Three Stages of Ethical Poetry in Europe". (July 8.) Report of a debate on the relative merits of Virgil and Horace which the Chairman opened on

DEBATER *(cont.)*

behalf of Horace (July 22). No. 17. Nov. *St. Francis of Assisi.* A poem.

1893. No. 18. Feb. "With this number *The Debater* ceases to exist." Report of speech in a debate on "Humour up to Date" (Oct. 7) and on "Short Stories and Short Story Writers of To-day" (Oct. 14). The Chairman proposed for debate: "That Advertisement should be to a greater extent restrained by Law." *Ave Maria.* A poem (570).

520. DUBLIN REVIEW

1914. Jan. Notes on Recent Books by their Writers: G. K. Chesterton on *Magic.*

1925. Jan./March. A Reply to *Roman Converts.* (See 728, and for Arnold Lunn's reply, see 729.)

521. EMPIRE REVIEW

1923. Oct. Pickwick and the English Peoples (110. A Shy Bird).

522. ENGLISH LIFE

1925. Jan. Dr. Hyde, Detective and the White Pillars Mystery (411A).

522A. ENGLISH REVIEW

1909. March. The Homelessness of Jones (18).

1922. Sept. The Myth of Arthur (54).

523. EVERYMAN

1914. Nov. The Triumph of the Degenerate (35).

524. EYE-WITNESS.

1911. July 13. Ballade of an Anti-Puritan (37). Aug. 17. Ballade of Great Rivers (373). 31. The Song of the Wheels (37). Sept. 14. Ballade of Cutting a Stick (373). 21. Ballade of Suicide (37). Oct. 12. Lepanto (37). Ballade of a Book Reviewer (unsigned) (548, 37). Nov. 16. Ballade to a Philanthropist (373). 23. Ballade of Monsters (373). Dec. 21. Sonnet with the Compliments of the Season (37). 29. Ballade of Dead Men. 1912. Jan. 11. Ballade of an Impartial Person (373). 25. Wonder

EYE-WITNESS (*cont.*)

and the Wooden Post (105). Feb. 8. Ballade of Reasonable
Inquiry (373). March 14. Ballade of a Stoic. April 11. Ballade
of the Grotesque (373). 25. Ballade of the First Rain (37). May
30. Anti-Christ or the Re-Union of Christendom. An Ode
(37). June 13. Last Ballade (with H.B., M.B., J.S.P., T.M.P.,
C.C. and XXX) (373). 20. The Shakespeare Memorial (37).
July 11. The Horrible History of Jones (37). 25. The New Free-
thinker (37).

525. FORTNIGHTLY REVIEW

1930. May. The Reaction of the Intellectuals (97). Sept. The
Spirit of the Age in Literature (91).

1931. April. The Return to Religion (97). Aug. George
Bernard Shaw (91).

1932. July. Walter de la Mare (108).

526. G.K.'s WEEKLY. Edited by G. K. Chesterton.

G. K. C. contributed signed and unsigned work of all kinds
from March 21, 1925 (Vol. I, No. 1) until his death in June
1936 (Vol. XXIII. No. 587). He usually, but not always,
wrote the editorials and, as with the contributions to the
New Witness, work that was not his was sometimes reprinted
elsewhere over his name. (See W. R. Titterton, *G. K.
Chesterton. A Portrait* (748), pp. 149–150.) The short, unsigned
articles headed *Top* and *Tail*, which appeared weekly from
Sept. 5, 1925 to August 10, 1929, were also written by G. K. C.
Most of these contributions are uncollected. The items recorded below are those that subsequently appeared in book
form together with certain other items such as reports of
speeches and debates.

1925. March 21. Vol. I. No. 1. The First Principle (unsigned
leader). *Answers to the Poets:* The Skylark Replies to Words-
worth (unsigned) (69). The Sea Replies to Byron (unsigned)
(69). The New Fiction (unsigned) (69). *Found Wandering:*
How I Tried to Boom this Paper. The World State (69). The
Old Gentleman in the Park (unsigned) (69). 28. *Answers to the
Poets:* Dolores Replies to Swinburne (unsigned) (69). How I
Got Inside this Paper. April 4. Regina Angelorum (65).
Answers to the Poets: From the Spanish Cloister (unsigned) (69).

G.K.'S WEEKLY (cont.)

How I Shall Deface this Paper. 11. The Judgment of England (69). 18. By a Reactionary (unsigned) (69). 25. The Modern Magic (unsigned) (69). On a Prohibitionist Poem (unsigned) (69). The Free Man and the Ford Car (64). May 2. Americanisation (unsigned) (69). The Namesake (unsigned) (69). The New Omar (unsigned) (69). *Answers to the Poets:* Lady Clara Vere de Vere replies to Mr. Alfred Tennyson (unsigned. Not collected). 9. *Answers to the Poets:* The Fat White Woman Speaks (unsigned) (69). By a Captain, or Perhaps a Colonel, or Possibly a Knight-at-Arms (unsigned) (69). May 16. To a Lady (69). 23. The Buried City (69). 30. *Answers to the Poets:* To a Modern Poet (unsigned) (69). July 4 (weekly to Nov. 28). *The Outline of Sanity* (64). To the Unknown Warrior (unsigned) (69). *Answers to the Poets:* Post-Recessional (unsigned) (69). August 8. Race-Memory (unsigned) (69). *Answers to the Poets:* Lucasta Replies to Lovelace (unsigned) (69). August 22. The Towers of Time (65). Sept. 5. To a Holy Roller (unsigned) (69). 19. The Temptation of St. Anthony. A play. Oct. 17. How to Write a Detective Story. Nov. 14. Commercial Candour (69). Dec. 5. (weekly to Nov. 20, 1926). *The Return of Don Quixote* (68). *The Turkey and the Turk* (87). Wishes (unsigned) (69. Some Wishes at Christmas). 12. The Apology of an Editor.

1926. Jan. 9. What You Won't. A Problem Play for a Progressive Audience. March 27. Jealousy (69). July 17. Propaganda. 24. A Patriotic Song (69). Sept. 25. The Outline of the Fall (79). The League Meets (Speech). Oct. 16. A Broad-Minded Bishop Rebukes the Verminous St. Francis (69). 23. Have we lost Liberty? (Speech). Nov. 27. The New Despotism (Speech). Dec. 11. The Composite Tool (105. The Professor and the Cook, I). 25. Can we Replace the Trade Unions? (Debate).

1927. Feb. 5. The Menace of the Busybody (Debate with Lady Rhondda). The Scientific Mind (105. The Professor and the Cook, II). April 23. Meeting on Buses and Barrows (Speech). May 14. A Grammar of Knighthood (97). June 18. The First Point about Poland (106). 25. The Hope of the New Nations (106). July 2. The Blunder of the Bolshevist (106. The Crime in Warsaw). 9. The Enemy of Poland (106). Aug. 20. All

G.K.'S WEEKLY (cont.)

through the Night (389). Nov. 5. Do We Agree? (Debate with Bernard Shaw) (352).

1928. Jan. 14. Inge *versus* Barnes (79). March 17. The Mediaevalism of Ibsen (110). April 28. What's Wrong with Coal? (Speech). May 26. The Mask of the Agnostic (79). Sept. 15. The Legend of the Sword (unsigned) (102). Oct. 27. The Usual Article (79). First Pages from a New Book (355). Nov. 3. On Two Allegories (79).

1929. May 11. Our Cure for Unemployment (Speech). Oct. 5. Alice Meynell (110).

1930. May 3. The Menace of Empire (Speech). June 28. The Menace of Prohibition (Debate with E. Scrymgeour). Nov. 15. On a Skyscraper (91). 29. The Artistic Side (105). Dec. 27. America Rediscovered (91. Which is the Government). 27. The Merger (Poem and cartoon).

1931. Jan. 3. A Plea for Prohibition (91). 10. The School for Swagger (91). On an American Best-Seller (Poem and cartoon). Feb. 14. The True Village Idiot (91). 28. A Preface on Praise (91). April 18. Bernard Shaw and America (91). 25. The Apology for Hustle (91). May 23. They are all Puritans (91). Dec. 12. Poem. "Irresponsible outbreak . . ." (105, 383. Bob-up-and-Down).

1932. Jan. 30. On Cleaning Up (106). March 5. The Right to Rob (106). May 28. The Higher Nihilism (97). June 4. The Ascetic at Large (97). 11. Third Thoughts are Best (106). 18. One Word More (106). July 9. Back in the Fog (97). 23. Levity or Levitation (97). Sept. 17. The True Case for Unity (Speech). Oct. 29. The Backward Bolshie (97). Nov. 12. Babies and Distributism (97). Dec. 31. The Scripture Reader (97).

1933. Feb. 11. John Galsworthy (obituary). March 2. Hiding an Earthquake (106). 9. The End of the Pacifists (106). April 20. The Heresy of Race (106). May 18. Who is Dictator? (106). 25. If it were England (106). June 9. The Don and the Cavalier (97). 15. The Opportunity for Communism (Speech). 29. The Pacifist as Prussianist (106). July 13. The Other Cheek (106). 20. The Judaism of Hitler (106). 27. The Return of Caesar (97). Aug. 24. The Last Taboo (97. The Don and the Cavalier). Sept. 7. Shocking the Modernists (97). Nov. 9. Sex and Property (97).

23. The Umbrella Question (106). Dec. 14. The New Luther (97).

1934. August 2. Austria (97). Three Foes of the Family (97). Oct. 18. Europe and the Press (Speech). Dec. 20. Christmas and the First Games (105).

1935. May 2. The Case of Claudel (97). 16. Killing the Nerve (97). July 4. The Right to Strike (Speech). Oct. 10. On War Books (106).

1936. March 19. Hitler *versus* History (Signed leader) (106). 26. To the Jesuits (Spain 1936). May 21. The Truth about Tribes (106). June 11. In Reply to Critics. [G. K. C. *died on June 14.*] Nov. 5. The Common Man (108).

527. GOOD WORDS

1904. Jan. Studies in Shakespeare. I. *Love's Labour's Lost.* Sept. and Oct. *A Midsummer Night's Dream*, I and II (108).

528. GRANTA

1908. Oct. 17. Ballade of the Renaissance of Wonder. Reprinted in *The Eye-Witness*, April 11, 1912, as Ballade of the Grotesque and collected under that title in *One Hundred and One Ballades* (373).

529. HEATON REVIEW

1934. Vol. VII. A Note on Father Brown.

530. HERITAGE

1956. Jan. A Beaconsfield Ballad (103).

531. IDLER

1904. June to Dec. *The Club of Queer Trades.* Illustrated by the author (8).

532. ILLUSTRATED LONDON NEWS

Our Note-book. G. K. C. contributed a weekly essay under this heading from 1905 until his death in 1936. The series was interrupted only by illness or absence abroad. The essays appeared in the issues dated: Sept. 30, 1905, to Nov. 9, 1907; Nov. 23, 1907 to Oct. 9, 1912; Oct. 23, 1912 to June 21, 1913; July 5, 1913 to Nov. 21, 1914; May 22, 1915, to Nov. 2, 1918; Nov. 23, 1918; Dec. 7, 1918, to Jan. 10, 1920; May 29, 1920,

ILLUSTRATED LONDON NEWS (*cont.*)

to Jan. 22, 1921; May 21, 1921, to April 21, 1923; May 5, 1923, to June 9, 1923; June 23, 1923, to May 1, 1926; May 22, 1926, to June 20, 1936.

The issue dated June 20, 1936, contained, in addition to the last contribution to *Our Note-book*, a reprint of G. K. C.'s first essay in the series from the issue of Sept. 30, 1905.

In all there were 1,535 essays in the series. Of these, 362 were afterwards collected in the following books: *All Things Considered, The Uses of Diversity, Fancies versus Fads, Generally Speaking, All is Grist, Come to Think of It, All I Survey, Avowals and Denials, As I Was Saying, The Common Man, A Handful of Authors,* and *The Glass Walking-Stick.* The essays thus collected were given titles for the first time on their appearance in book form. The titles are listed below in alphabetical order with the date of first appearance of each in *The Illustrated London News* and in parentheses the reference number of the book in which it is collected.

Abolishing Sunday. 29.ix.29 (86). About Christianity. 17.viii.35 (111). Abraham Lincoln. 17.xi.28 (86). Abraham Lincoln, Myself on. 23.ii.29 (86). Age of Reason, The. 23.x.26, 16.x.26, 13.xi.26 (111). Alphabet of Giants, The. 19.vii.24 (111). America. 14.xii.29 (86). American Morals. 5.ii.27 (75). American Revolt Against Americanism, The. 30.iii.29 (86). Anonymity and Further Counsels. 12.x.07 (12). Archaeology. 25.xi.22 (75). Architecture. 7.viii.26 (75). Atheist Museum, On the. 19.xi.32 (95). Bad Comparisons, About. 29.vi.35 (100). Bad Poetry. 18.iii.31 (93). Bad Word for Guild, On the. 5.i.29 (89). Baroque and Gothic Architecture. 12.iii.27 (111). Bath. 31.i.25 (75). Beggars and Soldiers. 22.xii.34 (100). Behaviourist, On the. 5.vii.30 (89). Beliefs, About. 29.ix.34 (100). Bigness and America. 10.xi.28 (86). Blake and his Critics. 21.x.33 (95). Blake and Inspiration. 23.xi.29 (110). Blondes, About. 26.i.35 (100). Books for Pessimists. 18.ii.33 (95). Boredom of Butterflies, The. 15.vii.22 (56). Boy, The. 10.xi.06 (12). Boys. 27.x.28 (86). Brevity and Wit. 21.v.32 (93). Broadcasting. 7.v.27 (75). Buddhism. 13.x.23 (75). Business Education. 29.iii.30 (89). Byron and Tom Moore. 18.iii.22 (75).

Carols. 25.xii.26 (75). Censor, About the. 17.ii.34 (100).

Censorship for Literature. 23.iii.29 (86). Change, About. 13.vii.35 (100). Change, On. 16.iii.29 (86). Changes in Taste. 17.xii.27 (75). Changing Human Nature. 9.vi.34 (100). Chaucer, Mr. Geoffrey. 26.xii.31 (93). Child, On the. 5.iii.32 (93). Christian Science. 22.x.10 (50). Christian Science, On. 18.x.30 (89). Christmas. 29.xii.06 (12). Christmas, On. 3.i.25 (75). Christmas that is Coming. 23.xii.33 (95). Classicism of Terror, On the. 6.v.33 (95). Classics, On the. 10.viii.29 (86). Closed Conspiracy, On the. 15.xii.28 (86). Cockneys and their Jokes. 1.ix.06 (12). Code Napoleon, The. 21.v.21, 17.vi.22 (111). Colour of Spain, The. 19.vi.26 (111). Comic Spirit, On the. 10.xii.27 (75). Conceit and Caricature. 16.xii.05 (12). Condiments and Conduct. 21.ii.31 (89). Contiguous Past, On the. 3.ix.32 (93). Court of Camelot, The. 16.xii.22 (111). Crank and the Cad, On the. 14.i.33 (95). Creative and the Critical, On the. 11.iv.31 (93). Cryptic and the Elliptic, On the. 15.vi.07 (12). Current Claptrap. 31.viii.29 (86). Cyrano and Chanticleer. 5.iii.10 (111).

Dante and Beatrice. 22.iii.30 (89). Darwinism. 2.ii.35 (100). Dead Poet, A. 30.xi.07 (12). Deceptibility of Youth, On the. 20.i.34 (95). Demagogues and Mystagogues. 11.i.08 (12). Dependence and Independence. 28.xi.31 (93). Detective Novels. 15.viii.22 (75). Detective Story Writers. 17.viii.29 (86). Dialect and Decency. 16.xii.33 (95). Dickens Again. 21.xii.12 (50). Dickens and After. 22.ix.28 (86). Dictatorships. 2.ii.29 (86). Dogs with Bad Names. 26.xi.32 (95). Domestic Servants. 30.vi.23 (75). Dreams. 4.ii.33 (95). Dress and Decorum. 13.ix.30 (89). Duke of Marlborough, On the. 28.x.33 (95). Duty of the Historian, The. 24.ix.10 (50).

Eatanswill Gazette, The. 10.viii.07 (12). Eating and Sleeping. 4.iv.31 (93). Education, About. 15.vi.35 (100). Education, On. 28.v.32 (93). Edward VII and Scotland. 3.xi.06 (12). *Edwin Drood*, On. i.vii.22 (75). Egoists and Egoists. 3.xi.28 (86). Egyptian Influence. 17.ii.23 (75). Electric Houses. 17.iii.28 (75). Encyclopaedias. 14.vii.28 (86). Englishman Abroad, On the. 11.vi.27 (75). Epstein, On Mr. 15.vi.29, 22.vi.29 (86). Eric Gill. 10.vi.33 (95). Error of Impartiality. 20.iv.07 (12). Essay on Two Cities. 29.vi.07 (12). Essay, On

ILLUSTRATED LONDON NEWS (*cont.*)

Letter-Bag Novel, On the. 8.iv.33 (95). Liberties and Lotteries. 1.iv.30 (89). Limericks and Counsels of Perfection. 5.x.07 (12). Literary Cliques. 6.vi.31 (93). Literary Parallels. 20.vii.29 (86). Living for Posterity. 31.v.30 (89). Logic and Lunacy. 27.vi.31 (89). Loneliness. 30.xi.29 (86). Love. 2.v.31 (93). Loving Germans, About. 5.v.34, 26.v.34 (100). Lying in State. 1.ii.36 (111).

Macaulay, On the Innocence of. 28.xii.29 (86). Mad Metaphors. 10.viii.35 (100). Maid of Orleans, The. 14.iii.08 (12). Making Good. I. 23.i.32. II. 27.ii.32 (93). Maltreating Words. 21.v.27 (75). Mammoth Portraiture. 31.x.31 (93). Man: Heir of all the Ages. 7.i.33 (95). Man on the Spot, On the. 26.viii.33 (95). Melodrama, On a. 11.ii.33 (95). Mencken and Fundamentalism, Mr. 14.vi.30 (89). Meredith, About. 12.v.34 (100). Meredith, George. 22.v.09 (50). Merits of Shakespeare's Plots, The. 18.x.19 (111). Merry Monarch, The. 21.xi.31 (93). Methuselahite, The. 23.xii.05 (12). Misunderstanding, On. 29.ix.23 (75). Modern Girls. 24.ix.34 (100). Modern Martyrs. 25.i.08 (12). Modern 'Paganism'. 7.v.32 (93). Monsters. 22.viii.08 (50). Monsters. 16.i.32 (93). Monsters and Logic. 6.i.34 (95). More Thoughts on Christmas. 27.xii.13 (50). Mormonism. 29.xi.10 (50). Morris, About. 17.iii.34 (100). Movies, On the. 27.viii.27 (75). Much Too Modern History. 4.ii.22 (56). Mythology of Scientists, On the. 26.i.29 (86).

Narrowness of Novelty, The. 12.xi.32 (111). National Anthem, The. 15.vii.11 (111). National Spirit, The. 25.xii.20 (111). Negation, On a. 3.v.24 (75). Negative Morality. 1.x.32 (93). New Capitals. 9.vii.27 (75). New Insularity, On the. 25.iv.31 (89). New Poetry, On the. 25.viii.28, 6.x.28, 13.x.28 (86). New Prudery, On the. 11.iii.33 (95). New Religion Coming, On the. 13.iv.29 (86). New Tax, A. 23.v.31 (93). Note on Old Nonsense, A. 8.vii.22 (56). Nudists, On the. 10.i.31 (89).

Old Men who Make Wars. 24.ix.32 (93). Old Nurse, The. 4.iv.36 (111). One Party System, The. 27.i.34 (95). Open Conspiracy, On the. 16.vi.28 (86). Optimism and Scepticism. 24.xi.30 (89). Original Sin. 1.ix.28 (86). Oxford from Without. 3.viii.07 (12).

ILLUSTRATED LONDON NEWS (*cont.*)

2.ix.22 (56). Seriousness. 17.i.14 (50). Shakespeare. 1.x.27 (75). Shamelessness. 16.xii.33 (100). Shaw and his Black Girl. 31.xii.32 (95). Shaw's Puritanism, Mr. 7.ii.31 (89). Shirts. 31.iii.34 (100). Shockers. 28.vii.34 (100). Sightseeing. 29.ii.31 (89). Silver Goblets, The. 10.ix.10 (50). Simplicity of Asia, On the. 13.vi.31 (93). Solar System, On the. 11.vii.31 (93). Spirits, The. 30.viii.19 (50). Spiritualism. 26.v.06 (12). Stage Costume. 27.v.11 (50). Staleness of Revolt, On the. 17.x.31 (93). Standardisation of Stevenson, On the. 24.x.31 (93). Street Cries and Stretching the Law. 14.x.22 (56). Suicide: North and South, On. 16.iv.32 (93). Superstition of School. 26.iv.30 (108). Sweepstakes and Gambling. 2.vii.32 (93). Swift, On Jonathan. 15.x.32 (93). Swinburne, On Algernon Charles. 25.i.30, 1.ii.30, 21.iii.31 (89).

Taffy. 2.ix.11 (50). Telephone, About the. 19.i.35 (100). Tennyson. 14.viii.09 (50). Terror of a Toy, The. 7.i.22 (56). Teutonic Theory, On the. 3.x.31 (93). Thoughtless Remarks. 22.x.32 (93). Thoughts around Koepenick. 27.x.06 (12). Thoughts in Canada. 15.xi.30 (89). Thrills of Boredom, On the. 3.v.30 (89). Timid Thinkers. 9.xi.29 (86). To Praise, Exalt, Establish and Defend. 19.viii.33 (111). Tom Jones and Morality. 27.iv.07 (12). Tom Jones and the Escorial. 5.vi.26 (111). Total Abstinence. 7.i.28 (75). Touchy Realist, On the. 4.iii.33 (95). Tradition of Toledo, The. 12.iv.26 (111). Traffic. 6.iv.35 (100). Travel's Surprises. 8.xi.30 (89). Tricks of Memory. 12.ii.10 (111). Trollope: Historian, On Anthony. 15.iii.30 (89). True Artist, On the. 25.xi.26 (111). Truth of Legends, On the. 14.ii.31 (89). Turning Inside Out. 5.viii.22, 12.viii.22 (56). Turnpikes and Mediaevalism. 12.iii.32 (93). Twilight Sleep. 2.xi.29 (86).

Vachel Lindsay. 19.iii.32 (93). Victorians, The. 6.vi.36 (111). Voltaire. 25.xi.33 (100). Vote and the House, The. 6.i.06, 24.ii.06 (12). Vulgarity. 8.vi.29 (86).

Walking Paradox, The. 26.iii.27 (111). War Memorials. 7.xi.31 (93). Way of the World, On the. 30.viii.30 (89). What Might Have Been. 27.iv.29 (111). What We would do with Two Million (If We Had It). 21.ix.29 (86). White Fronts. 22.iv.35 (100). 'Who Killed John Keats?', On.

ILLUSTRATED LONDON NEWS (cont.)

27.vii.29 (86). Widows. 14.ix.35 (100). Wine When it is Red. 6.iv.07 (12). Wishes. 22.xi.13 (50). Wolfe and the Midshipman. 26.ii.10 (111). Woman. 24.iii.06 (12). Women who Vote. 13.v.33 (95). Wordsworth. 30.xii.33 (95). Workers, About the. 30.vii.35 (100). Worship of the Wealthy, The. 16.ii.07 (12). Writing of History, On the. 23.vi.23 (75).

Young Idea, On the. 18.ii.28 (75).

Zola Controversy, The. 4.iv.08 (12).

533. **INDEPENDENT REVIEW**

1906. June. The New Humility (13).

1909. The Moral Philosophy of Meredith (110).

534. **JOHN O' LONDON'S WEEKLY**

1951. Jan. 5. The Macbeths. ("This brilliant and characteristic article was written for J. M. Dent and Co. some years ago and not published . . ."—Editorial note.)

535. **LANSBURY'S LABOUR WEEKLY**

1926. Dec. 25, and 1927, Jan. 22. Social Reform versus Birth Control (67).

536. **LISTENER 1932–1936**

The text of G. K. C.'s regular broadcasts usually appeared in The Listener two weeks after the broadcast. The date given in parentheses is that when the broadcast was delivered.

1932. Nov. 9 (Oct. 31.) Some Famous Historical Characters. A review of: Philip of Spain by David Loth; William of Orange by G. J. Renier; Prince Charlie by Compton Mackenzie; Bonnie Prince Charlie by Clennell Wilkinson; Talleyrand by Duff Cooper; Napoleon by Jacques Bainville; The King of Rome by R. McNair Wilson.

Nov. 23. (Nov. 14.) A Batch of Memories. A review of: Reading, Writing and Remembering by E. V. Lucas; My Own Way by His Honour Sir Edward Parry; Under Czar and Soviet by John W. Hird; A Princess in Exile by Marie, Grand Duchess of Russia; Memoirs of a British Agent by R. H. Bruce Lockhart; Episodes in a Varied Life by Lord Conway of Alington; Writ in Sand by R. B. Cunningham Grahame.

LISTENER (*cont.*)

Dec. 7. (Nov. 28.) *Travellers' Tales*. A review of: *Argentine Tango* by Philip Guedalla; *Northern Lights* by F. Spencer Chapman; *Tiger-Man* by Julian Duguid; *Kabluk of the Eskimos* by Lowell Thomas; *The Way of the Lancer* by R. Boleslavski and H. Woodward; *Wings over Poland* by K. M. Murray.

Dec. 21. (Dec. 12.) *The Day Before Yesterday*. A review of: *The Life of Joseph Chamberlain, Vol. I*, by J. L. Garvin; *The Life of Lord Oxford and Asquith* by J. A. Spender and Cyril Asquith; *Battle: the Life Story of the Rt. Hon. Winston S. Churchill* by Hugh Martin; *No Phantoms Here* by James Lansdale Hodson; *A Candle to the Stars* by W. R. Titterton.

1933. Jan. 4. (Dec. 26, 1932.) *Books of the Week*. A review of: *Reminiscences of a Specialist* by Greville Macdonald; *The Week-End Calendar* compiled by Gerald Barry; *Passage Through the Present* by George Buchanan; *Our Mothers* by Alan Bott and Irene Clephane; *1933 and Still Going Wrong* by J. B. Morton.

Jan. 18. (Jan. 9.) *Architecture in Search of a Style*. A review of: *How to Look at Buildings* by Darcy Braddell; *Purpose and Admiration* by J. E. Barton; *Rome of the Renaissance and To-Day* by Sir Rennell Rodd; *Pugin* by Michael Trappes-Lomax.

Oct. 4. (Sept. 25.) *Understanding France*. A review of: *French Revolution* by J. Mills Whitham; *Marie Antoinette* by Stefan Zweig; *Napoleon's Love Story* by R. McNair Wilson; *Napoleon III* by Robert Sencourt; *Napoleon III* by Graham Brooks.

Oct. 18. (Oct. 9.) *Prophets and Poets*. A review of: *William Blake* by J. Middleton Murry; *William Blake* by Alan Clutton-Brock; *The Lord Fish* by Walter de la Mare.

Nov. 1. (Oct. 23.) *Truth About Ourselves*. A review of: *A Wandering Minstrel* by Sir Henry Lytton; *Freeman of Stamboul* by Professor Freeman; *Trekking On* by Deneys Reitz.

Nov. 15. (Nov. 6.) *Cavaliers and Roundheads*. A review of: *Charles the First, King of England* by Hilaire Belloc; *John Hampden's England* by John Drinkwater; *John Hampden* by Hugh Ross Williamson.

Nov. 29. (Nov. 20.) *Both Sides of the Looking-Glass*. A review of: *Selections from the Letters of Lewis Carroll to his Child*

LISTENER (cont.)

Friends edited by Evelyn M. Hatch; *Life of Hans Christian Andersen* by Signe Toksvig.

Dec. 13. (Dec. 4.) *Rebels and Reactionaries.* A review of: *Memories of a Victorian* by Edgar Jepson; *Twice Seven* by H. C. Bainbridge; *Female Pipings in Eden* by Dame Ethel Smyth; *Reaped and Bound* by Compton Mackenzie; *What Me Befell* by J. J. Jusserand.

1934. Jan. 31. (Jan. 1.) *Seven Days' Hard.* (874.) A talk in a series so named.

Oct. 3. (Sept. 26.) *The Return of the Hero.* A review of *Marathon and Salamis* by Compton Mackenzie; *The Cid and his Spain* by Ramon Menendez Pidal; *Bertrand of Brittany* by Roger Vercel; *Barlow's Journal* edited by Basil Lubbock; *The Hundred Days, 1815* by Philip Guedalla; *The Baton in the Knapsack* by Laurence Currie; *The First War in the Air* by R. H. Kiernan.

Oct. 17. (Oct. 10.) *Popular and Party Heroes.* A review of: *Robert Bruce; King of Scots* by Agnes Muir Mackenzie; *William Cecil, the Power behind Elizabeth* by Alan Gordon Smith; *Oliver Cromwell* by John Buchan; *Cromwell* by Hilaire Belloc.

Oct. 31. (Oct. 24.) *Eighteenth-Century Gains and Losses.* A review of: *Marlborough; His Life and Times, Vol. II,* by Winston Churchill; *Sir Richard Steele* by Willard Connely; *Fox* by Christopher Hobhouse.

Nov. 14. (Nov. 7.) *Revolutionists and Revivalists of the 19th Century.* A review of: *Maximilien Robespierre* by Reginald Somerset Ward; *The Rossettis and their Circle* by Frances Winwar; *The Wilfred Wards and the Transition, Vol. I,* by Maisie Ward; *Dostoievsky* by Nicholas Berdyaev.

Nov. 28. (Nov. 21.) *Nothing to Shout About.* A review of: *Make it New,* essays by Ezra Pound; *Men Without Art* by Wyndham Lewis; *Treatise on Right and Wrong* by H. L. Mencken; *Experiment In Autobiography* by H. G. Wells; *Calling All Countries* by Geoffrey West.

Dec. 12. (Dec. 5.) *Documents of the Twentieth Century.* A review of: *A Time to Keep* by Halliday Sutherland; *Nomad* by C. J. McGuiness; *I'll Go No More A-Roving* by Charles Ladds; *Destination Unknown* by Fred Walker; *Round the Corner* by

LISTENER (*cont.*)

Percy Brown; *I Was a Tramp* by John Brown; *I, James Whittaker* by James Whittaker.

Dec. 26. (Dec. 19.) *Victorian Frames and Picture.* A review of: *The Bleak Age* by J. L. and Barbara Hammond; *Early Victorian Novelists* by David Cecil; *Dickens* by André Maurois.

1935. Jan. 9. (Jan. 2.) *The Stuarts.* A review of: *Prince Charlie and his Ladies* by Compton Mackenzie; *Charles II and Madame* by Cyril H. Hartmann; *The England of Charles II* by Arthur Bryant; *Prince Rupert the Cavalier* by Clennell Wilkinson.

Jan. 23. (Jan. 16.) *War and Post-War.* A review of: *Our Own Times 1913–1934* by Stephen King-Hall; *A History of the Great War 1914–18* by C. R. M. F. Cruttwell; *Crisis in Europe* by George Slocombe.

Feb. 6. (Jan. 30.) *Remembering Far-Off Things.* A review of: *Charlemagne* by Douglas Woodruff; *The Emperor Charles IV* by Bede Jarrett, O.P.: *The Mind of Napoleon* by R. McNair Wilson; *India—Minto and Morley 1905–1910* by Mary, Countess of Minto.

Feb. 20. (Feb. 13.) *Back to Reason.* A review of: *The Deliverer of Helen Keller; Anne Sullivan Macy* by Nella Braddy; *Experience* by Desmond MacCarthy; *Return to Philosophy* by C. E. M. Joad; *Portraits by Inference* by Humbert Wolfe; *Suburban Columbus* by John Gibbons; *A Modern Columbus* by S. P. B. Mais.

March 6. (Feb. 27.) *Attitudes to Poverty.* A review of: *The Exemplary Mr. Day* by Sir S. H. Scott; *Time to Spare* by Eleven Unemployed; *Russia's Iron Age* by W. H. Chamberlin; *Among the Wolves* by Father Icilio Felici.

March 20. (March 13.) *Things We Don't Know about European History.* A review of: *An Outline of European History*, Part I by Oliver J. G. Welch, II by P. C. Gordon Walker, III by H. E. Howard, IV by J. C. Pennethorne Hughes.

June 19 (June 11.) *The Liberty That Matters.* Broadcast in the series entitled "Freedom" and collected in book form with the same title (404).

The appearance of the text of G. K. C.'s broadcast in *The Listener* set off a long controversy in the correspondence columns in which Dr. Percy Scholes and Dr. G. G. Coulton participated. This developed into a duel between G. K. C. and

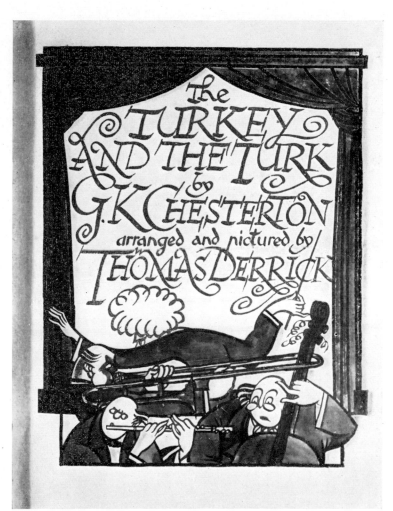

The Turkey and the Turk, 1930. Decorated title, p. (9).

LISTENER (*cont.*)

Dr. Coulton that was still unfinished at the time of the former's death. Dr. Coulton had proposed, and G. K. C. had agreed, to reprint a selection of the letters together with statements from themselves in book form. The letters to be included were:

July 10 (Dr. Percy Scholes, G. K. C.); 17 (G. K. C.); 31 (Dr. Scholes); Aug. 14 (G. K. C.); 28 (Dr. Scholes, Dr. Coulton, G. K. C.); Sept. 11 (G. K. C.); 18 (Dr. Coulton); 25 (Dr. Scholes); Oct. 2 (G. K. C.); 9 (Dr. Coulton); 23 (G. K. C.); 30 (Dr. Coulton); Nov. 13 (G. K. C.); 20 (Dr. Coulton); Dec. 4 (G. K. C.); 11 (Dr. Coulton); 1936. March 25 (Dr. Coulton).

At the time of his death, G. K. C. had written 6,000 words of the 7,000-word contribution that he had undertaken to write for the book. The book did not appear.

Nov. 27. (Nov. 16.) *Who Should Bring Up Our Children?* A debate between Bertrand Russell and G. K. Chesterton.

1936. March 18. (March 15.) *"We Will End with a Bang"*, Broadcast in *The Spice of Life* series.

April 1. (March 27.) *What the Middle Ages Meant to Europe.* A broadcast to schools.

The following broadcasts were delivered but not published:

1931. Dec. 25. *Dickens and Christmas.* Broadcast to America.

1935. March 20. *England and Patriotism.* July 8. *Meet the Detective.*

537. LONDON MERCURY

1920. Feb. The Romance of Rhyme (56).

1921. Dec. Milton and Merry England (56).

1928. June. An Apology for Buffoons (97).

1929. Oct. Three Sonnets in Summer Heat (378A).

1931. Feb. If Don John of Austria had married Mary Queen of Scots (108, 379).

1933. Jan. The End of the Moderns (108).

538. MANCHESTER EVENING NEWS

1936. May 8. Personal View.

539. MERRY-GO-ROUND
    1923. Dec., and 1924, Jan. The Best Game in the World.
    (The Toy Theatre.)

540. NASH'S MAGAZINE
    1915. Divorce *versus* Democracy (41).
    1921. Jan. The Fantastic Friends (77). Feb. The Finger of
    Stone (77). May. The Yellow Bird (77). Dec. The Shadow of
    the Shark (77).
    1922. July. The House of the Peacock (77).
    1923. Dec. The Oracle of the Dog (63).
    1924. Feb. The Dagger with Wings (63). May. The Miracle
    of Moon Crescent (63).
    1925. May. The Curse of the Golden Cross (63). June. The
    Doom of the Darnaways (63). July. The Arrow of Heaven
    (63).

541. NATION
    1907. Dec. 7. Louisa Alcott (110).
    1908. March 14. How Pleasant to know Mr. Lear (110).
    Dec. 5. The Genius of Gilbert (110).
    1909. Dec. 18. The Revolutionist: or, Lines to a Statesman (37).
    1911. Jan. 21 and 28 and Feb. 4. Private Members and the
    Cabinet. (Three letters.) (107, 782.)

541A. NEOLITH
    1907. No. I. The Secret People (37).

542. NEW AGE
    The Chesterton-Belloc-Wells-Shaw Controversy.
    1907. Dec. 7. (Thoughts about Modern Thought. By Hilaire
    Belloc, M.P.)
    1908. Jan. 4. Why I am not a Socialist. (Jan. 11. About
    Chesterton and Belloc. By H. G. Wells) (715). Jan. 25. On
    Wells and a Glass of Beer. (Feb. 8. "Not a Reply". By
    Hilaire Belloc.) (15. Belloc and Chesterton. By G. Bernard
    Shaw) (741). 29. The Last of the Rationalists. A Reply to Mr.
    Bernard Shaw. (March 21. A Question. By Hilaire Belloc.)
    (March 28. An Answer. By H. G. Wells.)

NEW AGE (*cont.*)

The Chesterton-Bax-Shaw Controversy.

1908. Nov. 5. (Spiritual Spoof. By E. Belfort Bax. A review of *Orthodoxy*.) 26. The Solemn Spoofer. A reply to Mr. Belfort Bax. (Dec. 10. Smart-Paradox Spoof. By E. Belfort Bax. On Miracles: a Retort to Mr. Chesterton. By G. Bernard Shaw.) 31. The Shawbax.

1909. Jan. 7. (Chesterton Facing-both-Ways. By G. Bernard Shaw.) (Jan. 14. The Chestershaw. By E. Belfort Bax.) Feb. 25. A Summary of Sects.

543. NEW QUARTERLY

1908. Oct. Rabelaisian Regrets (108).

544. NEW STATESMAN

1916. (May 13. The Case Against Chesterton. A long review article by Bernard Shaw of *G. K. Chesterton* by Julius West.) June 3. G. K. C. replied to Shaw and the exchanges continued in the issues dated June 10, 17 and 24 and July 15 and 29.

545. NEW WITNESS. Edited by Cecil Chesterton.

1912. Nov. 7. Sonnet. ("If you have picked your lawn of leaves and snails") (37). 14. A Song Against Grocers (31). 28. The Song of the English (31). Dec. 5. To a Turk (2). 19. A Song of Songs (31). 26. The Neglected Child (2).

1913. Jan. 2. The Song of the Good Rich Man (31). 9. The Aristocrat (2). 23. A Song of Strange Drinks (31. The Song of Right and Wrong). 30. Song of the Happy Vegetarian (31. Pioneers, O Pioneers). Feb. 6. Song of the Temperance Hotel (31. "The Saracen's Head"). 20. The Song of the Strange Ascetic (31). 27. The Song of the Second Deluge (31. Wine and Water). March 13. When I came back to Fleet Street (37) 27. The Song of Cosmopolitan Courage (not collected). April 17. The Crusader Returns from Captivity (37). 24. On Righteous Indignation (37). Sept. 11. A Song of Dietetic Logic (31. The Logical Vegetarian). 25. A Song of Temperance Reform (31. The Rolling English Road). Oct. 23. The Song of the Alternative Explanations of the Curvature of the English Country Road (31. The Road to Roundabout). Nov. 27. The Song of the Dog Named Quoodle (31). Dec. 25. A Christmas Song for Three Guilds (37).

NEW WITNESS (*cont.*)

1914. Feb. 5. In Memoriam P. D., Nice, Jan. 30, 1914 (37). May 7. The Higher Unity (37). July 16. Lines to an Old Pro-Boer (69). Aug. 13. "1914". Alliterativism (69). 27. The Wife of Flanders (37). Oct. 8. Blessed are the Peacemakers (37). 1915. Aug. 12. The Battle of the Stories (69). Dec. 15. The Peace of Petrol (69).

1916. Sept. 7. The Ballad of St. Barbara (54). [Oct. 19, Vol. VIII, No. 207. *G. K. C. becomes Editor.*] Dec. 7. Autobiography of a Bad Editor. 14. The Yule Log and the Democrat (50).

1917. Jan. 4. How Mad Laws are Made (56). 25. The Prudery of the Feminists (56). Feb. 15. The Innocence of Criminals (56). March 15. The Lawlessness of Lawyers (50). 29. The Secret Society of Mankind (56). July 19. The Evolution of Emma (50). 1918. March 8. A Sketch of George Wyndham (50). 22 and 29 and April 5, 12, 19. *The Superstition of Divorce* (47). June 14. The *New Witness* League. (Speech at first public meeting.) Oct. 11. Two Stones in a Square (46). 25. The Lost Joke against us (46. The Family and the Feud). Nov. 1. The Fenians and a Fallacy (46). 15. The Dreamland of Belfast (46). 29. Ireland *versus* Internationalism (46).

1919. Jan. 17. The Home of the Unities (56). Feb. 7. Wings and the Housemaid (56). 14. Strikes and the Spirit of Wonder (56). April 25. Sherlock Holmes and the Moonlighters (46. An Example and a Question). May 2. Weddings in War-time (54). July 11. Education Lyrics, I (54). 18. Songs of Education, II (54). 25. Songs of Education, III (54). The Suffragette and the Strikers (56). Aug. 1. Songs of Education, IV (54). 8. Songs of Education, V (54). Nov. 28. Tagtug and the Tree of Knowledge (105).

1920. June 25. The Nightmare and the Novelist (56. Hamlet and the Psycho-Analyst, II). Sept. 10. Logic and the Missing Link (56. Is Darwin Dead?). 24. New Dreams for Old (56. Hamlet and the Psycho-Analyst, I). Oct. 1. The Brotherhood of Beans (56). Dec. 10. Note on Nursery Rhymes (56). *Old King Cole* (49 and 69. Variations of an Air). 24. The Meaning of Mock Turkey (56).

1921. Feb. 18. The Statue and the Irishman (53). March 11. A Defence of Interviewers (53). 18. A World of Wood (53).

NEW WITNESS (cont.)

April 8. A Caution about Coats and Canes (53). 15. The March to Main Street (53). 29. On Dollars and Day-dreams (53). May 6. On Making Friends for England (53). 13. Diplomacy and Dixie (53). 20. The Case for the Englishman (53). 27. On an American Critic (53). June 10. The Republican in the Ruins (53). July 22. The Extraordinary American (53). 29. The American King and the English President (53). Aug. 12. Is America Young? (53). Sept. 16. Mr. R. J. Campbell and the Cabman (53). Nov. 25. Concerning a Strange City (108). Dec. 9. A Christmas Carol (54).

1922. May 12. To Captain Fryatt (54). Freedom and the Film (56). June 2. Hamlet and the Humanitarians (56. Hamlet and the Psycho-Analyst, III). 23. The Mercy of Mr. Arnold Bennett (56). July 14. Stonehenge and the Modern Myth (56). 21. At the Caxton Hall (Speech). Oct. 6. On Household Gods and Goblins (105). 13 and 20. A Grave Allegation (Speech). Dec. 1. Shakespeare and the Legal Lady (56).

1923. April 21. More about "G.K.C.'s Weekly". 28. An Open Letter to Hilaire Belloc (413). May 5. The End of the World's End.

546. OBSERVER

1916. March 5. Henry James (108).
1920. June 6. Dickens after 50 Years (48).
1932. April 14. Reply to Mr. Ivor Brown's review of *Chaucer* (743).
1940. Feb. 17. Prayer in Darkness. (See 547.)

547. OCCASIONAL PAPERS

1904. July. Translation of a sonnet of Du Bellay (37).
1905. May. Prayer in Darkness. (This early poem was re-printed in the *Observer* on Feb. 17, 1940.)

548. ODD VOLUME

1908. Ballade of a Book Reviewer (37).
1912. A Cider Song (37).

549. OLD VIC MAGAZINE

1926. Jan. Prologue to the Old Vic Pantomime for 1925.

550. OUTLINE
     1928. Jan. 21 and 28. Why I am a Catholic (341).

551. OUTLOOK
     1899. March 4. A Chord of Colour (2).

552. PALL MALL MAGAZINE
     1902. April. Victor Hugo (110). July. Bret Harte (14).
     1913. March. The Absence of Mr. Glass (32). May. The
     Purple Wig (32). June. The Head of Caesar (32). July. The
     Strange Crime of John Boulnois (32). Aug. The Paradise of
     Thieves (32). Sept. The Man in the Passage (32). Oct. The
     Mistake of the Machine (32). Nov. The Sword of Wood (76).
     Dec. Song of Gifts to God (37).
     1914. June. The Perishing of the Pendragons (32). July. The
     Salad of Colonel Cray (32). Aug. The Duel of Dr. Hirsch (32).
     Sept. The God of the Gongs (32).
     1928. May. The Drift from Domesticity (79).
     1929. March. Am I a Prig? (91). May. On Calling Names (91).
     July. On Keeping Your Hair On (91). Sept. The True
     Victorian Hypocrisy (91).

553. PARENTS' REVIEW
     1897. Dec. The Nativity. (511 and 37. A much-revised version.)
     1900. Dec. The Feast of the Snow (511 and 37).
     1904. March. The Education of Children.

554. QUARTO
     1896. First Series. A Picture of Tuesday. (G. K. C. refers to
     this in a letter to E. C. Bentley quoted in *Gilbert Keith
     Chesterton*, by Maisie Ward, p. 71.)
     1897. Third Series. A Crazy Tale.

555. RADIO TIMES
     1933. Dec. 22. Laughter (108).

556. REVIEW OF REVIEWS
     1932. The New Groove (108).

556A. SCRIP. The University of Notre Dame Quarterly. Notre
       Dame, Indiana.
       1937. Jan. Vol. 8, No. 2. A special issue commemorating
       G. K. Chesterton and containing a poem, *The Arena*, written
       at the time of his visit to the University in 1931. (Not
       collected.)

557.   SHAKESPEARE REVIEW
       1928. May. Shakespeare and Shaw (91).

558.   SPEAKER
       1892. Dec. 17. The Song of Labour. This poem marks
       G. K. C.'s first public appearance. See *Debater* (519), *Academy*
       (501) and *Clarion* (510).
       1897. Aug. 7. The Earth's Shame (2).
       1898. May 28. To them that Mourn (2).
       1899. Jan. 7. To a Certain Nation (2).
       1900. Oct. 20. An Election Echo (37). Dec. 1. St. Francis of
       Assisi (4). 22. William Morris and his School (4).
       1901. Feb. 2. Nonsense (3). 16. The Philosophy of Farce (3).
       March 9. Defence of Rash Vows (3). 16. Defence of Penny
       Dreadfuls (3). 23. Defence of Ugly Things (3). 30. Defence of
       China Shepherdesses (3). April 13. Defence of Humility (3).
       20. Defence of Skeletons (3). 27. Defence of Slang (3). May
       11. Defence of Planets (3). 18. Defence of Heraldry (3). A
       Denunciation of Patriotism (3). 25. Baby-Worship (3). June
       1. Patriotism and Ethics (A letter). 15. The Catholic Puritan
       (4). 22. The Value of Detective Stories (3). July 27. The Last
       Hero (37). Aug. 3. The Literature of Information (3). 17. The
       Bones of a Poem (110). 24. Dreams (105). 31. Materials (105).
       Sept. 28. Lost (37). Oct. 26. The Heroines of Shakespeare
       (110).
       1904. Sept. 24. Dr. Barry's Life of Newman (110).

559.   SPECTATOR
       1908. June 27. Anonymity in Journalism (Speech).
       1928. Centenary Number. The Popularity of Dickens (91).
       1932. Feb. 27. St. Thomas Aquinas (390).

560.   STANDARD (Dublin)
       1942. Dec. 4. God. (Poem from an early notebook.)

560A. STAR
1911. Oct. 16. Lepanto (37).

561. STORYTELLER
1910. Sept. The Blue Cross (24). Oct. The Secret Garden (24). Nov. The Queer Feet (24). Dec. The Hammer of God (24). 1911. Jan. The Wrong Shape (24). Feb. The Sign of the Broken Sword (24).
1919. Oct. The Garden of Smoke (55).
1920. July. The Face in the Target (55). Sept. The Vanishing Prince (55). Oct. The Soul of the Schoolboy (55).
1921. July. The Bottomless Well (55). Oct. The Fad of the Fisherman (55).
1922. Aug. The Temple of Silence (55. The Fool of the Family.) Oct. The Vengeance of the Statue (55).
1924. Feb. The Tower of Treason (55). June. The Unpresentable Appearance of Colonel Crane (60). July. The Improbable Success of Mr. Owen Hood (60). Aug. The Unobtrusive Traffic of Captain Pierce (60). Oct. The Elusive Companion of Parson White (60). Nov. The Exclusive Luxury of Enoch Oates (60). Dec. The Unthinkable Theory of Professor Green (60).
1925. Jan. The Unprecedented Architecture of Commander Blair (60). March. The Ultimate Ultimatum of the League of the Long Bow (60).
1927. Jan. The Vanishing of Vaudrey (71). April. The Red Moon of Meru (71).
1929. March. The Purple Jewel (77). July. The Honest Quack (83). Sept. The Crime of Gabriel Gale (77).
1930. May. The Loyal Traitor (83).
1932. Oct. The Point of a Pin (96).
1933. Oct. The Five Fugitives (96. The Blast of the Book). Nov. The Scandal of Father Brown (96).
1934. Feb. The Quick One (96). June. Mr. Blue and Mr. Red (96. The Pursuit of Mr. Blue). Sept. The Crime of the Communist (96).
1935. March. The Insoluble Problem (96). July. The Three Horsemen of the Apocalypse (104). Nov. When Doctors Agree (104). Dec. Ring of Lovers (104).
1936. Feb. A Tall Story (104). July. The Crime of Captain

STORYTELLER (*cont.*)
Gahagan (104). Aug. The Terrible Troubadour (104). Sept. Pond the Pantaloon (104).

562. STRAND MAGAZINE
1936. Aug. The Vampire of the Village. (The last Father Brown story. Collected in the 1953 edition of the omnibus volume, *Father Brown Stories* (861).)

563. STUDIES
1932. Sept. The Mission of Ireland (92).

564. STUDIO
1930. April. Eric Gill and No Nonsense (110).

565. T.P.'s WEEKLY
1907. Christmas Number. A Scheme for Reading for 1908 (108. On Reading).
1910. April 29. On the Death of Mark Twain (110).
1913. March 21. How I Began.

566. T.P.'s AND CASSELL'S WEEKLY
1926. Jan. 23. In the Days of my Youth.

567. TABLET
1946. June 15. Frances. Xmas 1900. (An unpublished poem reproduced in facsimile from the fly-leaf of the copy of *The Wild Knight* given by G. K. C. to his fiancée in 1900.)
1953. April 4. From the Notebooks of G. K. Chesterton (*c.* 1893). Dec. 26. Three letters to Maurice Baring.

567A. TIME AND TIDE
1926. Dec. 3. Candida and a Candid Friend (414). A reply to a series of articles in *Time and Tide*, called "Women of the Leisured Class".

568. TIMES
1911. March 9. On Imperialism. (A letter.)
1932. Feb. 17. Ballade of Devastation. Signed: "G.K.M.B.C." Written with Maurice Baring during a sitting for "Conversation Piece" by James Gunn (now in the National Portrait Gallery.) (782.)

569. TRIBUNE

1906. Feb. 9. W. W. Jacobs (110).

570. UNIVERSE

1926. Nov. 3. On False Sentiment (79. The Hat and the Halo).

1927. May 20. On Ignorance of Ignorance (79. The Call to the Barbarian). Aug. 12. Logic and Lawn Tennis (79). Sept. 23. If they had Believed (79).

1928. Feb. 13. On Courage and Independence (79). 24. The Nordic Hindoo (79). March 16. Dean Inge's *Protestantism* (79. *Protestantism*: a Problem Novel). July 20. The Roots of Sanity (79). Sept. 21. The Protestant Superstition (79). Nov. 30. A Simple Thought (79).

1929. Jan. 11. A Problem from Scotland (79. The Idols of Scotland). Feb. 8. The Case of Conspiracies (79. Who are the Conspirators?). March 1. Thanks to the Sceptic (79. The Optimist on Suicide). 22. The Outline of Liberty. (108). April 12. Emancipation and Conspiracy (97). June 14. What We Think About (79).

1930. April 4. The Establishment and the Anglican Clergy (108. The Erastian and the Establishment). Aug. 8. The New Case for Catholic Schools (108).

1932. July 8. The Fluttering of the Flags (92). 15. The Island of Christendom (92). Aug. 22. This was Real Democracy (92). 29. The Phoenix in Phoenix Park (92).

1934. Sept. 28. *My Six Conversions* (97). I. Germany's Race Religion. Oct. 26. II. When the World Turned Back. Nov. 30. III. The Surrender upon Sex. Dec. 21. IV. The Prayer-Book Problem.

1935. Jan. 18. V. The Collapse of Materialism. Feb. 15. VI. The Case of Spain. March 15. The Well and the Shallows (97). May 17. Thomas More (97). Aug. 2. Where is the Paradox? (97).

1936. April 9. A Very Catholic Encyclopaedia (108). June 5. Strange Talk of Two Victorians (108).

1953. Dec. 4. *Ave Maria*. (An early poem. See 519.)

571. WEEK-END REVIEW

1930. April 26. Bernard Shaw and Breakages (91). Dec. 20. A Note on Notting Hill (388).

572. WEEKLY REVIEW
       1938. May 12. Earthquake Esquire. (An early story.)

573. WESTMINSTER GAZETTE
       1908. Oct. 24. Translation from Charles Guérin. (Prize poem
       in a competition.) (250A.)

574. WESTMINSTER REVIEW
       1901. March. Queen Victoria (14).

D

BOOKS AND PERIODICALS CONTAINING
ILLUSTRATIONS BY G. K. CHESTERTON

The place of publication is London unless otherwise stated.

1900

601. *The Speaker*. General Election Supplements. Sept. and Oct. Front-page cartoons.
602. *Greybeards at Play* (1).
603. *Nonsense Rhymes*. By Cosmo Monkhouse. Cover design and illustrations by G. K. Chesterton. Brimley Johnson. Uniform with 602.

1903

604. *The Great Inquiry* (Only Authorised Version). Faithfully reported by H. B. Reporter to the Committee, and Ornamented with Sharp Cuts Drawn on the Spot by G. K. C. Duckworth.
605. *The Speaker*. Dec. 12. Two illustrations to *An Annual Problem. Books for Children*, by E. V. Lucas. Three illustrations to *What a Child Wants*, by Hilaire Belloc.

1904

606. *Emmanuel Burden*. By Hilaire Belloc, with 34 illustrations by G. K. Chesterton. Methuen.
607. *The Speaker*. Dec. 10. Seven illustrations to *Children's Books*, by E. V. Lucas.

1905

608. *The Club of Queer Trades* (8).
609. *Biography for Beginners*. Being a Collection of Miscellaneous Examples for the use of Upper Forms. Edited by E. Clerihew, B.A. With 40 Diagrams by G. K. Chesterton. T. Werner Laurie. Reprinted in *Clerihews Complete*, by E. Clerihew Bentley. Methuen, 1951.
609A. *The Speaker*. Dec. 9. Five illustrations to *On Children's Books*, by Hilaire Belloc.

1909

609B. *Fairy Tales from the German Forests*, by Frau Arndt. Everett. (n.d.) Coloured frontispiece, "The Dwarf", and coloured title-page by G. K. C. The title-page is also pasted on the front cover within blind borders.

1911

610. *Strand Magazine*. April. Drawing: *Dons Disproving the Sea-Serpent*.

611. *The Odd Volume*. Edited by John O. Wilson. Four drawings: *Villains Plotting:—Mr. Pecksniff and Rashleigh Osbaldistone; Count Fosco and Mr. Quilp; The Master of Ballantrae and Bill Sykes: Eugenics.*

1912

612. *The Green Overcoat*, by Hilaire Belloc, with illustrations by G. K. Chesterton. Bristol. Arrowsmith.

1914

613. *The British Review*. Aug. Illustrations to *Eccles of Beccles*, by Wilfred Ward.

1922

614. *The Mercy of Allah*, by Hilaire Belloc. Chatto and Windus. Drawing on dust jacket by G. K. C.

1924

615. *Stampede!* by L. de Giberne Sieveking. With illustrations by G. K. Chesterton. Cayme Press.

615A. *The Granta and its Contributors, 1889–1914.* (326A.) A drawing: *After the Bump Supper.*

1925

616. *Mr. Petre*, by Hilaire Belloc. With 22 drawings by G. K. Chesterton. Arrowsmith.

617. *G.K.'s Weekly.* Dec. 5. Two illustrations to *The Turkey and the Turk* and one to *The Return of Don Quixote.*

1926

618. *The Emerald*, by Hilaire Belloc. With 21 drawings by G. K. Chesterton. Arrowsmith.

619. *G.K.'s Weekly*. Feb. 27. *A Biography for Beginners*. March 6. *Another Biography for Beginners*. 13. *A Third Biography for Beginners*. 20. *A Fourth Biography for Beginners*. 27. *A Fifth Biography for Beginners*.

1927

620. *The Haunted House*, by Hilaire Belloc. Twenty-five illustrations by G. K. Chesterton. Arrowsmith.

1928

621. *But Soft—We are Observed*, by Hilaire Belloc. With 37 drawings by G. K. Chesterton. Arrowsmith.

1929

622. *More Biography*, by E. Clerihew Bentley. Illustrated by G. K. Chesterton, Victor Reinganum, Nicolas Bentley and the Author. Methuen. G. K. C. contributed 15 drawings. Reprinted in *Clerihews Complete*, Methuen, 1951.

623. *The Missing Masterpiece*, by Hilaire Belloc. With 41 drawings by G. K. Chesterton. Arrowsmith.

1930

624. *The Man Who Made Gold*, by Hilaire Belloc. With 17 drawings by G. K. Chesterton. Arrowsmith.

625. *G.K.'s Weekly*. Dec. 27. *The Merger*. Poem and cartoon.

1931

626. *G.K.'s Weekly*. Jan. 10. *On an American Best-Seller*. Epigram and cartoon.

1932

627. *The Postmaster-General*, by Hilaire Belloc. With 30 drawings by G. K. Chesterton. Arrowsmith.

628. *Reading, Writing and Remembering*, by E. V. Lucas. Reprints two illustrations to the *Speaker* article (605) and an epitaph and sketch *Sacred to the Memory of E. V. Lucas* in facsimile of G. K. C.'s holograph.

629. *G.K.'s Weekly*. Dec. 10. Front-page cartoon.

1933

630. *Pauline and Old Pauline*, by H. A. Sams (399). Two drawings.
631. *G.K.'s Weekly*. Dec. 7. Front-page cartoon.

1934

632. *G.K.'s A Miscellany* (400). Reprints three drawings from *G.K.'s Weekly*.
633. *G.K.'s Weekly*. Oct. 11. Cartoon.
634. *G.K.'s Weekly*. Dec. 13. Front-page cartoon.

1935

635. *Programme*. Tessa Richardson Concert in aid of Beaconsfield Children's Convalescent Home. Drawing.
636. *G.K.'s Weekly*. March 21. Tenth Birthday Number. Cartoon.
637. *G.K.'s Weekly*. July 11. Front-page cartoon.
638. *G.K.'s Weekly*. Oct. 10. Front-page cartoon.
639. *G.K.'s Weekly*. Oct. 17. Front-page cartoon.
640. *G.K.'s Weekly*. Nov. 7. Front-page cartoon.

1936

641. *The Hedge and the Horse*, by Hilaire Belloc. With 40 illustrations by G. K. Chesterton. Cassell.

1938

642. *The Coloured Lands* (105).

1941

643. *As it Happened*. An Autobiography by Maurice B. Reckitt. Dent. One page of doodles by G. K. C.

1944

644. *Gilbert Keith Chesterton*, by Maisie Ward (782). Reproduces an early self-caricature and two pages of figures from the toy theatre.

1952

645. *Return to Chesterton*, by Maisie Ward (811). Six pages of drawings.
646. *Catholic Herald*. Dec. 5. Eleven illustrations to *A Vision of Edens* (509).

647. *Catholic Herald.* Dec. 26. *From the Cradle to the Grave.* A page of unpublished drawings.

1957

648. The *Listener.* Jan. 3. *The Viking and the Very Tame Lion* (see 826).
649. *The Eye of the Beholder,* by Lance Sieveking (829). Three drawings: "Mr. Chesterton discovers he is twenty years late for school" (drawn for Lance Sieveking in 1912); an illustration from *Stampede* (615); and *The Viking and the Very Tame Lion* (826).

CHRISTENDOM
IN DUBLIN

✝

"So careful of the Type she seems":
She mends what Man so foully makes:
Searching for five minute misprints
    In a forest of mistakes.

FF F (in form) dictated this
You will agree, at any rate,
Some things are here which you believe
And I did not Dictate.

As you were better than a friend
    In more than friendship we agree —
Friendship at best may be a bond:
And Truth has made us free.

Who enters by that Door alone,
    However dubious or afraid
For that one hour is that one Mind
For which the World was made..

...So let them blare... Creed, rack and rod
    Torture and Torquemada's Chain...
...That was the hour when souls were free
That now are friends again ——

Inscription in a copy of *Christendom in Dublin*, presented by
G. K. Chesterton to Miss Dorothy Collins, 1932

E

BOOKS AND ARTICLES ABOUT
G. K. CHESTERTON

The place of publication is London unless otherwise stated.

1900

701. Edward Chesterton. Reviews of *Greybeards at Play*: (*a*) *Speaker*. Oct. 6. (*b*) *Parents' Review*. Dec.

1903

702. C. F. G. Masterman. G. K. Chesterton. An Appreciation. *Bookman*. Jan.

1907

703. George Knollys. Mr. Gilbert Chesterton and his Toy Theatre. With the outline of a play written by Mr. Chesterton. And directions for those who would like to enjoy a fascinating pastime. *Girls' Realm*. June.
    The article is illustrated with excellent photographs of the "Battersea Problem Theatre", scenes and characters. The play is "St. George and the Dragon".

1908

704. [Cecil Chesterton.] *G. K. Chesterton—A Criticism*. Alston Rivers. (Published anonymously.)
705. H. G. Wells. About Chesterton and Belloc. *New Age*. Jan. 11 (542 and 715).
706. G. Bernard Shaw. The Chesterbelloc: A Lampoon. *New Age*. Feb. 15 (542 and 741).
707. Fr. Joseph Keating, S.J. Faith Found in Fleet Street. Mr. Chesterton's "Orthodoxy". *Month*. Nov.

1909

708. G. Bernard Shaw. Chesterton on Shaw. (A review of *George Bernard Shaw* by G. K. Chesterton.) *Nation*. Aug. 25 (741).

1910

709. *Bookman.* May. Special Chesterton number. Contains an article by Henry Murray with many photographs of G. K. C. and four illustrations by G. K. C. Also a portrait on the cover from a life-size painting by Alfred Priest and a presentation plate portrait from a crayon drawing by Alfred Priest.

710. André Chevrillon. Une Apologie du Christianisme, in *Nouvelles Études Anglaises,* pp. 213–70. Paris. Hachette.

1912

711. Rev. William T. Scott. *Chesterton and other Essays.* Cincinnati. Jennings and Graham.

1913

712. Horace J. Bridges. *Mr. G. K. Chesterton as Theologian.* Philadelphia.

713. H. J. Massingham. Mr. Chesterton's "Black Magic". *Nation.* Nov. 15.

1914

714. Wilfred Ward. Mr. Chesterton among the Prophets. In *Men and Matters.* Longmans.

715. H. G. Wells. About Chesterton and Belloc. (542.) Collected in *An Englishman Looks at the World* and reprinted in *The Works of H. G. Wells.* Atlantic Edition, Vol. IX, London, 1925.

1915

716. Julius West. *G. K. Chesterton; A Critical Study.* Secker.

1916

717. G. Bernard Shaw. The Case against Chesterton. *New Statesman.* May 13 (741).

1917

718. Edwin E. Slosson. G. K. Chesterton. In *Six Major Prophets.* Boston, U.S.A. Little, Brown.

719. G. Bernard Shaw. Something Like a History of England. *Observer.* Nov. 4 (741). (A review of *A Short History of England.*)

1918

720. G. Bernard Shaw. How Free is the Press? *Nation.* Feb. 9 (741).

1920

721. Joseph de Tonquédec. *G. K. Chesterton, ses idées et son caractère.* Paris. Nouvelle Librairie Nationale.

1921

722. Alan Handsacre. *Authordoxy.* Being a discursive examination of Mr. G. K. Chesterton's "Orthodoxy". John Lane.
723. Rose Macaulay. Personalities and Powers. Mr. G. K. Chesterton. *Time and Tide.* Feb. 4.

1922

724. Patrick Braybrooke. *Gilbert Keith Chesterton.* The Chelsea Publishing Company. Enlarged edition, 1926.
725. Louis Untermeyer. *Heavens.* New York. Harcourt, Brace. (Pp. 7–16. See also caricature on cover.)
726. G. Bernard Shaw. Chesterton on Eugenics and Shaw on Chesterton. *Nation.* March 11 (741).
726A. K. H. Andersen. *Chesterton.* Copenhagen.

1923

727. Gerald Bullett. *The Innocence of G. K. Chesterton.* Cecil Palmer.

1924

728. Arnold Lunn. G. K. Chesterton. In *Roman Converts.* Chapman and Hall (520 and 729).
729. Arnold Lunn. "Roman Converts". A Reply to Mr. Chesterton. *Review of the Churches.* July (520).

1925

730. Karl Urms. *Gilbert Keith Chesterton.* Dortmund. Wolfram-Verlag.
      A critical study and a selection of prose extracts.

1926

731. Sister M. Paraclita, M.A. *Gilbert Keith Chesterton; Propagandist.* New York.

1927

732. *Tygodnik Illustrowany*. (Polish review.) Chesterton number. April 23.
733. J. C. Squire. Mr. Chesterton's Verse. *Observer*. July 3.
734. Monsignor John O'Connor. Chesterton as Poet. *Blackfriars*. Oct.

1928

735. Dorothy Edwards. G. K. Chesterton. In *Scrutinies* by various writers. Collected by Edgell Rickword. Wishart.

1929

736. Waclaw Barowy. *Gilbert Keith Chesterton*. Cracow. (In Polish.)
736A. Patrick Braybrooke. *The Wisdom of G. K. Chesterton*. Cecil Palmer.

1930

737. *Mr. Chesterton at Holy Cross*. The Lecture in Mechanics Hall. Dec. 12, 1930. Holy Cross College. Worcester, Mass., U.S.A. (Tributes from numerous people, including Paul Claudel)
738. Charles Williams. G. K. Chesterton. In *Poetry at Present*. Oxford. Clarendon Press.
739. *Canisius College Monthly*. Buffalo. Special Chesterton number. Nov.

1931

740. R. B. MacCullum. Mr. Chesterton as a Democrat. *Bookman*. Oct.

1932

741. G. Bernard Shaw. *Pen Portraits and Reviews*. Constable.
742. W. R. Titterton. G. K. Chesterton. In *A Candle to the Stars*. Grayson.
743. Ivor Brown. Bobbe-up-and-Doun. *Observer*. April 7. (This review of *Chaucer* drew a long letter from G. K. C. in the next issue of the *Observer*, April 14.)

1934

744. Roberto Arocena. *El sembrado de Chesterton*. A. Barreiro y Ramos. Montevideo.
744A. Karl Pfleger. *Geister, die um Christus ringen*. Salzburg. (See 747.)

1935

745. André Maurois. G. K. Chesterton. In *Magiciens et Logiciens*. Paris. Grasset. (See 746.)

1936

746. André Maurois. G. K. Chesterton. In *Poets and Prophets*. Cassell. (An English version of 745.)

747. Karl Pfleger. Chesterton, the Adventurer of Orthodoxy. In *Wrestlers with Christ*. Translated by E. I. Watkin. Sheed and Ward.

748. W. R. Titterton. *G. K. Chesterton. A Portrait*. Ouseley.

749. *Obituary Notices.*

Hilaire Belloc. G. K. C.: the Man and his Work. *Observer*. June 21. It was a Benediction to Know Him. *Universe*. June 19. Chesterton's Genius for Using the Right Word. *Universe*. June 26. G. K. Chesterton and Modern England. *Studies*. Sept. G. K. Chesterton. Portrait of a Friend. *American Review*. Oct.

E. C. Bentley. "G. K." *Listener*. June 20. (Broadcast on June 14.) "G. K. C." *Spectator*. June 19.

Arthur Bryant. Our Note Book. *Illustrated London News*. Oct. 31.

Emile Cammaerts. To G. K. C. (June 17, 1936). *Observer*. June 21.

B. R. Carter. Some Personal Recollections. *Millgate*. Aug.

R. Davies. Memories. *Pax*. No. 177.

G.K.'s Weekly. June 18. Contains: "Gilbert" by Hilaire Belloc; *In Memoriam* by Vincent McNabb, O.P.; The G. K. C. of Fleet Street by Mrs. Cecil Chesterton; Some Memories by W. R. Titterton. June 25. Contains: "Fide et Literis" by C. E. Baines; Happy Warrior by R. McNair Wilson; G. K. C.'s Mistake by W. K. Scudamore; The Playboy by H. D. C. Pepler. July 23. Contains: Gilbert Keith Chesterton. An epitaph by Walter de la Mare. Sept. 10, 17, 24. Contain: Personal Recollections of G. K. Chesterton by Ramon Dyboski.

A. G. Gardiner. Obituary notice. *English*. Vol. I, No. 3. Renée Haynes. Jongleur de Dieu. *Time and Tide*. June 20. Rt. Rev. Monsignor Ronald Knox. Panegyric on G. K.

Chesterton. Preached at Westminster Cathedral, June 27.
G.K.'s Weekly. July 2 (771). Chesterton the Prophet. *Catholic Herald*. June 28.

Robert Lynd. Laughing Cavalier of Controversy. *News Chronicle*. June 15. Y.Y. (Robert Lynd). "G. K. C.". *New Statesman*. June 20.

E. J. Macdonald. G. K. Chesterton. His Life and Work. *Universe*. June 19.

Gregory Macdonald. G. K. C. A Pen Portrait. *Catholic Times*. June 21. Obituary notice. *Month*. Aug.

Manchester Guardian. A Great Literary Figure. June 15.

Monsignor John O'Connor. G. K. Chesterton. Only a Memory. *Downside Review*. Vol. LIV.

Tablet. June 20. Contains: obituary article by D(ouglas) W(oodruff); a sonnet, Death of a Biographer, by R. A. Knox; and memorial notices by Hilaire Belloc, Alfred Noyes, the Abbot of Buckfast, the Rev. C. C. Martindale, S.J., Sir Henry Slesser and T. S. Eliot. June 27. Contains further tributes by Douglas Jerrold, Arnold Lunn, A. Hungerford Pollen and T. S. Gregory.

Times. Obituary. June 15. Further notices on June 16, 17 and 22.

Humbert Wolfe. Poem. "G. K. Chesterton". *Observer*. June 21.

750. E. C. Bentley. The Last Chesterbelloc. *G.K.'s Weekly*. Oct. 8.

751. Ernest Bramah. Father Brown. *G.K.'s Weekly*. Oct. 8.

752. Ronald Knox. Chesterton in his Early Romances. *Dublin Review*. Oct.

753. *Times Literary Supplement*. Nov. 7. G. K. Chesterton: Child and Man. The Making of an Optimist.

754. Sidney Dark. G. K. C. The Far Too Happy Warrior. *Church Times*. Nov. 8. (See 755.)

755. Clare Nicholl. An Attack on the Character of G. K. Chesterton. *Catholic Herald*. Nov. 20. (See 754.)

1937

756. Monsignor John O'Connor. *Father Brown on Chesterton*. Muller, and Burns, Oates.

757. Emile Cammaerts. *The Laughing Prophet*. The Seven Virtues and G. K. Chesterton. Methuen.

758. Sister Marie Virginia S.N.D. *G. K. Chesterton's Evangel*. Benziger Bros. New York.

759. Gretel Hoffmann. *Gilbert Keith Chesterton als Propagandist*. Dresden.

760. Elliott Dodds. The Man who fell on his Feet. *Congregational Quarterly*. Jan.

761. *Mark Twain Quarterly*. Spring. Special Chesterton number, with contributions from Alfred Noyes, Walter de la Mare, Bernard Shaw and others.

762. *Scripta*. Gibbons Academy, Baltimore, U.S.A. April. The first issue, devoted to G. K. C., has contributions by Hilaire Belloc and others.

762A. *Scrip*. The University of Notre Dame Quarterly. See 556A.

763. Hubert Waring. Prince of Essayists. *Fortnightly Review*. Nov.

1938

764. Monsignor Ronald Knox. G. K. Chesterton. In *Great Catholics*. Ivor Nicholson and Watson.

765. Raymond Las Vergnas. *Chesterton, Belloc, Baring*. Sheed and Ward.

766. D. de Pauw, O.P. *Gilbert Keith Chesterton*. 1874–1936. Antwerp. N.V. Standaard-Bockhandel.

767. Patrick Braybrooke. *I Remember G. K. Chesterton*. Epsom. Dorling & Co.

768. Herbert Palmer. G. K. Chesterton and his School. In *Post-Victorian Poetry* (Chapter XI). Dent.

1939

769. Maurice Evans. *G. K. Chesterton*. The Le Bas Prize Essay, 1938. Cambridge University Press.

770. Cyril Clemens. *Chesterton as seen by his Contemporaries*. With an Introduction by E. C. Bentley. Webster Groves, Missouri. The International Mark Twain Society.

770A. Heinz Kuhn. *Der Gemeinschaftsgedanke bei Chesterton*. Verlag Heinrich Pöppinghaus.

770B. A Menrad. *Der Fortschrittsgedanke bei G. K. Chesterton*. Inaugural dissertation. Freiburg, Goldschagg.

1940

771. Monsignor Ronald Knox. G. K. Chesterton. In *Captive Flames*. A Collection of Panegyrics. Burns and Oates (749).
772. Hilaire Belloc. *On the Place of G. K. Chesterton in English Letters*. Sheed and Ward.
773. E. C. Bentley. *Those Days*. Constable.
774. A. M. A. Bogaerts. *Chesterton and the Victorian Age*. Translated from the Dutch. Hilversum.

1941

775. Mrs. Cecil Chesterton. *The Chestertons*. Chapman and Hall.
776. Maurice B. Reckitt. *As it Happened*. An autobiography. J. M. Dent.
777. Ronald Knox. G. K. Chesterton: the Man and his Work. *Listener*. June 18.
778. *Times Literary Supplement*. Chestertoniana. July 5.
779. V. H. H. Green. Chesterton's "theology". *Theology*. Aug. and Sept.
780. Maisie Ward. G. K. Chesterton in *The Dictionary of National Biography*, 1931–40, pp. 171–175. Oxford, O.U.P.
781. Hugh Kelly. Chesterton: his Philosophy of Life. *Studies*. March.

1943

782. Maisie Ward. *Gilbert Keith Chesterton*. New York. (London, 1945.) Sheed and Ward.

1944

783. Ivor Brown. A Multiple Man. *Observer*. April 16.
784. E. C. Bentley. The Greatest Man of his Age. *John O' London's Weekly*. April 21.
785. *Times Literary Supplement*. G. K. Chesterton. Crusader for the Common Man. April 15.
786. J. C. Squire. The Most Remarkable "Person" since Johnson. *Illustrated London News*. April 29.
787. Hugh Kingsmill. G. K. Chesterton. *New Statesman and Nation*. May 6. (See 788.)
788. Gerald Barry. G. K. Chesterton. (A letter in reply to 787.) *New Statesman and Nation*. May 13.
789. John Murray. G. K. Chesterton: a New Approach. *Studies*. June.
790. Ashley Sampson. G. K. C. *Theology*. Dec.

1945

791. F. A. Lea. *The Wild Knight of Battersea. G. K. Chesterton.* Modern Christian Revolutionaries series. James Clarke. (n.d.)

792. *Times Literary Supplement.* The Pilgrimage of G. K. C. Nov. 3.

792A. K. H. Andersen. *G. K. Chesterton. Der muntre Strid.* Copenhagen. The second, enlarged, edition of 726A.

792B. Sir Francis Chisholm. *G. K. Chesterton and his Biographers.* With a prefatory note by Cyril Clemens. Webster Groves, Missouri. The International Mark Twain Society.

793. Aodh de Blacam. G. K. C. as Defender of the Faith. Chesterton's First Conversion. Chesterton as Pilgrim. Chesterton as Apologist. Last Words on G. K. C. *Irish Monthly.* Jan.–May.

1946

794. Father Brown. (Monsignor John O'Connor.) G. K. Chesterton. Recognita Decennalia. *Nineteenth Century and After.* June.

795. Douglas Woodruff. Chesterton after Ten Years. *Tablet.* June 15.

796. Walter Allen. Books in General. *New Statesman and Nation.* July 27.

797. James Stephens. The "Period Talent" of G. K. Chesterton. *Listener.* Oct. 17. (See 797.)

798. C. S. Lewis. Notes on the Way. *Time and Tide.* Nov. 9. (A reply to James Stephens (796), whose article Lewis considered "ungenerous and even unjust".)

799. Rev. N. H. Gascoigne, Ph.D. *The Path to Serfdom.* Wellington, N.Z. The C.W.M.

1947

800. Emile Cammaerts. Chesterton, the "Laughing Prophet". *Listener.* June 19.

1948

801. Hugh Kenner. *Paradox in Chesterton.* Sheed and Ward.

802. J. W. Poynter. An old Controversy Recalled. *Blackfriars.* Sept. (The *Clarion* Controversy.)

803. Christopher Hollis. Prophet of the Counter-Attack. *Listener.* Nov. 25. (A broadcast in the series *Famous Men.*)

804. Harold Robbins. The Last of the Realists: G. K. Chesterton and his Work. *The Cross and the Plough,* Vol. 15, Nos. 1–4.

1949

805. Robert Hamilton. The Genius of Chesterton. *Blackfriars*. June.

1950

806. Christopher Hollis. *G. K. Chesterton*. Writers and their Work series. Published for the British Council by Longmans, Green.

807. Maurice B. Reckitt. *G. K. Chesterton. A Christian Prophet for England To-day*. S.P.C.K. (816.)

808. *Times Literary Supplement*. Chesterton as Essayist. June 16.

809. A. N. Gilkes. G. B. S., G. K. C. and Paradox. *Fortnightly Review*. Oct.

1951

810. E. S. P. Haynes. *The Lawyer*. A Conversation Piece. Eyre and Spottiswoode.

1952

811. Maisie Ward. *Return to Chesterton*. Sheed and Ward.

812. Michael Asquith. G. K. Chesterton: Prophet and Jester. *Listener*. March 6.

812A. James M. Keane, O.S.M. *The Mariology of G. K. Chesterton's Poetry*. Rome. The International Marian Commission.

1953

813. W. S. Handley Jones. G. K. Chesterton and the Discovery of Christianity. In *The Priest and the Siren*. Epworth Press.

814. G. B. Stern. Bright Pledge. In *A Name to Conjure With*. Collins.

815. Alfred Noyes. The Centrality of Chesterton. *Quarterly Review*. Jan.

1954

816. Maurice B. Reckitt. Belloc and Chesterton: the Study of an Impact. In *The World and the Faith*. Faith Press.

1955

817. Hilaire Belloc. Gilbert Chesterton. In *One Thing and Another*. A Miscellany from his Uncollected Essays selected by Patrick Cahill. Hollis and Carter.

818. Margaret Clarke. Chesterton the Classicist. *Dublin Review*. First Quarter.

819. Lucy Masterman. The Private Chesterton. Poems for Every Occasion. *Manchester Guardian*. April 11.

820. Ferdinand Valentine, O.P. Father Vincent and Gilbert Chesterton. In *Father Vincent McNabb*, *O.P.* (pp. 264–280). Burns, Oates.

821. Maria Petrie. Father Brown and Concavism. More about the private Chesterton. *Manchester Guardian*. June 11.

822. Francis Edward Nugent (Ed.). G. K. Chesterton. In *A Vincent McNabb Anthology* (pp. 82–96). Blackfriars Publications.

1956

823. Grace Carey. To the Memory of a Great Man. G. K. Chesterton at Beaconsfield. *Heritage*. Jan.

824. Hesketh Pearson. G. K. Chesterton and Hilaire Belloc. In Snapshots of my Seniors series. *Listener*. June 28.

825. Helen Dwyer. *The Idealistic Realism of G. K. Chesterton*. Thesis for M.A. Fordham University, U.S.A. Privately printed. (n.d.)

1957

826. Lance Sieveking. "Mr. Tame Lion." Reminiscences of G. K. Chesterton. *Listener*. Jan. 3. Reproduces "The Viking and the Very Tame Lion", drawn by G. K. C. in Lance Sieveking's copy of *A Miscellany of Men*.

827. Robert Speaight. *The Life of Hilaire Belloc*. Hollis and Carter.

828. John Raymond. Jee Kaycee. *New Statesman and Nation*. March 23.

829. Lance Sieveking. *The Eye of the Beholder*. Hulton. Contains an expanded version of 826, and three drawings.

F

COLLECTIONS AND SELECTIONS

The place of publication is London unless otherwise stated.

1911

851. A DEFENCE OF NONSENSE and other Essays. New York. Dodd, Mead. Stiff green wrappers lettered: A/DEFENSE [*sic*] / OF NONSENSE. A gift book made up of essays reprinted from *The Defendant*, *Varied Types*, and *Tremendous Trifles*.

1913

852. THOUGHTS FROM G. K. CHESTERTON. Selected by Elsie E. Morton. Harrap. (n.d.) Sesame Booklets No. 50.

1916

853. THE G. K. CHESTERTON CALENDAR. A quotation from the works of G. K. Chesterton for every day in the year. Selected by H. Cecil Palmer. Cecil Palmer and Hayward.

854. A SHILLING FOR MY THOUGHTS. Being a selection from the essays, stories and other writings of G. K. Chesterton. Methuen. The selection was made by E. V. Lucas.

1925

855. G. K. CHESTERTON. The Augustan Books of Modern Poetry. Benn. Fifteen poems from *Poems* and *The Flying Inn*.

1926

856. A GLEAMING COHORT. Being selections from the writings of G. K. Chesterton. Methuen. The selection was made by E. V. Lucas.

857. THE MINERVA EDITION OF THE WORKS OF G. K. CHESTERTON. The Library Press. (n.d.) Nine

volumes in uniform binding, all originally published by Methuen: *Alarms and Discursions, All Things Considered, The Ballad of the White Horse, Charles Dickens, Fancies* versus *Fads, The Flying Inn, A Miscellany of Men, Tremendous Trifles, The Uses of Diversity.*

1928

858. G. K. CHESTERTON. (Selected Stories.) Harrap. *Short Stories of To-day and Yesterday.*

859. G. K. CHESTERTON. (Selected Essays.) Harrap. *Essays of To-day and Yesterday.*

860. A CHESTERTON CATHOLIC ANTHOLOGY. Compiled and edited by Patrick Braybrooke. Foreword by Fr. Owen Francis Dudley. Burns, Oates. (n.d.)

1929

861. FATHER BROWN STORIES. London. Cassell. An omnibus volume containing *The Innocence of Father Brown, The Wisdom of Father Brown, The Incredulity of Father Brown* and *The Secret of Father Brown.*
1947. Re-set, to include *The Scandal of Father Brown.*
1953. *The Vampire of the Village* included (562).
The American edition, N.Y., Dodd, Mead, 1933, was called *The Father Brown Omnibus.*

862. CHRISTMAS POEMS. Burns, Oates. Selected from *Poems* (37).

1933

863. G. K. CHESTERTON. (An anthology of his humorous writings.) *Methuen's Library of Humour.* Edited by E. V. Knox.

864. ON RUNNING AFTER ONE'S HAT AND OTHER WHIMSIES. N.Y., R. M. McBride & Co. American edition of 863.

1935

865. STORIES, ESSAYS AND POEMS. G. K. CHESTERTON. J. M. Dent. *Everyman Library*, No. 913.
"I may add that he (G. K. C.) has kindly co-operated in making this selection."—Introduction.

1936

866. G. K. CHESTERTON OMNIBUS. Methuen. Contains: *The Napoleon of Notting Hill, The Man Who Was Thursday* and *The Flying Inn.*

1937

867. THE MAN WHO WAS CHESTERTON. The best essays, stories, poems and other writings of G. K. Chesterton. Compiled and edited by Raymond T. Bond. New York. Dodd, Mead.

1939

868. ESSAYS BY G. K. CHESTERTON. Selected with a Preface by John Guest. Collins.

868A. POCKET BOOK OF FATHER BROWN. Philadelphia. The Blakiston Co. Seventeen Father Brown stories.

1947

869. THE PAULINE MUSES. Edited by Edward Pine. With a Foreword by Compton Mackenzie. Gollancz. Selections from G. K. C.'s verse and prose, pp. 228–243.

1949

870. SELECTED ESSAYS OF G. K. CHESTERTON. Chosen by Dorothy Collins. Introduction by E. C. Bentley. Methuen.

1953

871. CHESTERTON ESSAYS. Edited by K. E. Whitehorn. *Methuen's Modern Classics.*

1954

871A. THE AMAZING ADVENTURES OF FATHER BROWN. N.Y., Dell Publishing Co. Inc. (n.d.). Contains ten stories from four books.

1955

872. FATHER BROWN. Selected Stories by G. K. Chesterton. Introduction by Ronald Knox. Oxford University Press. *World's Classics*, No. 547.

873. NEW WORLD CHESTERTON. New York. Sheed and Ward. A collected edition in uniform binding: *Robert Louis Stevenson, Tremendous Trifles, The Poet and the Lunatics, The Flying Inn.*

1956

NEW WORLD CHESTERTON (cont.). *What's Wrong With the World, All Things Considered, Tales of the Long Bow, Chaucer.*

1957

874. G. K. CHESTERTON, An Anthology. Selected with an Introduction by D. B. Wyndham Lewis. O.U.P. *World's Classics*, No. 554.

TRANSLATIONS INTO FOREIGN LANGUAGES
OF BOOKS BY G. K. CHESTERTON

901. *CZECHOSLOVAKIAN*

1917

The Man Who Was Thursday. Poslovenil. Oton Župančiĉ.
Izdala in Zalozela, "Omladina".

1924

Manalive. L. Kuneir. Prague, Albert.
The Innocence of Father Brown. A. Srdoe. Prague.

1925

What's Wrong with the World. L. Kuneir. Prague, Albert.
Tremendous Trifles. Prague, Vaclav Petr.
Tales of the Long Bow. Prague, Albert.
The Superstition of Divorce. Prague, Vaclav Petr.
The Wisdom of Father Brown. Prague, Vaclav Petr.

1926

Alarms and Discursions. Prague, Aventinum-Zizkov.
The Incredulity of Father Brown. F. Borowy. Prague.
The Return of Don Quixote. F. Borowy. Prague.
Kamarád Ŏtvertek. Fantasticka Komedie. L. Kuneir. Prague.
(The dramatised version of *The Man Who Was Thursday*.)

1927

The Everlasting Man. Prague, Vaclav Petr.

1936

St. Thomas Aquinas. Prague, Vyshrad.

1947

The Secret of Father Brown. R. Uhl. Prague, Albert.

902. *DANISH*

1931

The Everlasting Man. Copenhagen.

1938

Erindringer. (Autobiography.) W. Petersen. Slagelse, Asas Forlag.

1945

Mørk Middelalder. (*St. Francis of Assisi* and *St. Thomas Aquinas* in one volume.) P. Schindler. Copenhagen, Sankt Ansgers Forlag.
The Secret of Father Brown. Copenhagen, Frimodt.
The Incredulity of Father Brown. Copenhagen, Frimodt.
The Wisdom of Father Brown. Copenhagen, Frimodt.
The Flying Inn. Copenhagen, Frimodt.
Magic. Copenhagen, Frimodt.

1949

The Man Who Knew Too Much. Copenhagen.

903. *DUTCH*

1925

The Superstition of Divorce. Amsterdam, Bockhandel E. Van der Vecht.

1926

Five Stories from *The Innocence of Father Brown.* Dr. N. Zwager. Amsterdam, J. B. Walters.
The Everlasting Man. H. Reyner. Karkrade.

1927

The Catholic Church and Conversion. Amsterdam, Uitgevers en Boekhandel Forscholte.

1947

Waar Het Om Gaat. (The Thing.) D. Houtman. Brussels, Sheed and Ward.

1948

The End of the Armistice. Amsterdam, Forscholte.

1952

Charles Dickens. P. J. M. Boezeman-Droog. Antwerp, Uitgevery "Het Spectrum". Utrecht, Prisma-boeken.

1953
De Man die Teveel Wist. Dr. E. Brongersma. Utrecht, Prisma-boeken. (Eight stories from *The Man who Knew Too Much* and five from *The Paradoxes of Mr. Pond.*)

1954
Orthodoxie. P. Kerstens. Amsterdam, N.V. Uitgevers-Maatschappij, "Fidelitas". Antwerp, Het Spectrum.

904. *ESPERANTO*
1937
La Naiveco de Pastro Brown. Dr. Cecil Bean. Rickmansworth, Herts. Esperanto Publishing Co.

905. *FRENCH*
1909
Charles Dickens. A. Laurent et L. Martin-Dupont. Paris, Gallimard.

1911
Le Nommé Jeudi, Un Cauchemar. J. Florence. Paris, Gallimard.

1912
Le Napoléon de Notting Hill. J. Florence. Paris, Gallimard.

1914
La Barbarie de Berlin, Lettres à un vieux Garabaldien. I. Rivière. 1914. London, Imprimé par Eyre and Spottiswoode. 1916. Paris, Gallimard. 1944. Montreal.

1916
Les Crimes de l'Angleterre. C. Grolleau. (Introduction by Charles Sarolea.) Paris, G. Crès.

1919
La Clairvoyance du Père Brown. Émile Cammaerts. Paris, Perrin.
Hérétiques. T. J. Serruys. Paris, G. Crès.

1920
Orthodoxie. C. Grolleau. Paris, L. Rouart et J. Watelin.

1921
La Sphère et la Croix. C. Grolleau. Paris, G. Crès.

1927
L'Homme Éternel. M. Vox. Paris, Plon.

1928
Le Retour de Don Quichotte. Paris, Blond & Gay.

1930
La Vie de William Cobbett. M. Agobert. Paris, Gallimard.
La Vie de Robert Browning. L. Guilloux. Paris, Gallimard.
Le Secret du Père Brown. Mme F. Maury. Paris, Gallimard.
Hérétiques. J. S. Bradley. Paris, Plon.
Petite Histoire d'Angleterre. A. Osmont. Paris, G. Crès.

1931
Divorce. J. Fournier-Pargoire. Paris, Editions Saint-Michel.
Le Poète et les Lunatiques. J. Fournier-Pargoire. Paris, Gallimard.
The Flying Inn. Paris, Gallimard.

1932
L'Incrédulité du Père Brown. Mme F. Maury. Paris, Gallimard.

1933
Lumières sur Deux Villes. (Sidelights.) H. Thies. Paris, Nouvelle Revue Critique.

1934
Saint François d'Assise. I. Rivière. Paris, Plon.
La Nouvelle Jérusalem. J. Fournier-Pargoire. Paris, Perrin.

1935
Saint Thomas d'Aquin. M. Vox. Paris, Plon.
Also a de luxe edition.

1936
La Sagesse du Père Brown. Y. André. Paris, Gallimard.
Supervivant. (Manalive.) M. Rouneau. (n.d.) Paris, Desclée de Brouwer.

1937
Chaucer. R. Bourdariat. Paris, Gallimard.

1938

Poèmes Choisis. Mme E. M. Denis-Graterolle. Paris and Brussels, Cahiers des Poètes Catholiques.
Autobiography. Paris, Desclée de Brouwer.
The Well and the Shallows. Paris, Gallimard.

1946

Le Livre Maudit. J. Fournier-Pargoire. Paris, Editions du Bateau Ivre.
"Le titre anglais . . . est 'The blast of the book'"—a story in *The Scandal of Father Brown.*

1947

Le Club des Fous. (Tales of the Long Bow.) P. A. Gruennais. Paris, Editions du Bateau Ivre.

1948

Ce qui Cloche dans le Monde. (What's Wrong with the World.) J. C. Laurens. Paris, Gallimard.

906. *GAELIC*

The Innocence of Father Brown. Seán O Liatáin. Dublin, Government Printing Office. (n.d.)

907. *GERMAN*

1909

Der Mann der Donnerstag War. (The Man Who Was Thursday.) B. Sengfelder, Munich. H. von Weber Verlag. 1947. Wiesentheid, Dromersche Verlags-anstalt.

1914

Magie; eine phantastische Komödie. R. Kommer. Berlin, Oesterheld.

1924

What's Wrong with the World. Musarion Verlag.
The Wisdom of Father Brown. E. S. Stein.
Tremendous Trifles. E. S. Stein.

1925

The Man Who Knew Too Much. Munich, Musarion Verlag.

1926

The Incredulity of Father Brown. Munich, Musarion Verlag.
1930. Bremen, Schunemann.
Manalive. Munich, Musarion Verlag.

1927

Ein Pfeil von Himmel; Kriminalerzahlüngen. (Six Father Brown
stories.) D. S. Kellner. Berlin, Die Schmiede.
St. Francis of Assisi. Munich, Kasel.

1928

Das Geheimnis des Pater Brown. (The Secret of Father Brown.)
R. Nutt. Frankfurt and Hamburg, Fischer Bücherei.

1929

The Return of Don Quixote. C. Thesing. Bremen, Schünemann.

1930

Do We Agree? R. Kayser. Bremen, Schünemann.
Das neue Jerusalem. Bremen, Schünemann.
The Everlasting Man. Bremen, Schünemann.

1932

Wie denken Sie darüber? Untersuchungen, und Betrachtungen.
Tages—und Ewigkeitsfragen. (Essays, mainly from *Come to
Think of It.*) C. Thesing. Bremen, Schünemann.

1933

The Wisdom of Father Brown. C. Meitner. Munich, Musarion
Verlag.

1936

Dickens. H. E. Herlitschka. Vienna, Phaidon Verlag.

1937

Autobiography. Vienna, Phaidon Verlag.
St. Thomas Aquinas. Vienna, Phaidon Verlag.
A Short History of England. Vienna, Phaidon Verlag.

1945

Verteidigung. (The Defendant.) P. Schifferli. Olten, Switzer-
land, Otto Walter.

1948

Wer war der Täter? (*The Scandal of Father Brown.*) K. Demmer.
Vienna, Amandus.

1952

Der Mann mit dem goldenen Schlüssel. (Autobiography.) Dr. H. Schiel. Freiburg, Verlag Herder.

908. *HUNGARIAN*

1925

St. Francis of Assisi. Cleveland, Ohio, Franciscan Monastery.

1936

The Wisdom of Father Brown. Franklin-Tarsulat.

909. *ITALIAN*

1914

Berlino barbara. Harrison & Sons, printers.

1925

L'Ortodossia. R. Ferruzzi. Brescia, "Morcelliana".

1930

La Chiesa Cattolica e la Conversione. (The Catholic Church and Conversion.) G. Barra. Brescia, "Morcelliana". *Il Candore di Padre Brown.* R. Constanzi. Milan, Rizzoli.

1931

Il Segreto di Padre Brown. I. Lori. Milano, Bietti.

1933

Le Avventure d'un Uomo Vivo. (Manalive.) E. Cecchi. Milano-Roma, Treves.

1935

The Everlasting Man. M. Feruzzi, La Nuova Italia.

1937

San Tommaso D'Aquino. A. Ruhl—Ripamonti & G. Datta. Florence, Agnelli.

1938

Autobiografia. A. Castelli. Milano, Istituto di Propaganda Libraria.

1939

La Chiesa viva. (The Thing.) F. Ballini. Alba, Edizione Pavline.

1945
Piccola storia d'Inghelterra. N. de Feo. Rome, Atlantica.

1946
Lepanto. M. Piattoli. Cairo.

1948
The Well and the Shallows. Rome, Editrice A.R.C.

1949
Lo Scandalo di Padre Brown. E. Pivetti. Milan, Garzanti.

1950
S. Francesco d'Assisi. A. del Vecchio. Milan, Istituto di Propaganda Libraria.

1952
La Resurrezione di Roma. I. Ballini. Milan, Istituto di Propaganda Libraria.

Il Poeta e i Pazzi; Episodi tratti dalla vito di Gabriel Gale. (The Poet and the Lunatics.) F. Ballini. Milan, Istituto di Propaganda Libraria.

La Saggezza di Padre Brown. G. Dauli. Milan, Istituto di Propaganda Libraria.

L'Osteria volante. G. Dauli. Milan, Istituto di Propaganda Libraria.

L'innocenza di Padre Brown. G. Dauli. Milan, Istituto di Propaganda Libraria.

Il Club dei mestieri stravagantri. G. Dauli. Milan, Istituto di Propaganda Libraria.

La Sfera e la Croce. S. Cornaghi. Milan, Istituto di Propaganda Libraria.

L'Uomo che fu detto Giovedi. M. Pettvello. Milan, Istituto di Propaganda Libraria.

1953
L'Incredulità di Padre Brown. Guintavalle. Balsamo, Edizioni Paoline.

1954
Magia. S. Cormagi. Milan, Editrice La Fiaccola.

1955
L'Uomo Comune. (The Common Man.) F. Ballini. Alba, Edizione Paoline.

1956

Un Prete Detective Padre Brown.
Contains: L'Innocenza di Padre Brown (G. Dauli); L'Incredulita di Padre Brown (M.I. Quintavalle); La Saggezza di Padre Brown (E. de Carli); Il Segreto di Padre Brown (E. de Carli). Milan, Editrice A.A.S.

910. *JAPANESE*

1933

Dickens. Tokyo, Kenkyusha Publishing Co.

1951

As I Was Saying. Fifteen essays from *As I Was Saying* in English with Introduction and Notes in Japanese by H. Ogata. Tokyo, Daigakushorin.

1952

The Invisible Man. Four stories from *The Innocence of Father Brown*: The Invisible Man, The Honour of Israel Gow, The Wrong Shape, The Three Tools of Death. In English with Introduction and Notes in Japanese by N. Kanayama. Tokyo, Osaka Kyoiku Tosho Co.
The Man Who Was Thursday. (In Japanese.) F. Matsumoto. Tokyo, Hayakawa shobô.
The Innocence of Father Brown. Three stories from *The Innocence of Father Brown*: The Blue Cross, The Secret Garden, The Queer Feet. In English with Introduction and Notes in Japanese by J. Ogawa. Tokyo, Osaka Kyoiku Tosho Co.

1954

Tremendous Trifles. Twelve Essays from *Tremendous Trifles* in English with Introduction and Notes in Japanese by H. Hirohashi. Tokyo, Nan' Un-Do.
The Wisdom of Father Brown. Toshirô Murazaki. Tokyo, Hayakawa shobô.
The Innocence of Father Brown. Toshirô Murazaki. Tokyo, Hayakawa shobô.

911. *NORWEGIAN*

1946

The Everlasting Man. Aschong.

912. *POLISH*

1927
The Innocence of Father Brown. Mme Ziemilska. Drukarnia Torunska.

1928
The Everlasting Man. Vienna, Renaissance Verlag.
The Flying Inn. Vienna, Renaissance Verlag.
The Secret of Father Brown. Towarzystwo Wydawnioze. 'Roj.'
The Wisdom of Father Brown. Bibljolaka Groszown.

1929
Charles Dickens. M. Godlewaka. Ksiegarnia Robotnicza.
The Return of Don Quixote. Vienna, Renaissance Verlag.
The Incredulity of Father Brown. Dru Karnia Ksiegarnia.

1947
The Blue Cross. Translated into Polish by E. Arthurton-Barker and N. Reh. Duns, Caldra House. Bi-lingual edition.

1948
Manalive. Zygmunt Jakimiak. Warsaw.

1950
Krotka Historia Anglii. (A Short History of England.) A. Doboszynski. London, Biblioteha Polska.

1955
Manalive. Z. Jakimiak. Warsaw, Pax.

1956
Adventures of Father Brown. (Eight stories from four books.) Warsaw, Wydawnictno Pax.

913. *PORTUGUESE*

1932
The Everlasting Man. S. America, Livaria do Globo.

1933
Return of Don Quixote. S. America, Livaria do Globo.
The Superstition of Divorce. S. America, Livaria do Globo.

1939

Autobiography. S. America, Livaria do Globo.

1942

O Homem Que Era Quinta-Feria. (The Man Who Was Thursday.) D. Arouca. Lisbon, Portugalia Editora.
St. Francis of Assisi. Lisbon, Libraria Cruz.

1945

The Wisdom of Father Brown. Lisbon, Libraria Cruz.
The Incredulity of Father Brown. Lisbon, Libraria Cruz.
The Barbarism of Berlin. Lisbon, Libraria Cruz.

1946

St. Thomas Aquinas. Lisbon, Libraria Cruz.

914. *RUSSIAN*

1923

The Innocence of Father Brown. V. Krymar. Berlin, "Argus".

915. *SPANISH*

1915

Sobre el Concepto de Barbarie. H. Oriol. (Con un Prologo de Miguel de Unamuno.) Barcelona.

1917

Ortodoxia. A. Reyes. Madrid, Calleja.

1920

Pequeña historia de Inglaterra. Version castellana de A. Reyes. Madrid.

1926

St. Francis of Assisi. (Catalan.) Barcelona, M. Manent.

1927

The Everlasting Man. (Catalan.) Barcelona, M. Manent.

1928

The Return of Don Quixote. Madrid, Editorial Cosmopolis.

1929

What's Wrong with the World. (Catalan.) La Nova Revista.
The Poet and the Lunatics. Madrid, Editorial Poblet.
La Supersticion del Divorcio. Eduardo Toda Valcarcel. Madrid, Poblet.

1932

Herejes. M. J. Barroso Bonzon. Madrid, Poblet.

1933

Chaucer. Madrid, Editorial Poblet.
El hombre eterno. F. de la Mille. Livraria do Globo.

1934

Santo Tomás de Aquino. H. Muñoz, O.P. Madrid, Espasa-Calpe.

1936

La Sabiduria del Padre Brown. A. Nadal. Barcelona, Biblioteca Oro.

1938

El hombré que fué jueves (pesadilla). A. Reyes. Buenos Aires. Editorial Losada.

1939

Autobiografia. A. Marichalar. Buenos Aires, Espasa-Calpe.

1940

La Esfera y la Cruz. M. Azana. Buenos Aires, Espasa-Calpe.
Las Paradojas de Mr. Pond. Buenos Aires, Espasa-Calpe.

1941

El Napoleon de Notting Hill. M. L. de Uduando, M. C. Padilla and J. Devoto. Buenos Aires, C.E.P.A.
Las Quintaesencias. A study and a selection by Ramon Setantí. Madrid and Barcelona, Ediciones de la Gacela.

1942

La Incredulidad del Padre Brown. I. Abello de Lamarca. Barcelona, Editorial Tartessos.
La Hosteria Volante. (The Flying Inn.) M. Pineda. Barcelona, Libreria Editorial Argos.

1943

Robert Browning. S. Santaines. Barcelona, Lauro.
Vida de Dickens. E. G. Orbaneja. Madrid, Editorial Summa.
Cuentos Del Arco Largo. (Tales of the Long Bow.) F. J. Eastaway. Barcelona, Al Monigote de Papel.
William Cobbett. L. Nonell. Barcelona, Colección Historia.

1944

El Hombre que Sabia Demasiado y Otras Historias. (The Man Who Knew Too Much.) R. Berenguer. Barcelona, Colección Historia.

1945

Charlas. (Generally Speaking.) J. L. de Isquierdo. Buenos Aires. Espasa-Calpe.

El Fin del Armisticio. (The End of the Armistice.) G. Y. L. Gossé Clayman. Barcelona, José Janés.

1946

El Candor del Padre Brown. A. Reyes. Barcelona, José Janés.

El Escandalo del Padre Brown. F. G. Taujis. Barcelona, José Janés.

Also in this uniform edition: *La Sabiduria, El Secreto, La Incredulidad* and *El Hombre que Sabia Damasiado.*

1950

Chesterton; Maestro de Ceremonias. (G. K. C. as M.C.) M. M. Conde. Buenos Aires, Emecé.

El Almirante Flotante. (The Floating Admiral by Dorothy L. Sayers, G. K. C., Victor L. Whitechurch *et al.*) Maria Antonia Oyuela. Buenos Aires, Emecé.

1951

La Reina de Las Siete Espadas. (The Queen of Seven Swords.) C. P. de Saravia. Buenos Aires, Plantin. Bi-lingual edition.

1952

El Perfil de la Cordura. (The Outline of Sanity.) M. R. Bengolea. Buenos Aires. Emecé Editores.

1956

Father Brown Stories. Published separately in a uniform edition. El Hombre del Pasaje (The Man in the Passage); La Maledicion de los Pendragon (The Perishing of the Pendragons); La Cabeza de Cesar (The Head of Caesar); El Dios de los Gongs (The God of the Gongs); La Peluca Purpurea (The Purple Wig); El Cuento de Hadas (The Fairy Tale of Father Brown).

Maria Antonia Oyuela de Grant. Buenos Aires, Editorial La Isla.

1952-6

G. K. *Chesterton*. Obras Completas. Barcelona, José Janés.
Vol. I. Autobiografia (trans. A. Marichalar) Herejes (M. J. Barroso Bonzon), Ortodoxia (A. Reyes), Lo que esta mal en la mundo (M. Amadeo); La supersticion del divorcio (E. Toda Valcarsel); Alarmas y disgresiones (T. Reyles); Charlas (Generally Speaking) (J. Louis de Izquierdo); Enormes minucias (Tremendous Trifles) (R. Calleja); El hombre eterno (F. de la Mille).
Vol. II. El candor del Padre Brown; La sabiduria . . .; La incredulidad; El secreto . . .; El escandala; El hombre que sabia demasiado; Los arboles del orgullo (R. Berenguer); El jardin del humo (R. Berenguer); El cinco de espadas (R. Berenguer); La torre de la traición (R. Berenguer); El poeta y los lunaticos (M. B. Barrett)
Vol. III. El hombre que fue jueves (A. Reyes); La esfera y la cruz (M. Azana); El regreso de Don Quijote (C.F.); La hosteria volante (M. Pineda); El Napoleon de Notting Hill (M. B. Barrett); Cuatro granujas sin tacha (Four Faultless Felons); El club de los negocios paros; Cuentos del arco largo (P. J. Eastaway).
Vol. IV. Robert Browning (S. Santaines); Vida de Dickens (E. G. Orbaneja); San Francisco de Asis (M. Manent); Chaucer (M. J. Barroso-Bonzon); William Cobbett (L. Nonell); George Bernard Shaw (J. M. Herrera); Santo Tomas de Aquino (P. H. Munoz. O.P.); Robert Louis Stevenson (P. Romeva).

916. *SWEDISH*

1926

Manalive. Stockholm, Soderstrom.
The Everlasting Man. Stockholm, Wessman.
St. Francis of Assisi. H. Hultenberg. Stockholm, Wessman.

1928

The Secret of Father Brown. Published in Finland. Soderstrom.

1933

Charles Dickens. Karl Ragnar Gieron. Stockholm, Norstedt.

1937

The Paradoxes of Mr. Pond. Stockholm, H. Gebers.

1947
The Return of Don Quixote. A. Bonnier. Stockholm, Norlin Forlag.

1948
Thomas Av Aquino. S. Stolpe. Stockholm, Norlin Forlag.
Isa Brownin Salaisus. (The Secret of Father Brown.) A. Lehto. Helsinki, Pellervo Seura.

1949
Charles Dickens. A. Bonnier. Stockholm, Norlin Forlag.

1950
Fader Brown. (Twenty stories from five Father Brown books.) T. Zetterholm. Stockholm, Albatross Norstedt.

H

G. K. C. MISCELLANY

951. *Portraits, etc.*

(*a*) *Busts*

(i) A bust in bronze by Maria Petrie, 1936. Now in the National Portrait Gallery. A photograph of the bust is on N.P.G. Post-card No. 3240. The verso has a "miniature biography" of G. K. C. by an anonymous hand.

(ii) A bust by Thomas Murphy. Now in the White Hart, Beaconsfield.

(*b*) *Portraits*

(i) A portrait in oils by Baccari, *c.* 1881. Now in the collection of Miss Dorothy Collins. Reproduced in 782.

(ii) A portrait in oils by Hugh Rivière, *c.* 1905. Reproduced in 811.

(iii) A silhouette by Eric Gill. 1930. In the collection of Miss Dorothy Collins.

(iv) A portrait by William Rothenstein. Reproduced, with an appreciation of G. K. C. in *Twenty-four Portraits*. Second Series. Chatto and Windus. 1923.

(v) Conversation Piece. G. K. Chesterton, Maurice Baring and Hilaire Belloc. An oil painting by James Gunn, 1932. Now in the National Portrait Gallery. A photograph of the picture is on N.P.G. Post-card No. 3654. It was also used for the dust jacket of 765.

(vi) A study by James Gunn, inscribed "G. K. C. sketching illustrations for Belloc's *Postmaster General* while sitting for Conversation Piece. James Gunn. '32." National Portrait Gallery, 1956.

(vii) Another study by James Gunn for Conversation Piece, 1932. National Portrait Gallery, 1956.

(*c*) *Caricatures*

(i) A self-caricature. Slade School period. Reproduced in 782.

(ii) By Max Beerbohm.

1907. *A Book of Caricatures*. No. XL. Mr. Hilaire Belloc

striving to win Mr. Gilbert Chesterton over from the errors
of Geneva.

1909. Drury Lane Souvenir. Matinee for the Queen's
Sanatorium, Davos. May 11, 1909. *Leaders of Thought. Mr.
Shaw and Mr. Chesterton*.

1911. Aug. *Bookman*. Mr. G. K. Chesterton.

(iii) By David Low.

1928. *Lions and Lambs*. With interpretations by "Lynx".

(iv) By J. H. Dowd.

1929. *Bibliophilus Maximus*. Frontispiece to 80.

(v) By Thomas Derrick.

1934. Frontispiece to 400.

(vi) By Albert Morrow.

1934. Dust jacket of 400.

952. *Parodies*

(i) 1912. Max Beerbohm. *A Christmas Garland*. Heinemann.
Contains: Some Damnable Errors about Christmas. By G. K.
Ch*st*rt*n.

(ii) 1920. J. C. Squire. *Collected Parodies*. Hodder and Stoughton. Contains: How They Do It. No. 5. Mr. G. K. Chesterton. I. Verse. II. Prose.

(iii) 1925. Humbert Wolfe. *Lampoons*. V. Beautiful Letters.
VII. The Poets.

(iv) 1928. Reginald Arkell. *Meet These People*. Herbert
Jenkins.

953. *Miscellaneous*

(i) 1910. Hilaire Belloc. *Verses*. Duckworth. Contains: Lines
to a Don.

(ii) 1920. Humbert Wolfe. *Shylock Reasons with Mr. Chesterton
and other Poems*. Oxford, Blackwell.

(iii) 1939. *The Christ Child*. Unison carol. Words by G. K.
Chesterton (from *Collected Poems*). Music by J. Meredith
Tatton. Deane & Sons. The Year Book Press Ltd.

(iv) 1957. Manchester Public Libraries. *G. K. Chesterton.
1874–1936. Manuscripts, Drawings, Cartoons. First Editions*.
Catalogue of an Exhibition, April 10–May 4, 1957.

954. *Memorials*

(i) Cast-bronze tablet on 32 Sheffield Terrace, Kensington, W. Inscribed:

Gilbert Keith
Chesterton
was Born Here
29th May 1874

Donor, Mr. Edward T. Moldram. May 1952.

(ii) Plaque on 11 Warwick Gardens, London, W.14 (where G. K. C. lived from 1881 until his marriage in 1901). Inscribed:

Gilbert Keith Chesterton
Poet, novelist and critic. 1874–1936

Plaque put up by the London County Council and the Royal Society of Arts on 27 March 1952.

(iii) Tablet in the porch of the Church of St. Teresa and the English Martyrs, Beaconsfield. Inscribed:

This Church was completed
as a Memorial to Gilbert
Keith Chesterton, an illustrious
parishioner, through the
generosity of his friends and
admirers throughout the world.

(iv) Monument, carved by Eric Gill, over the grave at Beaconsfield inscribed:

Pray for the soul of Gilbert Keith Chesterton
Born May 29 1874   Died June 14 1936
& of Frances His Wife
Born June 28 1869   Died Dec 12 1938
Vitam Sine Termino Nobis Donet in Patria

A photograph of the monument appears as the frontispiece to 782.

GILBERT KEITH CHESTERTON

Knight of the Holy Ghost, he goes his way
Wisdom his motley, Truth his loving jest;
The mills of Satan kept his lance in play,
Pity and Innocence his heart at rest.

WALTER DE LA MARE.

INDEX

Note: The numerical references are to sections and not to pages.

Entries in small capital letters (e.g. ALARMS AND DISCURSIONS) refer to works by Chesterton himself.